Promoting Children's Rights in European Schools

Also available from Bloomsbury

Austerity and the Remaking of European Education, edited by Anna Traianou and Ken Jones

Children's Rights Education in Diverse Schools and Classrooms: Pedagogy, Principles and Practice, Lee Jerome and Hugh Starkey

Educating for Peace and Human Rights: An Introduction, Maria Hantzopoulos and Monisha Bajaj

Education as a Human Right: Principles for a Universal Entitlement to Learning, Tristan McCowan

Ethics and Research with Young Children, edited by Christopher M. Schulte

Identity, Culture and Belonging: Educating Young Children for a Changing World, Tony Eaude

Issues and Challenges of Immigration in Early Childhood in the USA, Wilma Robles-Melendez and Wayne Driscoll

Race, Education and Educational Leadership in England: An Integrated Analysis, edited by Paul Miller and Christine Callender

Rethinking Children's Rights: Attitudes in Contemporary Society, Phil Jones and Sue Welch

Schooling for Social Change: The Rise and Impact of Human Rights Education in India, Monisha Bajaj

The Bloomsbury Handbook of Global Education and Learning, edited by Douglas Bourn

Transforming Education: Reimagining Learning, Pedagogy and Curriculum, Miranda Jefferson and Michael Anderson

Promoting Children's Rights in European Schools

Intercultural Dialogue and Facilitative Pedagogy

Edited by
Claudio Baraldi, Erica Joslyn and Federico Farini

BLOOMSBURY ACADEMIC
LONDON • NEW YORK • OXFORD • NEW DELHI • SYDNEY

BLOOMSBURY ACADEMIC
Bloomsbury Publishing Plc
50 Bedford Square, London, WC1B 3DP, UK
1385 Broadway, New York, NY 10018, USA
29 Earlsfort Terrace, Dublin 2, Ireland

BLOOMSBURY, BLOOMSBURY ACADEMIC and the Diana logo are
trademarks of Bloomsbury Publishing Plc

First published in Great Britain 2022
This paperback edition published in 2023

Copyright © Claudio Baraldi, Erica Joslyn, Luisa Conti, Federico Farini,
Vittorio Iervese, Chiara Ballestri and Angela Scollan, 2022

Claudio Baraldi, Erica Joslyn, Luisa Conti, Federico Farini, Vittorio Iervese,
Chiara Ballestri and Angela Scollan have asserted their right under the Copyright,
Designs and Patents Act, 1988, to be identified as Author of this work.

Cover image © Rawpixel/iStock

All rights reserved. No part of this publication may be reproduced or transmitted
in any form or by any means, electronic or mechanical, including photocopying,
recording, or any information storage or retrieval system, without prior
permission in writing from the publishers.

Bloomsbury Publishing Plc does not have any control over, or responsibility for,
any third-party websites referred to or in this book. All internet addresses given
in this book were correct at the time of going to press. The author and publisher
regret any inconvenience caused if addresses have changed or sites have ceased
to exist, but can accept no responsibility for any such changes.

A catalogue record for this book is available from the British Library.

Library of Congress Cataloging-in-Publication Data

Names: Baraldi, Claudio, author.
Title: Promoting children's rights in European schools: intercultural
dialogue and facilitative pedagogy / Claudio Baraldi [and six others].
Description: London; New York: Bloomsbury Academic, 2022. |
Includes bibliographical references and index.
Identifiers: LCCN 2021025509 (print) | LCCN 2021025510 (ebook) |
ISBN 9781350217782 (hardback) | ISBN 9781350217799 (ebook) |
ISBN 9781350217805 (epub)
Subjects: LCSH: Multicultural education–Europe. | Culturally relevant
pedagogy–Europe. | Children's rights–Europe.
Classification: LCC LC1099.5.E85 B37 2022 (print) |
LCC LC1099.5.E85 (ebook) | DDC 370.117094–dc23
LC record available at https://lccn.loc.gov/2021025509
LC ebook record available at https://lccn.loc.gov/2021025510

ISBN: HB: 978-1-3502-1778-2
PB: 978-1-3502-1782-9
ePDF: 978-1-3502-1779-9
eBook: 978-1-3502-1780-5

Typeset by Integra Software Services Pvt. Ltd.

To find out more about our authors and books visit www.bloomsbury.com
and sign up for our newsletters.

Table of Contents

List of Illustrations vi
List of Figures vii
List of Tables viii

1 The SHARMED Project: The Conceptual Framework 1
2 Grounding Innovative Pedagogy: Social and Educational Experiences of Children 15

Part 1 Facilitation of Children's Participation

3 Use of Photographs 29
4 Production of Narratives 47
5 Meanings and Methods of Pedagogical Innovation 67

Part 2 Managing a Community of Dialogue in the Classroom

6 Children's Initiatives in the Classroom 91
7 Dealing with 'Intercultural Issues' 113
8 Conflicts in the Classroom 133

Part 3 SHARMED Evaluation and Outcomes

9 Improving Pedagogical Work: Evaluation 153
10 SHARMED Training: Design and Practice 173
11 The SHARMED Participatory Digital Archive 193
12 Conclusion: General Reflections on SHARMED as Innovative Pedagogy 217

References 228
Index 240

Illustrations

1	Great-Grandmother	107
2	Child and Grandfather	107
3	Baptism	108
4	Marriage	108
5	Child in a snowy village	109
6	Sisters	109
7	Meeting Grandpa	110
8	A trip to America	110
9	Looking after my chair	111
10	River Thames Cruise	111
11	Wedding Day	112
12	Snowman	112

Figures

10.1	Facilitator toolbox	174
10.2	The RARA Model of reflection (Scollan 2009)	188
11.1	Picture, connected to the files with the written and oral descriptions	199
11.2	Access to SHARMED archive	201
11.3	Degree of participation in SHARMED archive	202
11.4	Visual search (left); Search filters (right)	208
11.5	Browse by map	209
11.6	Browse by timeline	210

Tables

2.1	Children	15
2.2	Parents	16
9.1	How much did you enjoy (% very much)	165
9.2	During the activities (%)	166
9.3	How did you feel with facilitator (%)	167
9.4	How would you define the facilitator (%)	168
9.5	During the activities the facilitator (% very much)	168
10.1	Example of initial reflections	189

1

The SHARMED Project: The Conceptual Framework

Claudio Baraldi Erica Joslyn and Federico Farini

1.1 Introduction

The Shared Memories and Dialogues project (SHARMED) is a project funded by the European Commission (Erasmus +, Key-action 3, innovative education), coordinated by the University of Modena and Reggio Emilia (Italy), in partnership with University of Jena (Germany) and University of Suffolk (England). The project was conducted between 2016 and 2018.

The SHARMED project was designed to promote intercultural dialogue in multicultural classrooms and explore innovative learning and teaching approaches that amplify all children's voices within multicultural communities. The SHARMED philosophy is underpinned by a belief that children's empowerment and their contributions in social and educational settings are a determining mechanism for building strong and inclusive communities for young people.

In its design, the SHARMED project was concerned with the production of narratives based on children's memories and the ways in which these narratives are constructed and negotiated in classroom interactions. Children participating in the SHARMED project were aged eight to thirteen years, and the project purposefully included children from both migrant and non-migrant backgrounds from selected schools in three European countries – Germany, Italy and the United Kingdom (particularly in England). While in Italy and Germany the project involved primary and secondary schools children, covering the full range of educational levels considered by the project, in England only primary school children participated in the project. The choice to work exclusively with primary school children was motivated by three considerations: (1) the results-driven and competitive vocation of secondary education in England made teachers less prepared to waive teaching time for the project's activities than primary school colleagues; (2) primary school curricula include a subject-*personal, social and health education*-where learning is project-based and collaboration with external partners are more familiar to teachers; (3) primary education in England extends over six years, compared to five years in Italy and four years in Germany. Grade 6 children in England are in primary schools, but they are in lower-secondary schools (middle schools) in Italy and in secondary schools in Germany.

The parents of participating children were invited to support their children's participation through choice of photographs or other artefacts and to provide their written consent about their child's inclusion into the SHARMED school project. Later, they were also involved in filling a questionnaire (see Chapter 2) and finally in commenting the project results. Headteachers and teachers were invited to collaborate in the project, and these volunteers were key to the success of the project especially in supporting and motivating children and their parents. In particular, teachers organized and supervised the classroom activities planned by the project. These activities involved some facilitators, which were hired by the three university partners with the task of enhancing children's active participation and dialogue among children, with particular attention of participation of children with migrant background. Finally, researchers documented the activities included in the project in order to provide a methodologically oriented evaluation. This book is based on this research activity.

1.2 Theoretical Constructs Embedded within the SHARMED Philosophy

The SHARMED philosophy is based on a unique combination of six conceptual dimensions that inform and shape the methodological and analytical design of the project:

1. An anti-essentialist view of intercultural communication and cultural identity;
2. Personal narratives as a mechanism for personal empowerment;
3. The significance of meanings attributed to photographs and other artefacts;
4. The influence of memory, relating to narratives and photographs;
5. The value of facilitation as a means to create communities of dialogue;
6. A recognition of potential conflict situations inherent in multicultural settings.

1.2.1 Intercultural Communication and Cultural Diffusion

Often, the definition of 'multicultural' is based primarily on the presence of participants from a variety of cultural backgrounds (Mahon & Cushner 2012). Studies show that there are a variety of ways for handling cultural meanings and identity (Gay 2000; Gundara 2000; Gundara & Portera 2008; Herrlitz & Maier 2005; Mahon & Cushner 2012). Importantly, these studies show that both social and self-identity are commonly associated with communication within specific cultural groups (Hofstede 1980; Schell 2009; Spencer-Oatey & Franklin 2009; Ting-Toomey 1999). This is an essentialist perspective which 'presents people's individual behaviour as entirely defined and constrained by the cultures in which they live so that the stereotype becomes the essence of who they are' (Holliday 2011: 4). However, according to Baraldi (2015b), essentialism takes for granted that cultural identities are determined before intercultural communication. Baraldi argues that the essentialist ideology is a feature of 'othering' – a process whereby the Western world attempts to legitimize its hegemony at the expenses of 'others' (Holliday 2011). Essentialism emphasizes internal cultural stereotypes and Guillherme (2012) argues that it interprets dialogue as enrichment based on acknowledgement of differences among predefined cultural identities (Alred et al. 2003; Grant & Portera 2011; Portera 2008).

The anti-essentialist view stresses the prefix '*inter*', which indicates the importance of relationships and communication, and warns against insisting on predefined cultural identities which are based on an essentialist representation of cultural belonging (Byrd Clark & Dervin 2014). Identity is seen as fluid, malleable and contingently constructed in communication (Dervin & Liddicoat 2013; Piller 2007; Tupas 2014). Some authors conclude that the primacy of cultural identity is replaced by the construction of hybrid identity (Jackson 2014; Kramsch & Uryu 2012; Nair-Venugopal 2009), which means that identity is always negotiated in communication processes through the manifestation of personal cultural trajectories (Holliday & Amadasi 2020).

The SHARMED project is grounded within an anti-essentialist perspective and is focused on the construction of narratives within communication processes. Thus, it replicates the importance of social participation and communication in the development of a genuine intercultural understanding in educational settings. In seeking to promote intercultural education, this study is focused on building classroom relationships and promoting dialogue. Hybridity is conceived as the outcome of a complex intertwining of interactions designed to 'open up many possibilities for how narratives can intertwine and express themselves'

(Holliday & Amadasi 2020: 11). In this anti-essentialist perspective, classrooms are the setting for sharing narratives about personal cultural trajectories – the production of '*small cultures*' (Holliday 1999).

Thus, in SHARMED, the classroom is 'multicultural' since it supports the production of a variety of small cultures rather than being the sum of individuals with different, predefined cultural identities. A theoretical point with pivotal implications for the aims of the project is that communication is intercultural when it produces narratives of cultural varieties (Baraldi 2015b). SHARMED aims to enhance children's participation via innovative participatory pedagogies. SHARMED does not aim to generate intercultural communication because, according to the project's theoretical foundations, intercultural communication may or may not constructed by participants in interaction through their choices. The promotion of agency may support intercultural communication because it creates the condition for participants' choices; however, if agency is taken seriously, intercultural communication is not necessarily a consequence of agency. The same is true for participants' identities: SHARMED does not aim to support the preservation or the change of cultural identities. Children's participation may or may not lead to the construction of cultural identities in interaction.

For SHARMED, promoting children's participation means promoting children's choices. SHARMED rejects instrumental approaches to the promotion of children's participation that would reduce children's agency. An important theoretical, methodological and ethical aspect of SHARMED is that *using* children's participation to achieve any pre-determined objective, including the construction of intercultural communication, contradicts the conditions of children's agency because children's choices are subordinated to adults' agenda.

1.2.2 Narratives

The production of personal narratives as a means to empowerment was at the centre of the SHARMED project and draws on two perspectives. First, narration in the context of interpreting and assessing communications (Fisher 1987; Somers 1994), and second, narrative as storytelling (Norrick 2013: 200).

According to Fisher, all forms of communication are stories, situational, as well as historically and culturally grounded. He suggests that 'narration is the context for interpreting and assessing all communication' as it is omnipresent in communication (Fisher 1987: 193). The SHARMED project accepts this definition and recognizes narratives as social constructions, in which the observed reality is interpreted and 'storied' in different ways. Similarly, Somers (1994) describes ways of narrative construction – differentiating narratives of the self (ontological narratives), public narratives, conceptual narratives (including scientific concepts) and metanarratives concerning 'the epic dramas of our time' (Somers 1994: 619). The SHARMED project draws on her distinction between ontological narratives and narratives concerning the wider society (public narratives, metanarratives).

Secondly, Norrick (2007) argues that public narratives as storytelling do concern not only the story content but also the rights associated with the activity of narrating. For the SHARMED project, the construction of public narratives based on autobiographical memory provided the opportunity to highlight meanings and identity of narrating participants (Bamberg 2005, 2011). In the telling of their narratives, participants 'create and recreate' their past in the light of their 'present needs and concerns' (Norrick 2007: 139). Within the SHARMED context, activities of narration were structured around three features (Norrick 2007, 2013):

- First, each participant contributes to constructing and negotiating a narrative in interactions as teller, co-teller, listener or elicitor of new narratives.
- Second, narratives can be either first-person narratives or vicarious narratives.
- Third, narratives can receive different comments from different participants; in particular, each narrative can be followed by response narratives that refer to it, and this enhances the production of interlaced stories.

1.2.3 Narratives, Photographs and Memory

In SHARMED, the construction of narratives was stimulated by personal photographs, propelling storytelling and other forms of collaborative engagement. The construction of these public narratives helped children to connect the image of a photograph with insight about situations and circumstances that lie behind the image. According to Baraldi and Iervese (2017) narratives can focus on both the image in photographs and the situations and circumstances behind and beyond photographs. This focus enables images to explore social and cultural contexts of photographs as well as to create new stories linked to images.

Use of photographs in the SHARMED project relied on the premise that the interactional production of narratives depends on past actions (taking pictures) that were designed for other purposes and only later do they become important in the specific context of remembering. While photographs allow access to captured moments of personal lives, to revisiting personal feelings and to preserving memory, they can also enhance and invite connections. In the SHARMED project, photography was not only understood as a technology for documenting life; photographs were also used as a powerful medium for social engagement and collaboration.

Research by Moline (2011) and Baraldi and Iervese (2017) have confirmed that the use of visual materials can positively engage children in creative workshops and that photographs are a powerful medium to stimulate personalized and interactive narratives in educational settings. Within the SHARMED project, photographs did not only elicit children's responses to visual inputs, but they also provided colloquial talking points – invigorating participation in classroom dialogue. In other words, children were able to fully participate in a range of conversations through, about and with photographs – engaging and building intercultural understandings and friendships in the process.

The SHARMED project recognized that memory does not only depend on people's awareness of their past, but also on the reflection of the past in the context of present social and cultural experiences. Against this interpretation of memory, the SHARMED project was designed to use photographs (and other artefacts in few cases) as triggers for recall and the exploration of individual comprehension and insight of captured memory.

1.2.4 Facilitation Designed to Create 'Communities of Dialogue'

Research has shown the Initiation-Response-Evaluation (IRE) sequence (Mehan 1979; Sinclair & Coulthard 1975) of teacher-initiated questions, student responses and teacher evaluation reproducing hierarchical structures (Farini 2011; Margutti 2010; Seedhouse 2004; Walsh 2011) that often limit the opportunities of children to participate (James & James 2004; Wyness 1999). For the SHARMED project, this traditional approach to classroom practice was rejected because it was accepted that the hierarchical IRE approach would children's agency and children's dialogue primacy within the classroom as required by the aims of the project.

It was crucial to the SHARMED project that classroom practice was designed to support co-equal relationships across all participants. It was essential that children's voices, their social and cultural identities and intercultural engagement should be made possible through the structure and conduct of the classroom. To this end, interactive classroom practice was designed to support non-hierarchical relationships between children and between children and the facilitator and included ways of evaluating the delivery and conduct of these interactions.

The facilitative pedagogy was designed to promote personalized versions of cultural meanings (Abdallah-Pretceille 2006) enabling the creation of small cultures through dialogic negotiation among participants. It was a key strategy designed to support two project imperatives – to mitigate hierarchical forms of teacher and child relationships and to fortify children's agency.

A number of writers promote the notion of children's agency (James 2009; James & James 2008; Oswell 2013). In this perspective, children's actions are not simple outputs of children's experience of adults' inputs. Showing agency means showing the availability of choices of action, opening different possible courses of action, so that a specific course of action is one among various possibilities (Baraldi 2014a; Harré & van Langhenove 1999). The project recognized children's agency as children's active participation enhanced through the availability of choices of action, which subsequently enhance alternative actions, and therefore change in the interaction. While children's active participation can happen anytime in communication, the achievement of agency needs the promotion of a child's right to active participation in relation to choice and construction of meaning. In the SHARMED project, by seeking children's agency and recognizing a child's right to construct their own narrative we enabled participants to contribute to collaborative and cultural understandings within their classroom communities – enabling them to gain epistemic authority (Heritage & Raymond 2005).

Some researchers argue that analysis of agency must focus on its social conditions and structures (Bjerke 2011; James 2009; Leonard 2016; Mayall 2002; Moosa-Mitha 2005). This research shows that structural limitations can be imposed on individual participation and these can be particularly inhibitive for children, who are often included within a hierarchical generational order (Alanen 2009).

Research on teacher–children interactions has highlighted some mitigation of hierarchical forms of epistemic status and authority, depending on adults' promotional actions (e.g. Mercer & Littleton 2007; Walsh 2011), such as actions of scaffolding (Seedhouse 2004; Sharpe 2008) or re-utterings (O'Connor & Michael 1996). Research has also highlighted a more radical change, based on facilitation of children's agency (Baraldi 2014a, 2014b; Baraldi & Iervese 2017; Hendry 2009; Wyness 2013). Baraldi (2014a) argues that facilitation is achieved in specific interactions, including organized sequences of adults' actions that enhance children's agency, and children's actions that display agency.

1.2.4.1 Facilitative Pedagogy and Dialogue

This study defines dialogue as a specific form of communication, which 'implies that each party makes a step in the direction of the other', while it does not imply 'that they reach a shared position or even mutual warm feelings' (Wierzbicka 2006: 692). In adult–children interactions, dialogue is 'the starting point, whereby children are consulted and listened to', ensuring that 'their ideas are taken seriously' (Matthews 2003: 268). In facilitation, adult's active participation supports children's self-expression, takes children's views into account, involves them in decision-making processes and shares power and responsibility with them (Shier 2001; Wyness 2013).

By combining the energy of dialogue and a model of facilitation, The SHARMED project activated agents of change designed to facilitate children's authorship of stories and their empowerment. Research by Baraldi and Iervese (2017) indicates that facilitation of narrative production can be analysed as dealing with children as agents who can choose the ways and contents of narratives regarding their perspectives and experiences, thus influencing the social situations in which they are involved. Facilitation also enables the construction of new, alternative narratives with respect to existing ones (Winslade & Monk 2008; Winslade & Williams 2012), thus enhancing communities of dialogue.

1.2.4.2 Facilitative Pedagogy and Conflict

The project recognized that by enhancing children's choice of action, facilitation can also heighten the potential for the emergence of conflict involving children. Luhmann (1995) suggests that conflicts may block or challenge the existing conditions of communication. However, conflicts may also provide a starting point for new conditions of communication, through conflict management.

The project also recognized that conflicts are often managed through judgemental actions, for example siding with a 'right' party against a 'wrong' party. Across the project, facilitation was designed to avoid the use of judgemental actions, enabling parties to settle their disputes rather than imposing a judgement (Mulcahy 2001). This approach interprets facilitation as a way of co-ordinating conflicting parties, dealing with their opposing preferences and modifying their relationship, i.e. including conflict mediation. Facilitative actions can enhance conflict mediation as empowerment and transformation of relationships (Bush & Folger 1994), and mediation between different narratives, giving voice to children's first-person stories (Winslade & Williams 2012). Facilitators may actively intervene as providers of opportunities to talk, dealing with conflicts and constructing narratives of these conflicts. Thus, facilitators may encourage participants' contributions, check reciprocal understanding and avoid dominance behaviours, which can block communication.

1.3 SHARMED: A European Project

The SHARMED project was designed to influence and contribute to European policy and practice in relation to educational inclusion, enhancement of acceptance and promotion of participation for children with migrant backgrounds into European schools. For this purpose, SHARMED was developed and implemented in three countries (Gemany, Italy and the United Kingdom), with different social and cultural settings. These different contexts provided different educational experiences for children with migrant backgrounds – based on different types and forms of educational policies. SHARMED was implemented in a variety of situations, which was wide enough to allow the elaboration of models to be potentially adaptable to other situations and countries in Europe. As a European-wide project, the study sought to simultaneously engage a range of integrated educational capabilities across all three countries:

- pedagogical innovations and training for teaching,
- technological support for intercultural learning and
- evaluative research on classroom facilitation and children's participation.

SHARMED has produced new knowledge, training and recommendations to support the education of children with migrant backgrounds, as well as children with non-migrant backgrounds. Ultimately, the contribution of the SHARMED project to European education policy and practice is based on the successful development of educational facilitative strategies including the combined use of:

(1) shared cultural memories,
(2) visual materials,
(3) methodologies of facilitation and dialogic teaching,
(4) non-essentialist forms of intercultural learning and adaptation and
(5) advanced technologies for learning and dissemination.

In terms of sustainability, SHARMED has produced guidelines for a facilitative methodology, a package for teacher's training made available as a Massive Open Online Course (MOOC), and a web exchange system. This includes an archive of visual materials, representing the cultural richness which can be produced in the classroom. The SHARMED outcomes converge to influence the attitudes of decision-makers, to extend methods of teaching, improve quality of education for all children and provide guidelines for practices in Europe. Its influence extends through the micro-level (teacher–student communication), the meso-level (educational institutions) and the macro-level (educational system and educational policy). SHARMED may affect the European educational culture by enhancing the understanding of European citizens as cosmopolitan citizens.

1.4 Methodology Preamble

The methodology was implemented in schools across three European countries. First, school meetings were organized with principals and teachers to explain the project. The participating classes were chosen by the schools, according to teachers' interest and the inclusion of children with migrant backgrounds. In each country, the project partners trained volunteer teachers to become facilitators to conduct SHARMED interventions.

The project activities were preceded by a survey, administered to investigate children and their parents' social and cultural background (see Chapter 2). The project activities included a preliminary as well as a final training for the involved teachers and facilitators (see Chapter 10), the collection of two sets of photographs (see Chapter 3): the first set included photograph collected from family or children's personal archives (digitally or printed); the second set included photographs taken by the children.

The project activities were centred around series of four meetings held in each classroom. In the first two meetings, children were invited to describe and discuss the first set of photographs, initially within small groups, subsequently with the whole classroom. Triggered by the photographs, both personal narratives and dialogue were enhanced through the interaction between children and facilitators. In the third meeting, children were invited to describe the photographs in a written form, guided by some loose guidelines. Although the descriptions of the photographs will not be analysed in this book, they provided further useful information to better understand the meaning of photographs for children. The fourth and last meeting was dedicated to the children's presentation of the second set of photographs. This meeting was rather similar to the first one, although children were asked to make short video-recordings to describe the photographs they took, supported by the facilitators where necessary. The aim of the production of video-recorded descriptions was to enhance children's autonomy in line with the upgraded role as authors of the photograph, whilst facilitating the more personalized narratives in the classroom.

Classroom activities were evaluated combining participants' views and analysis of interactions. With regard to participants' view on the activities, pre-test and post-test questionnaires, as well as a final short focus group, were administered to children. Audio-recorded interviews were administered to teachers and facilitators. The analysis of such research materials is discussed in Chapter 9. Regarding the analysis of interaction, half of the activities in the classrooms were video-recorded, and the recordings were transcribed and analysed to understand the efficacy of the activities in promoting innovative education. The analysis of the video-recorded interactions is discussed in Chapters 3–8. The most interesting materials emerging from the analysis of the activities, chosen according to their ability to document the educational meaning of the project, were archived in a secured section of the SHARMED website (see Chapter 11).

Throughout all its phases, the research followed the key principles of ethical research, securing the emotional well-being, physical well-being, rights, dignity and personal values of research participants. Research participants were fully informed regarding the purpose, methods and end use of the research, what their participation was going to involve and any foreseeable although remote risks associated with it. Safeguarding processes aiming to protect children were in place across the whole research process. All participants were provided an information sheet, with an informed consent form attached. The children were provided an appropriately simplified information sheet. In order to meet the possible needs of individual participants with English as an additional language, the researchers were available to explain the information sheet verbally. Contact with gatekeepers and teachers allowed the researchers to ascertain if any participant needed linguistic support to understand the information sheet and informed consent form. Although children were asked to participate, the researchers and facilitators were trained to constantly monitor verbal and non-verbal communication from children to ensure that they were willing participants, in line with the consideration for their right of self-determination.

Procedures were in place for the management of any form of data produced in the research. Questionnaires were anonymous, and the data produced through the use of questionnaires were collated and presented exclusively in an aggregated form. All questionnaires were stored in a secure, locked cupboard within each university's premises. Audio- and video-recorded data were encrypted and stored in password-protected computers. All researchers involved in the production and analysis were experienced professionals and committed to ensure confidentiality of data. The identity of the participants was, and will not be, revealed at any stage of the research, including dissemination of results. All data was securely kept for twelve months after the end of the research and destroyed after that. Nevertheless, a small amount of video-observations in the form of short clips was used as examples for reflective learning within the training package that the project was committed to produce for the European Union. The video clips were stored in a password-secured platform, administered by the project consortium. No interaction involving sensitive personal issues was selected as training material.

1.5 The Structure of the Book

This text is presented entirely in English but it is essential to recognize that data from Italy and Germany were obtained in the native languages of Italian and German respectively. The Italian and German data and results presented in the text are therefore translations of the original transcripts.

This chapter has introduced the SHARMED project and explored the conceptual foundations and methodology of this two-year project. It presented the rationale for the use of a facilitative pedagogy to stimulate intercultural understanding by creating communities of dialogue within classroom settings. The results of research into the social and cultural backgrounds of children and parents suggest that a focus on social relationships, both in the classrooms and between families and schools, is pivotal for achieving a better understanding of the educational experiences of children – particularly children from migrant backgrounds.

Chapters, 2, 3, 4 and 5 provide a detailed picture of the methodological principles and methods used by the SHARMED project to develop innovation in pedagogical practice. In Chapter 2 some key findings from this research are explored and analysed, and the chapter discusses how such an understanding can, in turn, enhance the use of and for innovative pedagogies in the classroom. Chapter 3 focuses on the use of photographs and examines the ways in which narratives can be generated from photographs. It explores three crucial aspects of the methodology developed for the SHARMED project – the specificity of photography as a medium, facilitative pedagogy around the use of photographs and the active participation of children. Chapter 4 explores how the production of narratives can promote children's participation and the negotiation of children's identities. This chapter presents an analysis of the different modes of narrative production (interactive production, co-production, intertwined narratives) and examines links to the different narrative forms (ontological, public and meta-narrative). It focuses on (a) methods by which narrative rights are linked to the direct or indirect experience of events as negotiated, (b) narratability as a conversation resource and as a risk for participants and (c) the ways in which narratives are structured according to the forms of participation activated in the classroom. Chapter 5 reports on children's stories and examines the contents and meanings of photographs and memories in classroom. This chapter discusses the results of the SHARMED classroom intervention and explores the use of dialogic communications, including examination of features such as comparing and sharing of photographs and stories.

Chapters 6, 7 and 8 explore practice in the classroom and the pedagogical management approaches used to develop SHARMED communities of dialogue. Chapter 6 explores children's unpredictable initiatives and deals with two aspects related to these initiatives: the types of initiatives taken by children during facilitative dialogue and facilitators' ways of dealing with these initiatives. These two aspects are particularly important since children's initiatives show their agency better than their other actions. Chapter 6 also examines ways of coordinating children's initiatives and managing children's interruptions and innovations. In Chapter 7 the concept of dialogic intercultural competence is examined, and in relation to pedagogical management the chapter explores the importance of intercultural competence for teachers. This chapter also presents dialogic intercultural competence as essential for developing intercultural understanding as a foundation for strengthening the fabric of multiculturalism in school communities. Chapter 8 explores how the project facilitated classroom interactions and examines classroom conflict in two ways – as narrative and as interactional disputes between children. This chapter argues that the extent to which conflicts arise depends on the school context and the strategies employed in facilitative pedagogy. The chapter also recognizes that facilitative pedagogy does not specifically help children to manage their conflictive relationships and must be managed effectively by facilitators.

Chapters 9, 10 and 11 explore some of the sustainable outcomes derived from the project and present the resulting learning materials that continue to be made available to educators in Europe and beyond. The SHARMED methodology remains a substantial feature of this three country project, and Chapter 9 explores methodological issues. It examines the project's initiatives and interventions in classrooms and schools and reflects on methodological innovations in the project. It questions assumptions and tendencies within pedagogical practice and embraces the possibilities of imagining new initiatives in practice. The project was designed to ensure sustainable outcomes, and Chapter 10 explores the application of the facilitation methodology to train facilitators and the development of a SHARMED model for training facilitators. It also reports on the results of developing an e-training manual and a sustainable MOOC with guidelines and a multimedia archive. Chapter 11 reveals the value and relevance of the SHARMED digital archive for teachers and practitioners and promotes the broad scope of use for this digital resource which is available free of charge.

Chapter 12 presents a condensed version of the conclusions drawn by the collaborating three research teams. This concluding chapter reflects on the achievements of the SHARMED project. It also explores the project's innovative pedagogy and its success in cementing intercultural understanding among diverse communities of young people.

2

Grounding Innovative Pedagogy: Social and Educational Experiences of Children

Claudio Baraldi and Federico Farini

2.1 Introduction

For any project of educational intervention, it is important to explore children's social and educational experiences in school and in the family that constitute the contexts of their participation. Dimensions of children's experiences such as language skills, cultural presupposition of classroom communication, peer relationships and others must be considered when planning educational project that will necessarily interact with them.

To explore children's experiences in the classroom and in the family for the development of educational activities, SHARMED proposed a survey to the forty-eight participating classrooms (see Chapter 1). In conclusion of the survey, 938 children as well as 1,004 parents/guardians had returned the questionnaires. The purpose of this chapter is to illustrate how data regarding the contexts of children participation can be important to construct innovative educational practices that are sensitive to the social and educational experiences of children. The first pieces of data presented in the chapter reveal some general characteristics of both participating children (Table 2.1) and parents (Table 2.2).

Table 2.1 Children

Country	Total number	Males (%)	Females (%)	Primary schools (%)	Secondary schools (%)	Speaking national language (%)	Speaking foreign language (%)	Bilinguals (%)
Italy	358	50.7	49.3	53.1	46.9	56.2	18.6	25.1
Germany	223	50.9	49.1	66.8	33.2	81.8	13.6	4.6
United Kingdom	357	51.3	48.7	100	-	34.2	65.8	

Table 2.2 Parents

Country	Total	Men	Women	Primary schools	Secondary schools	NSP	PSFLB	24–39	40–49	50+
Italy	455	42.9	56.8	52.5	47.5	62.6	37.4	29.9	54.9	15.2
Germany	302	33.4	66.6	69.5	30.5	80.1	19.9	61.6	30.1	8.3
United Kingdom	247	41.1	58.9	100	–	44.6	55.4	56.2	34.9	8.8

In SHARMED, the negligible difference between males and females indicates a balanced participation by gender. The age of participating children was not uniformly distributed in SHARMED. Whilst proportions between primary schools and secondary schools children were balanced in Italy, primary schools children were more numerous in Germany. In the UK, only primary schools were involved in the project (see Chapter 1), and this is reflected in the data.

The language most frequently used by participants was a pivotal piece of information for SHARMED, because it was not possible to ask a direct question about the nationality or the national background consequently to a veto imposed by German educational authorities. Data concerning the most used language at home were selected as an indicator of 'non-national' background of children in the context of SHARMED. Based on data, children were divided into three groups: the ones who only speak the national language, (National Speaking Children, NSC); the ones who speak exclusively another language, at least at home (Children Speaking Foreign Language, CSFL) and the ones who use the national language of their place of residence and at least an additional language when at home (Bilingual Children, BC).

The UK context is unique with regard to children's use of language: whilst children who report to have a first language other than English (defined as Speakers of Other Languages, SOL) are a quite large majority, nevertheless almost all of them can speak English very well or well, resulting in a high percentage of bilingual children (94 per cent of SOL). In Italy, CSFL and BC are a minority, with a prevalence of BC as many migrant children are long-term residents. In Germany, BC are very few and also CSFL are not many. The German data can be explained with a reference to the context of the German branch of SHARMED: the project, therefore the initial survey, took place in two federal states that were part of former GDR, where immigration processes are quite recent and consisting for a relevant part in the relocation of refugees.

A distinction is made between parents speaking only the national language of their place of residence (NSP) on the one hand and parents who speak exclusively another language, combined with parents who use the national language of their place of residence and at least an additional language when at home (PSFLB) on the other hand. It is possible to recognize that the use of language does not necessarily indicate a migrant status, because NSP may also be migrants, particularly in the UK due to the global status of the English language. In the UK, the percentage of PSFLB is lower than the percentage of CSFL+BC, suggesting a somehow limited engagement in the research. In Germany, a limited number of parents with migrant background returned the questionnaire, notwithstanding the availability of translated versions for non-German speakers. As a side comment, the German case suggests that preliminary research could offer pivotal information to SHARMED innovative education planning, for instance evidencing a limited engagement of parents, particularly parents with migrant background, inviting to consider the implications for future projects.

Young parents are more numerous in Germany and in the UK than in Italy. Even if the higher number of participating children in secondary education that characterizes the Italian branch of SHARMED can partially explain this piece of data, different parenting patterns can be considered. Most parents who returned the questionnaire were women, suggesting that mothers often represent the first line of parental involvement in children's education.

2.2 Social and Interpersonal Relationships in School and other Social Contexts

Children's positive assessment of relationships with teachers is rather frequent. However, at the same time the area of 'critical' assessment is not marginal, ranging between 17 and 30 per cent across the three contexts. Moreover, positive assessment of social relationships does not mean cultivating an interest in social relationship: a small minority of children indicate a preference for communicating with teachers. Rather, most of the children indicate friends and, albeit to less extent, classmates, as preferred interlocutors. Also, communication does not necessarily entail personal matters. Few children affirm not to talk about personal matters with others; communication about personal matters demands intense interpersonal communication: friends (more frequently in Italy and in the UK) and parents (more frequently in the UK and in Germany) are indicated as primary interlocutors. SHARMED data show ambivalent feelings towards communicating about personal matters: a slight majority of children in Italy indicate positive feelings (helpful, normal, funny) as opposed to a majority in the UK indicating negative feelings (embarrassing, strange, impossible, waste of time), whilst the proportion is balanced in Germany.

Children show positive perception of peers' attitudes to social relationships; peers are connoted as friendly, funny, helpful and nice. However, negative perception of peers (boring, nasty, aggressive and annoying) is chosen by a non-marginal minority of the returned questionnaires, particularly in the UK (above 40 per cent). The planning of SHARMED educational intervention could take advantage of data-driven knowledge concerning the ambivalence of children's representation of peers' attitude.

Producing data concerning social relationships between children and adults, in particular teachers and parents, is key for projects of educational intervention such as SHARMED. Most children who returned the questionnaire offer a description of adults as helpful as well as nice, particularly in Italy and in Germany. As a general interpretation of data, the perception of adults seems to be more positive in Germany. Many children describe adults as friendly and funny in the UK. However, 20–25 per cent of children describe adults as rarely or never friendly, more frequently in Italy and in the UK. Regarding negative assessment of relationships, adults are considered boring by a percentage of children ranging from 24 per cent (Germany) to 40 per cent (Italy), annoying by a percentage of children ranging from 11 per cent (Germany) to 35 per cent (UK). Potentially more problematic with regard to children's attitude towards the project is the perception of adults as always or often nasty (4 per cent in the UK, 12 per cent in Germany, almost 25 per cent in Italy) or aggressive (4 per cent in Germany, 6.4 per cent in the UK, about 10 per cent in Italy).

2.3 Problems and Disagreements

Interestingly, SHARMED data suggest that children experience relational problems with schoolmates and friends more often than with adults. However, except for a small minority, children do not consider cross-gender disagreement to be particularly relevant. Differences in cultural habits were considered problematic in Italy and Germany, where children seem to give importance to cultural characteristics more than what children do in the UK.

The survey also presented to the SHARMED team important data concerning classroom relationships: in particular, disagreement with classmates is experienced by a sizeable group of children across all contexts (around 30 per cent). Data thus indicate possible problems for peer-communication, with differences related to the national contexts. This is an important piece of information for an educational intervention.

Management of disagreements is a related aspect: in Italy and in Germany, almost half of the children try to understand others' point of view, while taking side is chosen by about 13 per cent of children in Italy and very few in Germany. Choices in the UK do not differ, although understanding is more frequent and taking side less so. Whilst respondents seem aware of disagreements, they are not particularly inclined to explore the underpinnings of disagreements, which would entail taking others' perspective in their reflection. Dialogue, including both understanding others' point of view and mediation, is preferred by a majority of children in Italy and Germany but only by a third in the UK. An understanding of management of disagreements as imposing opinions on others is very frequent across all contexts, and appear to be triggered by others' blaming, criticizing and failing to understand, with some variation across contexts.

2.4 Attitudes to Dialogue

Dialogue can materialise through several empirical actions. These actions include equality in participation; listening before talking; believing the interlocutors' words; awareness of the consequences of actions on others; asking for confirmation and clarifications; checking interlocutors' feelings before expressing own feelings; respecting and understanding interlocutors' opinions; lack of judgement; looking for shared solutions of disagreements. SHARMED questionnaire aimed to explore how often children experience dialogic actions in the classroom, because the familiarity with dialogic actions is a useful information to gather for a project like SHARMED, interested in promoting dialogic pedagogy. A large majority of children observe equality in the possibility of participation both with teachers and with classmates. However, this is largely context-dependent data with regard to the individual dialogic actions: equality was observed more frequently in the UK, less in Germany and to an even lesser extent in Italy.

With regard to the dialogic action 'listening before talking', children frequently listen to both teachers and classmates. However, this piece of data is context-dependent too, from a highest relevance in Italy, decreasing in Germany and reaching the lowest level in the UK, where data suggest that equality in participation is not necessarily associated with listening to others. Continuing with the discussion of how dialogic actions are relevant in children's experiences, a great majority of children believe what both teachers and classmates say, with the UK marking a partial difference as children believe classmates' words less than teachers' words. Children are aware of the consequences of their actions for others, another important component of dialogue, albeit less frequently so in the UK. The majority of children ask for confirmation of the correctness of their understanding or clarifications to classmates in Italy and in Germany, but not in the UK, where they represent a minority (42 per cent), suggesting that in the UK context communication with peers can be more challenging than communication with teachers. This is important data for a project like SHARMED, because the promotion of children's narratives in the classroom can take advantage from knowing children's experiences of communication with peers. Checking classmates' feelings is more frequent that checking teachers' feelings in the Italian and German data. This is important data that suggest limited emotional tuning with teachers in Italy and Germany, and with classmates in the UK. Respect of opinions was very frequently claimed by respondents both in communication with classmates and with teachers. Data suggest that lack of judgement is the dialogic action experienced with the greatest deal of difference across the contexts of the research. The majority of participating children report lack of judgements about classmates and teachers in the UK and in Italy, whilst in Germany a majority of children judge classmates and, less frequently, teachers. Another dialogic action such as looking for shared solutions to disagreement in communication with both classmates and teachers is frequent in Germany and less frequent in Italy and in the UK, although still advocated by a majority of respondents.

2.5 Differences Related to Language and Migration Background, School Grade and Gender

Differences Related to Language and Migration

Data concerning the effect of the use of different languages and migration background on social relationships and communication are important for a project of innovative education like SHARMED, where children's active participation to communication, in particular as authors of narratives, is considered an important indicator of agency.

For children participating in SHARMED, the effects of linguistic background and migrant background do not seem to be particularly relevant. For instance, no correlation between problems of communication and language or migrant background, was observed. Migrant children may have a more negative perception of peers' attitudes and peer relationships but they have a more positive perception of attitudes and relationships with adults, particularly with teachers. Management of disagreement is less frequently based on understanding and more frequently based on persuasion and taking side for children with migrant background.

Data concerning CSFL (Italy) as well as SOL (UK) indicate that communication with friends is less frequent for them than for other children. The same result is true for communication between CSFLB and classmates. Communication between CSFL and their classmates is frequent; however, CSFL dislike communication with classmates more frequently. It is less common for CSFL to listen to classmates, to check their feelings, to look for shared solutions and to refrain from judging. CSFLB are less inclined to see peers as helpful and nice, and more inclined to see them as nasty. CSFLB check classmates' feelings much less frequently, and share solutions to problems with classmates less frequently; they also understand classmates less frequently and disagree more often with them, as well as with friends outside of the classroom. SOL in the UK consider peers to be often nasty and annoying, and are less prepared to recognize them as helpful. SOL disagree more frequently with friends and classmates.

The results of the survey put communication between children and adults in more positive, albeit rather nuanced, light. CSFL consider adults as funny, nice, friendly, never boring and never annoying. However, CSFL also see adults as nasty more frequently than other children. Moreover, more CSFL and SOL assess relationships with teachers as critical. Nevertheless, CSFL and SOL see relationships with teachers as more intense than peers. SOL believe teachers' words much more frequently; they are more frequently active in asking to teachers, checking teachers' feelings and in understanding them. CSFL declare positive relations with teachers more frequently, observe equal relationships with teachers and listen to teachers more frequently than what they do with classmates. CSFL affirm to respect teachers more frequently than other children, and are more frequently active in asking them. CSFLB represent more frequently positive relations with adults, in particular with teachers, observing equal relationships and listening more frequently than with classmates, as well as respecting teachers more frequently that respecting classmates. However, CSFLB also perceive more adults' negative attitudes, are less prepared to define adults as nice and friendly, and are more inclined to define them as boring, nasty, annoying and aggressive. The results of the survey suggest team some ambivalence at the intersection between children's background and their assessment of social relationships; however, it made possible for the SHARMED team to make use of an important piece information in the implementation of the activities: CSFL, CSFLB and SOL experience less problems with teachers than with peers.

The results of the survey show the SHARMED team a nuanced picture with regard to the implication of migrant background: CSFL observe less frequently problems of communication, except with regard to communication with parents. CSFLB perceive less problems of communication as well, but they more frequently react to problems by forcing their own opinions on others, if they believe that others do not behave carefully or do not do the right thing. However, they also avoid judgements much more frequently.

Differences between Primary and Secondary Schools

As a general result, the analysis of data reveals that positive communication and relationships are less common when transitioning from primary schools to secondary schools. This is a very important piece of information to support the implementation of a research across different school levels. In primary schools, children consider peers as nice and helpful, never finding them boring, nasty and aggressive. On the contrary, children in secondary schools rarely find peers nice and helpful. Dialogue appears to be more frequent in primary schools, where children more frequently recognize equality with teachers and classmates. Primary school children also believe, respect and understand teachers, refrain from judging, actively ask to classmates and teachers, check classmates' feelings.

In secondary schools, disagreement is less frequent with friends, but much more common with adults. Children in secondary schools more frequently see relationships with teachers as critical. Talking of personal matters in secondary schools appears more difficult.

There are, however, some ambivalences. Relational problems are more frequently perceived in primary schools, suggesting that younger children are particularly sensitive towards these problems. While in Italy appreciation for talking with both classmates and teachers declines in secondary schools, in Germany the opposite can be observed. Equality with classmates and believing classmates are more frequent in German secondary schools, while shared solutions of disagreement with classmates are more common in Italian secondary schools.

Differences Related to Gender

The results of the SHARMED survey do not support the idea of important differences related to gender across the three contexts of the research. In all contexts, males prefer talking with friends and perceive more problems in communication. Females get along with everybody but also disagree more often with parents. Females experience more frequently dialogic actions, e.g. listening to and understanding classmates, believing classmates and teachers, finding shared solutions of disagreement with classmates.

Communication about personal matters with classmates in Italy and with parents in the UK is more common for females but communication about personal matters with teachers is more frequent among males in the UK. Males are more frequently critical of relationships with teachers in Italy, but this is true for females in Germany. Data suggest that females more often talk about personal matters, but either do not fully trust personal disclosure or do not discuss about *important* personal matters.

In Italy, females are less inclined to acknowledge peers as helpful, and more inclined to describe them as boring, nasty and annoying, while in Germany they see peers as helpful more frequently. In Italy and in the UK, females consider more frequently adults funny and friendly; on the contrary, in Germany females entertain a less positive image of adults. Data suggest that females offer a self-representation as more collaborative and nicer to others than males both in Italy and in the UK, but not so in Germany. Males declare to disagree with teachers more in Italy and above all in the UK, and to disagree with classmates more in Italy and Germany. Males manage disagreement by persuading and less frequently by understanding and asking for help both in Italy and in the UK contexts, where females show a more frequent interest in dialogue. In Germany, females are mindful about the consequences of their actions, avoid judgements and are proactive in asking classmates for support. In Italy and in Germany, females more frequently state to be active in asking teachers as well.

2.6 Integration of the family

Parents' experience of participation in communication can be used to produce a picture of their integration. The results of the survey indicate that a large majority of parents feel to be integrated in their social and cultural contexts. However, in Italy and particularly in Germany PSFLB seem to feel less integrated.

A large majority of parents in the UK and about half of the parents in Italy and Germany feel comfortable communicating with all neighbours. Relationships with neighbours are considered positively by a large majority of parents. Indifference is the prevailing negative aspect of parents' relationships with neighbours (30 per cent in Italy and 20 per cent in the UK), and it is more frequent among PSFLB in Italy and Germany. In Germany, lack of friendship and disagreement are other negative aspects of communication with parents. In Italy, tensions are frequently experienced, as well as exclusion, although the latter in a smaller minority of cases. Although problems in communication with neighbours do not necessarily depend on language and culture diversity, in Italy and Germany a relatively large minority of PSFLB experience problems of relationships with neighbours.

A large majority of parents feel comfortable in communication with all other parents, more often in the UK than in Italy and Germany. Almost all parents observe respect, understanding, trust, appreciation, harmony and agreement in communication with others. The most frequent negative aspects related to relationships concern indifference, lack of friendship and disagreement. Tensions, lack of respect and exclusion are observed more frequently among parents of children in primary schools. This piece of data suggested to the SHARMED team that relationships among parents could be more problematic in primary schools, with implications for the implementation of the project. Although the majority of PSFLB report not to have any problem in communication with others, the ones who experience difficulties do so more often in the context of school than in the neighbourhood.

In Italy as well as in the UK, the majority of parents feel comfortable communicating with all teachers; this is only partially true in the German context. Positive relationships with teachers are described by almost all parents across the contexts of the research. Whilst negative aspects seem to be marginal in Italy and Germany, PSFLB feel more frequently uncomfortable communicating with teachers, while SOL in the UK express more frequently positive assessment of communication with teachers. In Italy, parents feel more frequently uncomfortable communicating with teachers in secondary schools.

A vast majority of parents feel involved in the school community, although only a minority (one-fourth in Italy and one-third in Germany) feel *strongly* involved. In Italy, PSFLB both feel more frequently to be strongly involved and more frequently to be not involved than the average. In the UK, SOL parents less frequently affirm to be involved in the school community. Across all contexts, males are less involved. In secondary schools, parents feel less involved in school community. Although still high, the declining percentage of males and PFSLB/SOL who feel involved in school community as children move into secondary education indicates two potential areas of disengagement or marginalization, which represented a useful piece of information for the implementation of SHARMED.

2.7 Conclusion

Some general conclusions can be drawn concerning the importance for projects of innovative education of producing preliminary data on the social and cultural backgrounds of children and parents' experiences.

The results of the survey made the SHARMED team aware that social relationships and communication can be more problematic with classmates than with teachers. Moreover, relations and communication with classmates can be more frequently problematic for children with migrant background and linguistic difficulties. Positive relations with teachers flourish when they are based on mutual trust. Children with migrant background often refer good relationships with teachers, and less often with their classmates.

The second point emerging from the analysis of the survey is that the transition from primary school to secondary school can be problematic. Communication seems to be more difficult in secondary schools, with teachers as well as with classmates, although primary school children seem to be more sensitive towards relational problems. Gender differences have a limited impact on several relational aspects. A more positive attitude towards relationships among females can be observed, but the difference is not striking. A third point concerns parents with migrant background who signal to feel integrated in their social contexts displaying positive relations with all interlocutors (neighbours, other parents and teachers). However, a minority of parents feel to be affected by some relational problems, with indifference emerging as the main one. Parents' involvement in the school community is more common in primary school than in secondary school. As an overall observation based on data from the survey, the position of parents from migrant background appears to cohere around two extremes: full involvement or limited participation.

A fourth and final point concerns country-related differences which may be based both on organization of education and schooling and type of migration. In Italy, interpersonal relationships are more frequently seen as conflictive and difficult, are less frequently seen as equal. This could be related to the high number of secondary schools children in the Italian context, where inclusion of children with migrant background is more difficult and personal problems become more stringent. In the UK only primary school children participated in the activities but still, problems concerning interpersonal relationships in the classroom are perceived. In the UK, difference between migrants and non-migrant children are minimal, possibly due to more socially and culturally equipped migrant families as well as to almost absent linguistic problems for migrant children. In Germany, activities were undertaken in the East of the country, where teaching seems to be organized in a more traditional way and, at the time of the project, recent arrival of refugees, with language problems, created several difficulties in this otherwise monocultural context. This could explain why participants in Germany more frequently observed difficulties in interpersonal relationships. However, conflicts are very rare also in the German contexts.

Part One

Facilitation of Children's Participation

3

Use of Photographs

Vittorio Iervese

3.1 Introduction

In today's world, images have an immense power, which is particularly evident in photography, which gives the impression of taking over reality like no other medium. This authority can be attributed to two main factors: the great technological facility of producing and sharing images at any time of the day and the probative effect they apparently generate. Despite the many criticisms of the image's direct relationship with reality, photography is still acknowledged as having the capacity to witness something, whether it be an event, a revelation, a truth. These qualities allow the image to be part of a multimodal communicative process in which everyone can potentially participate, regardless of differences in gender, age or expertise. Therefore, pictures should not be treated separately from the practices they generate, as limited and fixed objects, but rather in order to understand how their use and meaning varies according to the contexts and communication processes in which they are embedded. According to Dinoi (2012: 12): 'the image is not so important for what it shows, but for what it becomes a relation of, for what it is able to relate and for the very form of that relation.' Starting from this reversal of perspective, the ways in which images can be addressed both as an object of study and as a research tool also vary. By academic tradition and according to the classical theories of representation, we have been used to researching the 'content' of images by asking ourselves questions such as: 'what does it mean?', 'what does it contain?', 'what is inside?', 'what does the author want to express?' A series of studies that have emerged since the end of the last century (Curtis 2010; Mitchell 2005) have generated an epistemological reversal in the study of images. The so-called pictorial turn has suggested, for example, that previous questions be added to or replaced with such as 'What is he asking? What is it looking for? Where does that image want to lead me?' Images are thus understood as part of a complex interplay between visuality, social systems, institutions, discourse, bodies and figurativity. Moreover, images become part of an inextricable network of cross-references between immaterial images (images) and material images (pictures) produced and exchanged daily (Iervese 2016). In this network, the iconic and narrative dimensions mix and mutually feed each other.

In SHARMED, images were treated as a medium and form of communication rather than as documents of a reality to be recognized and explained. The children were not asked to report on the meanings hidden behind the images they brought to class but to use the images as part of a system of interactions. The first interaction is that between the visual and narrative dimensions; the second is that which links to a communicative dimension in which other pictures and other participants are involved. Each picture refers to one or more images, which refer to a wider symbolic image inventory that we can call 'imagery'. This imagery unfolds in co-constructed narratives. In this regard, Walter Benjamin (1997) argued that history is dispersed through images and aggregated into narratives; each narrative uses as material to be put together mental and social images dispersed in a dense and complex network.

3.2 Photographs as a Tool for Promoting Children's Expression

Images are a particularly powerful and effective tool for activating children's narratives and participation. In particular, photographs can be considered 'condensed narratives' (Langford 2001) or 'stores of meaning' (Vaccari in: Panaro 2009). Both of these concepts suggest that photography has an implicit creative and cognitive potential that unfolds as it connects with the viewer's experience, transforming into narratives. As it does so, the image connects with an external imagery producing further associations and further images (Iervese 2017). In particular, photographs have been considered a powerful medium for triggering memories (Norrick 2013) and thus stimulating children's narratives of their experiences. To make the most of this activation capability, children were asked to talk not only about what they found within the frame but also about what could be reconstructed behind and around it. The narratives collected concerned, for example, the circumstances in which the photograph was taken or the relationships between the people portrayed in the photograph, going beyond the reading of the photographed image.

Thus, we move from a use of photography based on its self-evident informational value and its ability to be a 'transparent reflection of fact' (Samuel 1996) to an approach that is more concerned with eliciting questions than answers.

Looked at in this way, as evidence of something beyond itself, a photograph can best be understood not as an answer or an end to enquiry, but as an invitation to look more closely, and to ask question (Gourevitch & Morris 2009: 148).

The primary tool of this methodology is photo-elicitation (Kelly & Kortegast 2018), which involves conducting interviews or focus groups in which participants are asked to explain their images or react to images shared by researchers (Douglas 1998; Harper 2010; Harrington & Lindy 1998; Harrison 2002). Thus, photo-elicitation uses images as stimuli for discussion in a similar way to questions in an interview. In these cases, the researcher focuses primarily on the meaning attributed to the images or the information they display. An evolution of these methods can be found in some, recent research experiences that use the tool called photovoice, which puts participants in the role of experts (Latz 2012) called to relate images to their lived experiences. Photovoice attempts to step outside the frame of the image to investigate what is hidden or not immediately visible but related to the events experienced by the subjects involved in the research. Both photo-elicitation and photovoice restrict the method to the collection of opinions and interpretations that photographs can reveal. In SHARMED, on the other hand, photography was used as a medium capable of capturing moments of personal life, helping to express personal feelings and preserve memory, and as an enabler of interactions and relationships among participants. In SHARMED, photographs were used to unlock memories using images that had previously been produced and performed. Photographs reflect a lived past inviting recall, recreation and reminiscence. In this view, photographs can be considered as a perceptual medium of communication, which 'can be recognized only by the contingency of the formations that make them possible' (Luhmann 2000: 104). On the one hand, photographs are visual forms that can be transmitted across contexts and can be retrieved and manipulated via an array of resources. On the other hand, photographs are a medium that can take narrative forms and can be retrieved and manipulated through the construction of a narrative.

This use of photography in social research with children makes the interactive production of narratives conditional on past actions (taking photos) that were designed for other purposes and only later become important in the specific context of the interaction. Thus, the activation phase exposes itself to the risk of unpredictability of interaction outcomes and relies on the agency of children, who are asked to act as interpreters and mediators between past experiences and actions in the present.

That visual media can engage children in creative workshops and thus can be used in research settings is well established (Moline 2011). What is less obvious is how to move away from an informational and monological paradigm (gathering opinions and then analysing and confronting them) to a communicative and dialogical one (stimulating participation and observing their forms). The assumption of SHARMED was that, as illustrated in the previous sections, the photograph not only elicits children's comments or reactions to visual input but can also be the starting point for a participatory dialogue in the classroom. In other words, the SHARMED approach aims to promote children's participation in communication through, about and with photographs. More specifically, the way photography triggers memory narratives can be explained by a number of studies on autobiographical memory (Glenberg 1997; Rubin 2006; Sutton & Williamson 2014). These studies show that depictions of past experiences are formed in the interaction between multimodal elements, i.e. through the coordination of visual, auditory, spatial and linguistic cues of memory.

In this regard, the difference between studium and punctum (Barthes 1980) allows us to understand how, when faced with an image, we can apply both an analytical and an emotional gaze. The first term of the distinction suggests an interest of the observer in relation to his own knowledge: studium is an interest in the information contained in the photograph. The punctum in the Barthesian framework is what captures the viewer of the photograph, what penetrates him/her independently of his/her will and produces a feeling, an emotional turmoil. Studium is observation of the image in its totality, punctum is the separation of details, often apparently unremarkable, that emotionally characterize the image for the viewer. The co-presence of studium and punctum leads the viewer beyond what the image shows at first glance and allows the photograph to move the viewer (Barthes 1980: 60). Narratives can be activated from either the studium or a punctum, but the resulting stories take on different characteristics.

3.3 Turning Images into Narratives

By comparing the specialized literature in the area of memory studies (Berntsen & Rubin 2012; Conway & Pleydell-Pearce 2000) and the analysis conducted during the SHARMED project, three general ways in which children transform images into narratives can be found.

First of all, the declarative mode, which uses the informative evidence in or about the photograph to report facts, data, or specific events: 'from the unique perspective of the self in relation to others' (Nelson & Fivush 2004: 488) or by assuming the perspective of a third person or even by moving from the first to the third person (Chapter 3). This method usually starts with specific information in order to build an overview, thus moving from the micro to the macro dimension. In some cases this extension does not happen and the narrative remains at a superficial level. In these cases, the facilitator suggests insights and personalization. Second, the semantic mode deals with general knowledge of the world, in terms of facts, ideas, meanings and concepts. This mode is based on memories that are not strictly biographical but have a direct or indirect impact on the biography of the narrator or those close to him or her. Historical events, cultural identity representations, etc. are often the outline around which narratives gather. The movement is from the macro to the micro, but the narrative may remain on a level of abstractness or genericness. In these cases, facilitator efforts aimed at connecting the narrative with the narrator's personal memories. Third, the emotional mode takes its starting point from particular cues that provoke very intense feelings and emotions. In these cases, the punctum that triggers the remembrance is crucial and the background information reinforces and confirms the main narrative. The narrative movement goes from the inside to the outside: from an extremely personal and intimate reading to one that provides reasons and causes for the event that provokes emotions. The facilitator in these cases displays empathy for the children but at the same time encourages additional narratives and co-narratives related to that initiating event. In this way, the narratives are enriched with other accounts which often act to both reassure and support the narrator in his or her storytelling.

These ways of transforming images into narratives do not cover all the cases observed during the workshops with the children, but they highlight the main features of that delicate point of convergence between the cognitive level (memory) and the communicative level (narration). Moreover, these are not absolute and unique modalities: in a number of cases, thanks also to facilitation efforts, narratives have switched from one modality to another, overlapping and hybridizing. This eventuality is also reported by memory studies: Brown and Kulik (1977) define flashbulb memories as those vivid and persistent memories of the circumstances of a significant and highly emotional event. A high degree of surprise, the ability to produce relevant consequences on the individual's life and the emotional activation level are the fundamental components of this kind of memories (Finkenauer et al. 1998).

In flashbulb memories, the declarative and emotional modalities mix and reinforce each other. The tellers are in these cases able to recall and then narrate in detail not only the memory of the event itself, but also the circumstances in which they learned the news, the place where they were, the time of day, the activity being carried out, the source of the news, the emotional reaction experienced at the time, the other people present and their emotional reaction, and the immediate consequences of the event. The following examples report the 'putting into narrative' of memories activated by photographic perception. The analysis attempts to indicate the most important parts of the complex process of transition from images to narratives outlined above.

> **Example 1 (Italy, SS3, first meeting)**
>
> F: 'this photo represents the Dracula castle, I went there on holidays in two thousand fourteen, in Romania, and I wanted so much to visit that castle, and: I love this photo because first it's taken in Romania, so it's from where my mother comes, and because it was a long time I wanted to go there.'

Example 1 is the opening of a narrative by a child in an Italian school. The modality is declarative: the girl introduces some data about a specific place where her mother comes from. The studium of the photograph prevails over the suggestive details, but the motivations behind the choice of this photograph are linked to an affective dimension. The connection between the declarative mode and the presentation of the self is very frequent even without any emotions or private background being called into play. In example 2, the presentation is declarative and uses a set of information (name, date of birth, weight). The photograph is therefore considered as a document able to report objective data and which at the same time establishes a comparison between the past and the present ('I didn't weigh that much').

> **Example 2 (UK, PS2, second meeting)**
>
> F: This shows my name, my date of birth and how much I weigh (…) I look at it now and I didn't weigh that much.

The declarative mode is therefore not detached from the personal dimension and can also introduce a description of the self through the inclusion of contextual information, such as a particular atmosphere. In example 3, this connection seems most clearly.

Example 3 (UK, PS3, second meeting)

F: ((Looks out to and talks to class)) Well as you can see I was eating, I was drinking soup but as you can see I'm not a clean person, so I got it all over my face. And I chose this picture because it was funny and it brought a lot of memories to me. And I found it special because everyone in my family was laughing and I wondered why they were laughing.

In this example, the photograph does not depict an exotic place or a singular event. The little girl describes a quite ordinary private scene which, however, allows her to present some aspects of her person ('as you can see I'm not a clean person') in a funny way in line with the amusing context of the story ('everyone in my family was laughing and I wondered why they were laughing'). The function of the exogram is also highlighted by the admission of the narrator who states how that simple image brought back many memories.

The semantic mode emerges especially in cases where the description of the photograph is linked to abstractions or generalizing interpretations.

Example 4 (Germany, SS1, first meeting)

M: (this photo) is like, like a symbol of happiness, because all of us when we are together with our loved ones we feel safe and serene.

Even when using a semantic mode, children do not hide the personal, relational and emotional sides. Even the most abstract interpretations often contain a background of lived life that brings them to an empirical and emotionally involved level, as in example 6.

Example 6 (Italy, SS1, 2A, third meeting)

F5: In the picture there's the moon and it's evening, and I took it because, not for this project, because I knew I had to take the picture, but I could see that it's practically under my house, and there's, there's, there's my house, there's these two buildings and looking up you could see the moon and the sky with the clouds really well. i.e. I really just liked it, it's in front of my front door and and I made my mom wait there to take the picture, but it's one of my favorite pictures and I used it a lot for… I mean I showed it to several people and I used it, I don't know, like for mes- whatsapp profile. I looked up at the sky because I usually look up at it, because when I was little they used to tell me that my grandfather was in a star next to the moon and so I like to look up at the sky, and when I looked up at the sky I saw that you could see the moon really well.

The emotional mode, unlike the previous ones, focuses on the emotions from which the motivation for the choice of the photograph and the information that clarifies its dynamics and meaning are derived, as in example 8.

Example 8 (Italy, PS1, first meeting)

1	M4:	((shrugs)) (.) I was happy and: ((turning towards the photo)) this here is a a: photo from when my sister had come out of the hospital in ((place)) a few days ago, and: me:
2	FAC:	the hospital … because she was born there, or because ….
3	M4:	she had been born there
4	FAC:	so not because she had been ill
5	M4:	no
6	FAC:	ah ok she had just been born
7	M4:	she was just born two days and I: was very happy and there was mom telling me:: how she felt, what my sister's name was,
8	(…)	
9	M4:	instead my dad took my picture and: and I chose this picture because: m: I liked it: I didn't even ask my parents for their opinion
10	FAC:	it [was your choice
11	M4:	[I asked: can I take a picture and I took one, that picture
12	FAC:	and you left some others that (.) could have been brought too, if you could have brought more would you have brought more?
13	M4:	one more

14	FAC:	like what? What did it represent?
15	M4:	my sister who: with her game.
16	FAC:	so you have a strong relationship with your sister.
17	M4:	m: ((does so-and-so with her hand)) even though we fight often.

In example 8, the photograph is almost an excuse for the narration. Rather, a central role is played by the emotion and the backstory not visible in the photograph. It is almost possible to guess the punctum that animates the narrator (the sister with the game) from which a more articulate and complex relational narrative arises.

Special attention should be paid to the flashbulb memories that combine declarative reconstruction with a strong personal participation. However, it is above all the accounts of public or private events, ceremonies and moments of transition that allow us to recognize flashbulb forms in the children's narratives. In example 9, a bus trip and a traffic accident are recounted. Accidents are often brought up as flashbulb memories, that is, more or less traumatic memories that leave permanent imprints in the memory, vivid images and a number of apparently insignificant details.

Example 9 (UK, PS3, second meeting)

When I was like about five years old, I went on a coach to a seaside near a castle, and what happened with that the coach driver was a bit crazy about cigarettes. And apparently he nearly crashed into a car, and I was where the window was and I was like really scared, 'mum can you save me?', 'can we get out of this coach please?', I was scared. But then the coach driver stopped because of like a huge accident, because like a child who was really young and a man who was really drunk drove a car and he crashed, and it didn't go on fire and the child was safe and the man, everyone was safe. But the police were like shouting move, come on, why are you in my head, like mummy why are the police being mean, but it was because that they wanted us to be safe.

Despite its brevity and simplicity, this narrative is remarkably evocative and compelling. The account of the trip, the details about the driver ('he was a bit crazy about cigarettes'), the multisensory components ('the police were like shouting moves'), the personal trauma that reappears with an introspective dialogue ('why are you in my head') make this story at once precise and intense. As is typical of narratives that stem from flashbulb memories, the description of the context and its details is overlapped with the intimate perspective of the narrator ('I was where the window was and I was like really scared').

3.4 Starting from a Photograph and Moving Elsewhere

Like the 'Portkey' described in the Harry Potter adventures, photographs can have the power to transport the viewer from one place to another and from one dimension to another. To do so, as mentioned at the beginning of this chapter, it is necessary to go beyond the borders of each photograph and the traditional rules of formal analysis. In the SHARMED workshops, supported by the facilitator, the children showed great skill in using different strategies of 'playing' with the images. Some of these actions and dynamics have been recurrent and therefore its main characteristics can be outlined.

The first type of action is represented by invitations addressed to the children to talk about the photograph in question. This action may appear to be taken for granted, but it should instead be included within the whole process of interaction. Once the photographs had been collected and the first work of analysis had been carried out in small groups, the facilitators had the task of supporting the individual exposure in front of the class group. This step is prepared by the previous actions, but it represents a qualitative step in the research process and in the interaction between the participants. It is thanks to the trusting environment and the attention gained in the previous phases that it is possible to invite the individual participants to react to the solicitations of the facilitator and their classmates, who are considered co-facilitators.

What is interesting to note here are mainly those actions that use photographs to promote children's participation, i.e. those actions that do not simply analyse the true meaning or composition of a photograph.

The first type of action aimed at fostering participation is represented by invitations addressed to the children to talk about the photograph in question. This action may appear to be taken for granted, but it should instead be included within the whole process of interaction. Once the photographs had been collected and the first work of analysis had been carried out in small groups, the facilitators had the task of supporting the individual exposure in front of the class group. This step is prepared by the previous actions, but it represents a qualitative step in the research process and in the interaction between the participants. It is thanks to the trusting environment and the attention gained in the previous phases that it is possible to invite the individual participants to react to the solicitations of the facilitator and their classmates, who are considered co-facilitators. The invitations thus represent the transition from a collective and generic dimension to one of personal and intimate exposure. Each invitation has a personalized character that must take into account the sensitivities and characteristics of each child. Finally, invitations to children are addressed with targeted questions that allow for the possibility of acceptance or refusal to participate. The sequence and turns to speak are not predefined and the modes of presentation are free.

Example 2 (UK, PS3, third meeting)

FAC: Oh wow. So, we have a huge story from this picture. I was going to ask you actually why did you choose it but I think I know, I think I can see loads of happy memories coming out of it, out of your picture, loads of them. Does anybody want to ask about the picture, about anything they can see in the picture, about memories, has anybody got any questions that you might like to ask?
M: ((segna la fotografia)) How old were you?
F1: I think two and half.
F2: You look massive.
F1: I know
F2: Did you do your hair up on that day?
F1: No, I just brushed like crazy. I had my head upside down.
M: Was it like a traditional dance you did?
F1: No, I was doing my shaking
((risata))
FAC: Is that that you brought in, is that anything to do with it?
F1: ((tiene in mano una cartella e segna divers cose al suo interno)) Yeah, that's part of what I got from the goody bag. Someone gave it to me and it's like a folder, and I can just put my personal stuff inside, and this bit he's an elephant god called Ganesh and he (?) and these are silk fabric. And sometimes in weddings you will see these two people, which is (?) and when they got married that's a part of the celebration. So, at that time we celebrated the wedding, the groom and bride were doing a dance of this music but I was doing the wrong music.

This sequence opens with a long introduction by the facilitator, who openly expresses her point of view as well as appreciation for the photograph selected and for a previous contribution by a child. The facilitator then invites other children to participate by asking questions to the narrator, who then has the opportunity to enhance her narrative. In the last turn of this sequence in particular, it is possible to see how the questions asked allow capturing the essence of the photograph that was previously less understandable. This example introduces us to a second type of action consisting of questions of encouragement, expansion on the one hand, and distribution of participation on the other. Throughout the children's narration, facilitators frequently asked questions aimed at encouraging other children to add details, to expand further on points made, or to encourage them to question the narrator. These are almost always open questions not aimed at finding a right answer. In addition, these are questions that manifest interest in the narrative, trust in the narrator and avoidance of performance evaluation.

The promotion of participation from images was realized through actions finalized:

1. Describe the image and the 'content' of the photograph.
2. Tell the story of when the photograph was taken, by whom, the context, the occasion.
3. Examine the photograph (understood as a physical object).
4. State the reasons why that particular photograph was selected (its function).
5. Express the sensations or emotions to which the photograph is related.
6. Deduce information from the photograph
7. Find connections to other pictures and narratives.

This multiplicity of actions demonstrates the richness of the method and the complex work starting from the image. The description of the formal elements of an image refers to the tradition of iconographic analysis as described by Panofsky (1939) according to which the primary subject of the representation is described only on the basis of the viewer's immediate perception and practical experience. This is a recognition of the image that can lead to finding in a photograph what happened, where it happened and in what time, who the figures are, historical backgrounds, etc. Thus, one remains on the surface of the events indicated by the photograph. The identification of the inner substance and the deeper meaning of the subject represented would, again according to Panofsky, be the concern of iconological interpretation. The first point (Describing the image and the 'content' of the photograph) is thus fully within an important analytic and hermeneutic tradition.

There are many examples of this first type. The description of the photographs is done in great detail and listing the various elements that compose it.

> **Example 3 (Germany, SS1, first meeting)**
>
> M: emm, well we were at the zoo (?) Elephants, they were going like this the whole time (gestures the movement) and walked against the wall.

There is little to analyse in this type of description but to note that everything in the photograph, including the narrator himself, is described and performed. In fact, this type of description is usually preliminary to the actual narration in the most intimate and hidden aspects. On the other hand, the second point (telling the time when the photograph was taken, by whom, the context, the occasion, etc.) introduces the contextualization of the photograph by direct or indirect witnesses. 'Images are silent witnesses' (Burke 2013: 17) and as such require a description of their context of production, the authors, the hidden purposes, and any other data that can position that particular photograph in socio-historical terms. In SHARMED, we have gathered almost exclusively private or so-called vernacular photographs, an expression which includes all the images taken by common people (non-professionals) in everyday life situations, for personal use. In this regard, children initiated narratives about memories around the topical moment recorded by the photograph. Often these narratives are based on vicarious memories. Thus, on the one hand, the symbolic and emotional meaning of a memory is distinguished from the memory of the lived experience; on the other hand, the mediating function of a photograph is activated by connecting a non-directly lived experience with a first-person or vicarious narrative.

> **Example 4 (Germany, SS2, second meeting)**
>
> 1   M4:   well, this picture, well, this is the country Syria and the city is Aleppo and em on the first picture you can see that everything is still intact, that people are walking around and that there is a huge tower here and that em there are also cars, mopeds and everything is still fine. There are even some trees here. And it looks like a normal city.

2	M5:	and below it's em, there was definitevely a war, you can see a tank here and everything is broken there, so I believe- we believe that this one is a before photo and this one after. All of the houses are destroyed too and the tower is broken too.
3	M4:	so everything is just rubble and you can also imagine that people wouldn't like to live there or go there on holiday.

This interesting sequence is carried out simultaneously by two narrators who compare two images of the same place before and after a bombing. The description of the composition of the image gives way progressively to indications of context, of the events that took place and to a series of further inferences ('so everything is just rubble and you can also imagine that people wouldn't like to live there or go there on holiday'). The children describing the photograph are not direct witnesses of the events, but these events have produced important consequences on their personal and family lives. It is therefore an indirect memory but one that involves the two narrators in the first person.

Point 3 (Describing photography as a physical object) allows to come back to the difference between picture and image. The former has its own tangible, material, concrete reality that can contain information and narrative suggestions. Many of the photographs brought by the children were produced in dematerialized form, that is, as digital files that can be viewed through computers or other devices. In other cases, the selected photographs were printed on different media, with different formats and papers, some were in color and others in black and white, some contained writing and notes, etc. In these cases, the 'physical' aspects of the photograph are used as a source of information on which to build narratives and interpretations (it is an old photo, it is a rare photo, etc.). But even in the cases of digitized images, it was possible to detect some details regarding the production and technological components. The narratives created from the physical and tangible elements of the photographs brought to light elements that would probably have been hidden, namely the positioning, location and importance of a particular photograph in the private space from which it was taken (hung on a wall, placed on a bedside table, glued in an album, etc.).

Example 5 (Italy, PS1 4A, second meeting)

1	M2:	[it's a photo: smooth as oil
2	FAC:	it's a passport photo no?
3	M2:	eh smooth [as smooth as oil [without anything
4	FAC:	[to put [smooth as silk
5	M2:	((taps hand on leg and looks at teacher)) eh oh
6	FAC:	you wanted to add: something?
7	F9:	that: looks like M8's that looks: serious:
8	FAC:	((turns to look at the photo)) seems serious? (…) but were you serious or do you look serious?
9	M2:	((looks at the picture)) a bit serious
10	FAC:	a little bit serious because: you knew you had to go with the police
11	M2:	yes
12	FAC:	mh
13	M2:	I'm afraid
14	M?:	but did they arrest him?
15	FAC:	the police are a little scary
16	M2:	yes, I always feel that they put me in jail

The description of the textural and tangible part of a photograph is not frequently pointed out, but it provides interesting insights. In example 5, the child focuses on the texture of the surface of the photograph, while the facilitator looks at the format and function of the photograph. These two aspects are often related to each other. The description of a passport photo, for example, can lead to narratives related to migration experiences or with institutions and law enforcement. In this sense, even though they may appear to be distant and separate dimensions, it is possible to move effectively and immediately from the description of the photograph as an object (smooth as oil) to the lived experiences (the visit to the police station) and the feelings felt (the fear of being put in jail).

The fourth point focuses on the motivational element of the children's choice and therefore on their own autonomy. The reasons for the choice can be very different, but they are linked to the function that the image has in daily life. This point is often linked to the next one, that is, to the emotions triggered by the chosen photograph (point 5). The importance of a given photograph is almost always linked to its ability to create effects of fascination, emotion, amusement, pleasure, etc. Between the function of the photograph and the feeling that arises from it, there is the memory, understood as the action of connecting past events with effects in the present. The activation of emotions during the workshops created situations of strong involvement of the participants, who were able to share with each other similar experiences and empathy even starting from different stories with different subjects.

The last two points (deducing information from the photograph and finding connections to other images and narratives) indicate how we can move away from a given photograph to make connections to other images and other narratives. Because of the narratives made probable by a specific photograph, further communication becomes probable. This results in a process of dispersal or convergence of different narratives that can take many forms. Analysis shows that problems can arise with invitations to expand narratives either when they are generic and not sufficiently focused or when they are too specific, and thus the theme of expansion cannot be shared by all or valued as interesting in the classroom.

> **Extract 7 (Italy, SS2, first meeting)**
>
> In my opinion yes, it's like she said, she brought it (the photo) maybe because she is devoted to her dad and then it has a family value, because this photo represents the family, and then yes, you can see that in the photo they are all three happy, that's it.

From this example we can see how the description is based on deductions and on the search for a similar type of photo ('it has a family value because this photo represents the family'). During the workshops, the facilitators with the help of the participants ensured that some inputs became part of a common narrative. In these cases, inferences and connections were discussed in order to verify their real consistency and plausibility.

3.5 Conclusion

Describing the transition from images to narratives of memories means, on the one hand, questioning the shift from perception to meaning making, and, on the other hand, questioning how perception activates mnemonic traces. In particular, this transition can be divided into three moments: the perception of images, the move from images to memories and from memories to narratives. 'Engrams' and 'exograms' are the terms used in memory studies to refer to the operations of psychic and social systems starting from the perception and recall of directly or indirectly experienced past events. The combination of engrams and exograms allows for the narrative construction of these memories. Therefore, it is crucial to understand how certain images predispose to a specific narrative translation and what constraints and opportunities are presented to individual narrators and other participants. But it is not only an intrinsic quality of the images that makes them more or less available for narration; as we have tried to show in this chapter, the activity of transforming images into narratives can be facilitated by specific actions in support by both the adults and the children participating in the discussion.

4

Production of Narratives

Chiara Ballestri and Vittorio Iervese

4.1 Introduction

Promoting and supporting children's participation means first and foremost creating the conditions for children to express themselves as freely as possible. This aim needs to take into account above all the contextual conditions of participation and the processes of communication and interaction in which children and adults are involved. SHARMED has chosen to foster children's agency by creating opportunities for the narration of memories triggered by personal photographs. The children's participation should therefore be observed in three different but complementary moments: the selection of the photographs, the sharing of the stories with other participating children and adults, and the discussion raised by this storytelling. The use and importance of photographs as a tool to facilitate children's participation will be the topic of the next chapter. In this chapter we will deal with the forms and modes of children's narratives during the workshops.

The concept of narrative has been investigated by various authors from different perspectives. With regard to the social sciences, two main theoretical perspectives can be distinguished. The first, developed in the field of communication studies (Fisher 1987; Somers 1994), states that: 'narration is the context for interpreting and assessing all communication as it is omnipresent in communication' (Fisher 1987: 193). In this sense, every communication and every construction of information result in different and often competing narratives. Narrative can be understood as an inescapable condition of social life: it constructs identities, shapes experience, provides a repertoire of stories to narrate events and make sense of them, and guides people's actions in certain directions according to the repertoire of narratives available (Somers 1994: 614). Other authors (e.g. Norrick 2007) have combined the concept of narration with that of storytelling, stressing the interactional aspect of narrative construction. According to this perspective in face-to-face interactions everyone can participate in different ways in the narrative and with different roles (e.g. narrator, co-narrator, listener, initiator, facilitator). Narratives are constructed not exclusively by the narrating subject, but by the consultation and collaboration of all those present. Therefore, each narrative can be activated, sustained, continued, contradicted, etc. by the participants in the interaction in a specific context.

In the workshops carried out as part of the SHARMED project all participants, children as well as the facilitator, are to be considered co-constructors of the narratives recorded by the researchers. This research project looked at autobiographical memories as public narratives contextualized and actualized in the present moment. The methodology was aimed at promoting and facilitating the narration of the memories of the children involved in the research. First, the problem was how to activate narratives without imposing or predetermining them from the outside. On the one hand the problem was to bring out the memories that the children may have, and on the other hand to enable and support the storytelling in a context of peer interaction.

According to Higgins (1996) there are three basic principles of the memory activation process: availability, accessibility and applicability. These three principles are complementary to each other, but each requires the setting up of contexts suitable for expression and promoting participation. Availability concerns above all the possibility of the individual to recall his own or others' memories to be told. The greater the exposure to certain stories, the more they are 'available' to be told than others. The form and content of the narratives are therefore dependent on the stimuli to which each person is exposed. As far as this research is concerned, the focus on availability has meant addressing the question of how to enable the children involved in SHARMED to increase the availability of narratable memories, i.e. to access a variety of possible choices, thus increasing the sources and traces of memory available. Accessibility is concerned with the sources of memories that are not always readily available. The most engaging memories are not necessarily the most accessible ones but, on the contrary, may be linked to a lack of information or materials. According to Higgins: 'accessibility refers to the activation potential of available knowledge' (Leung et al. 2011: 66). Last, applicability refers to social contexts and its norms. Applicability refers to the adequacy of certain narratives to the norms of representation in a given setting. The relevance, pertinence and appropriateness of a story in a social context give it a specific degree of applicability or tellability. Applicability is thus both a constraint and a resource for participants who expose a part of their identity through their narrative in a socially situated interaction. The promotion of children's participation in storytelling cannot be separated from its activation, which is part of the facilitation actions. The process of activating narratives is therefore complementary to those supporting the narrator's different forms of expression and sharing with other participants. In the following paragraphs we will give some examples of how the right to narrate can be achieved in different ways and how the narration activity can be a complex and participatory one.

According to Nelson, 'memories become valued in their own right (…) because they are shareable with others' (1993: 12), and 'the process of sharing memories with others becomes available as a means of reinstating memory' (1993: 177). Narratives become means to connect remembering and communication. To this end, photo-histories were viewed within the project as a way to establish and communicate the position of the teller within a shared setting (Hoerl 2007; Norrick 2012), photographs which could be linked to personal preferences, interpersonal relationships or group memberships.

Exploiting photographs for constructing narratives of memories also means activating ideas through remembering that must be encoded in the language and narrative format (Norrick 2012). For what concerns this activation, two main types of narrative have been stressed (Berntsen & Rubin 2012; Williams et al. 2008; Conway & Pleydell-Pearce 2000):

1. Declarative narrative, referring to specific facts, data or events that can be recalled 'from the unique perspective of the self in relation to others' (Nelson & Fivush 2004: 488).
2. Semantic narrative, referring to general knowledge of the world, in terms of facts, ideas, meanings and concepts. Semantic narratives activate ideas through remembering but it is not part of an autobiographical narrative, rather it is a possible enrichment of this narrative.

Within this general distinction there are other specific forms of narration and ways of constructing them which will be presented in the following paragraphs.

4.2 Forms of Narratives

Right to tell is related to personal knowledge of the narrated events. In fact, events can be known by a single narrator, by a narrator and another participant and by different members of a group. For this reason, new members of a group first assimilate, then participate in the retelling of the group's origin story, while children retell the retold history of their parents' meeting and marriage. For the same reason, vicarious (reported) events are often co-narrated in groups, which can limit the right to narrate. In this hierarchy, only those involved in narrated events have the right to tell or co-tell a story, for example if the person involved is present he/she has the exclusive right to tell, but if he/she is not present, another person who was present has the right to tell the story (Norrick 2007).

Participants negotiate also tellability: to earn and keep the floor and avoid interruptions and negative evaluations, a narrator must choose a relevant story. Relevant means different things, all related to the specific context and participants: new to the specific audience or meaningful because to reminiscence. Thus, tellability falls between the lack of common experience and straying too far from that experience: is therefore a risk as well as a resource. Indeed, some stories may lead to negative consequences, for example, listeners may refuse to listen or may judge the narrator negatively. On the other hand, participants may tell a transgressive story to create intimacy, elicit admiration and change the relationship with listeners by promoting further narratives of the same type (Norrick 2007). In SHARMED narratives sometimes struggled with relevance because of a lack of significance to the audience or because of sensitive or taboo themes that conveyed the identity of a transgressive narrator. In the first case, narratives were insignificant because the child did not remember the events and did not ask about the story behind the picture he/she was carrying, or because he/she resisted telling the story of the picture. In the second case, the narratives involved sensitive topics that are usually censored in the school setting, and thus may lead to a negative evaluation of the narrator.

Storytelling production resources we have seen allow participants to construct different forms of narratives conveying different types of identities. Three main forms of narratives emerged in the SHARMED project: (1) ontological, (2) public and (3) metanarratives. Ontological narratives are about the narrators' selves and allow them define themselves, give meaning to their lives and decide how to act. In particular, the relevance of narrators as social actors is constructed through the organization of life events into episodes. Moreover, narrators' identities, being them ephemeral, ambiguous, multiple and conflicting, are constructed in relation to the spatial, temporal and relational context in which they are produced. Ontological narratives are therefore contingent and interpersonal: they exist only in temporarily situated social interaction.

Public narratives are connected to groups and thus can be stories of intersubjective networks, such as familial, friendship, but also religious or national (Baraldi & Iervese 2017).

Metanarratives are the fundamental and predominant narratives of a particular historical moment. They concern themes such as progress, industrialization, capitalism, the opposition between nature and culture or between individual and society. Being abstract constructs, metanarratives are closely related to conceptual narratives that provide an explanation of important forces in society (Somers 1994).

4.2.1 Ontological Narratives

Personal narratives are stories related to children's experiences, told in the first person and whose source is the child who lived them. First-person narratives can be either ontological or public, depending on whether they are used by children as a resource to convey their personal identity or that of a larger group in which they take part. In the first extract, F4 tells of a wedding in Thailand and the embarrassment she felt at hearing her mother argue with a policeman. Since the wedding was in Thailand, the facilitator asks some information about the kind of ceremony and then comments positively on the diversity of stories produced by different children on the same theme (marriage), highlighting the intercultural background of the group. By the end of the sequence (turn 13), encouraged also by the appreciation of the facilitator and inspired by F4's reference about her mother, M4 reports a transgressive action with the following reproach of the mother. M4 closes the narrative stating that, after eating the cake he ironically told his mother that it was time to go home, contributing to highlight his competence as a storyteller and his transgressive and autonomous identity. In conclusion, the facilitator compliments M4 for his story and for his ability to remember so many details despite the fact that at the time of the events he was only five years old (turns 18–21).

Extract 1 (UK, PS3, second meeting)

1   F4:   When was eight I went to a wedding there was some policemen in a car (?) (..) and my mum was talking to them (?)
2   FAC: You went into them and what did he say to you?
3   F4:   I felt embarrassed for the rest of the day

4	FAC:	What sort of wedding was it that you went to?
5	F4:	It was in Thailand
6	FAC:	In Thailand, you went to Thailand for a wedding. So and how did the wedding, how did the ceremony work in Thailand, what was it like?
7	F4:	The bride and the groom were colorful
8	FAC:	So, very colourful and elaborate outfits, yeah?
9	F4:	And it took place at a Temple (?) house
10	FAC:	Okay and where did you go to the wedding?
11	F4:	Groom's house
12	FAC:	So, very different to your wedding, the wedding that you went to. So, we've had some different, we've had some weddings in temples, in houses, in churches, in registry offices. There's a real mixture, everybody's been to kind of weddings all in different places. It's interesting to think about the different places they're in
13	M4:	((Smiles, use hands to show the 'whole ' cake)) I went to this wedding, my mum and my dad we went there with my brothers and sisters, and then I ate all of the cakes because I was really hungry, and then my mum was shouting because I have eaten the whole cake and I was eating with my hand, my face was full of chocolate
14	FAC:	You couldn't deny it
15	M4:	And then we went home and I said mummy can we go home now
16	FAC:	After you had eaten all of the cake?
17	M4:	Yes
18	FAC:	And can you remember that wedding very well?
19	M4:	Yeah
20	FAC:	How old were you?
21	M4:	I was five

In this example, the children put at the centre of their narrative not only an event but also the presentation of themselves in their relationship with their own mothers. Both F4's confessed embarrassment and M4's provocation are forms of claiming their autonomy and distinctiveness with respect to family norms.

4.2.2 Public Narratives

Within personal stories, it is possible to discern not only narratives about the narrator's self but also public narratives, that is, stories that fit events into a plot that depicts a specific group identity. The second example is also set at a wedding party, but in this case the action told is no longer individual but of a group. The transgression is in this case explicitly directed at the adults, who unaware continue to dance. The narrative is structured around a 'We' (the children) who act and a 'They' (adults) who are affected by those actions. The facilitator's comment at turn 6 helps solidify this narrative structure: children's enjoyment of weddings is very different from adults' and contemplates adventurous actions, potion-making and cucumber challenges. In addition, the facilitator stresses the topic of children's autonomy, asking several times if the adults were aware of and in agreement with what the children were doing (turns 4, 8 and 10).

Example 2 (UK, Transcript 2, Photo 2)

1   M3:   ((Waves hands around as speaking)) I've been to a wedding which basically there was plenty of juices at the far back. So, we got (..) we mixed all of the juices and we put pepper (?) and we were daring them to drink it. And I got another one which the cucumbers and then we got started fighting with the cucumbers
2   FAC: At the wedding?
3   M3:   ((smiles)) Yeah
4   FAC: And do you think the adults knew that you were doing all of this at the wedding?
5   M3:   Yeah
6   FAC: And was this a children's kind of, young people's lives at the wedding, what do you do, that's interesting, so you were doing potions and dares at the wedding?
7   M3:   Yeah and our parents were just dancing
8   FAC: And do you think the parents knew what you were doing all of the time, all of these potions and
9   M3:   Yeah
10 FAC: They did and they were okay with it?
11 M3:   Yeah
12 FAC: And who were you doing these potions with, were they people that you normally see?
13 M3:   ((smiles)) Yeah and some people that I don't normally see
14 FAC: So, would it be a member of your family or (..)
15 M3:   Friends and family
16 FAC: Both. Yeah, you see them every time there is an event

The following example shows how public and personal dimensions can be co-present in a single narrative. Location of past events in time allows the construction of a continuous self that exists through time. Therefore, narratives of memory allow the production of a picture of the past and through this process the development of identity. The narrative construction of identity can highlight either personal and autonomous responsibilities and choices (I–identity), or membership of groups (We-identity), e.g. as family identity, national identity, ethnic identity.

Despite the hilarity provoked by the image presented, M1 is not inhibited and does not give up participating (turn 2). The story is encouraged by the facilitator's interest and proceeds along a trajectory that moves from a detail (the hat) to a context (Afghanistan) and a religious event (Eid). The hat is therefore at first a marker of cultural belonging. Then, thanks also to the questions posed by the facilitator (turn 12) the central role of the affective relationship with the father becomes clear and how the memory of a past experience can shape the personal identity of the narrator in the present.

Example 3 (UK, PS3, second meeting)

1   FAC: When you choose a picture you never know what people are going to talk about, shall we see if we can get one more, I think there might be time for one more. Who's this?
2   ((laughter as picture appears on screen))
3   FAC: Who is coming up to share this picture?
4   M1:   You look like a girl! ((laughter))
5   M2:   ((steps up, his arms wave up in front of him))
6   FAC: Why did you choose to bring that in?
7   M2:   Because it was Eid in Afghanistan
8   FAC: So, it's in Afghanistan, so it's celebrating Eid
9   M2:   Yeah. All of our family was gathered around in this (?) park and my grandfather unfortunately had to bring his camera because he used to be a photographer, and I think he wanted me to wear this hat and he made me put it on and it made me smile (?) picture
10 FAC: Why did he make you wear that hat?
11 M2:   Because it was my dad's old hat
12 FAC: Oh, so your dad used to wear that hat as well and how does it link to Eid, how does that link to Eid?

13	M2:	Because he wore it on the same day as Eid
14	FAC:	And does it represent something, does it mean something?
15	M2:	It doesn't mean anything it's some hats that Afghans wear

4.2.3 Vicarious Metanarratives

Vicarious narratives are stories told in the third person, the source of which may be the child himself or someone else. In our data, they allow for public as well as metanarratives, as they can convey a group identity or underpin fundamental narratives. The fourth extract is an example of third person metanarratives: a historical narrative of M3's great-grandmother during World War II. This story inserts M3's personal family history into a villain vs. good war narrative. The triggering event is the theft of a pig by the German soldiers (turn 4) but the narrative is based on metanarratives of World War II, a time of abuses and violence, and of the Germans as negative absolute. Interrupting this stereotyped metanarrative, M3 introduces a positive character (turn 6), the leader of the Germans, as an exception to the rule that gives the story an unexpected development: the pig is partially returned the next day. However, the Evil versus Good metanarrative is confirmed because the Germans force the grandmother to accept the money (turns 12 and 16). In the plot, the counterpart of the violent Germans, with the sole exception of the 'good boss', is the great-grandmother who, with her courageous behaviour, first complains about injustice and then refuses to be reimbursed. The fact that M3, by entering into the details of the events, questions the relevant metanarrative shows how the latter often operates as a premise for the storytelling. For this reason, the facilitator supports M3 in his attempt to personalize his story, moving away from established narrative patterns.

Example 4 (Italy, SS1, first meeting)

1	FAC:	But are there other things that they told you about her?
2	M3:	Yes
		(.)
3	FAC:	[What

4	M3:	[That an episode happened during Second World War that e: she had a farm I mean her husband and: so basically the Germans have: they had stolen a pig from them
	(.)	
5	FAC:	[Ah
6	M3:	[And so e: then she de- e: had gone to the leader of the Germans in ((city)) and told him you stole my pig you have to give it back to me and that leader of the Germans was good I mean he wasn't bad
7	FAC:	Ah
8	M3:	And: so then she found
9	FAC:	Because there are good Germans [and less good Germans
10	M3:	[yes yes and: ((gesture with the hand indicating something past)) and so she found the day after the pig they gave it back to her but e:
11	M1:	Dead
12	M3:	A little because:: they had already eaten some parts and then they wanted to bring her the money (.) of the pig
13	FAC:	Ah
14	M3:	Be[cause
15	FAC:	[Just guess
16	M3:	To pay for it then my grandmother said no keep the money I don't want it and they said take the money or we shoot you
17	FAC:	Just guess!
18	M3:	Eh she took it ((smiles))

4.2.4 Transitions

Third-person narratives are often a resource for eliciting first-person or further third-person narratives about similar experiences. In particular, intertwined narratives are promoted through group discussion activities about pictures. During these activities, each group creates stories about classmates' photographs or tells other stories that the photograph brings to mind. Then, the owner, who has specific knowledge about that photograph, is asked to tell the 'real' story. In example 5, F1 tells a story about F10's photo, which depicts an old building with an unclear function and in an unclear place (turns 1–14). It is precisely on the basis of this lack of information that, in collaboration with the facilitator, the teacher and the other children, a story is drawn up based on hypotheses and deductions. F1's story highlights the emotional value of F10's photo and how the country of origin plays a role in defining a personal identity. At turn 13, the facilitator promotes the transition from third to first person, highlighting the constraint constituted by the rights to tell. Then, F10 starts telling the story of the picture, supported by facilitator's confirmation (turn 16) and teachers' questions (turns 14, 17, 19, 21, 23 and 25). It is also important to note that, in turn 12, the facilitator addresses all the children in order to show interest and trust in them. The facilitator's action is at the same time aimed at distributing participation by activating further narratives and encouraging the children to bring out other hidden memories.

Example 5 (Germany, SS2, second meeting)

1   FAC: Could you, I'd like to ask you to, em, it's about the stories and memories that each of you has and every memory is different, so please
2   M9:   (?)
3   T: Speak up please, none of us can hear a word you're saying
4   M9:   I think this picture was taken in Arabia
5   T: Arabian country
6   M9:   (?) emm, they took it before they went away
7   T: Mm-hm, do you think it's a residential building?
8   M9:   huh?
9   T: Was residential?
((children talk over one another))
10 T: What do you all think could be inside this building?
11 F1:   I believe, well I just think that the picture is of the building where they lived before they came to Germany, well before they fled and I think that the picture is just supposed to show that they, when they're in Germany, they don't live there anymore, that's how great my building was
12 T: I'm sure there are a lot of memories here. Mm-hm
13 FAC: Can you *plural* think of anything else? Shall we have the solution then. I think that was really interesting with that picture wasn't it
14 T: Whose picture is it then?
15 F10:   Here's my room and here is the kitchen
16 FAC: Mhm
17 T: That was your room, down there, and that was your *plural* kitchen. And what is up there, behind these beautiful windows? What was up there? Can you tell us what is up there?

18	F10:	Also rooms
19	T:	Those are rooms too, is that right? Was there a garden back there too?
20	F10:	Yes
21	T:	Nice, this is the building. Is it in a village or was it in a town
22	F10:	This is, err, small town, but they, they are very old
23	T:	And when did you *plural* take this picture then?
24	F10:	I don't know my granddad took it like this
25	T:	Mm-hm. Do you know if there are still, if any of your family live there now?
26	F10:	My granddad now is there, but this room now not my

4.3 Modes of Producing Narrative

Storytelling production is cooperative: participants can take part to a narrative as narrators, co-narrators, audience and activators of new narratives. Narrators usually signal their intention to take the floor and check the interest of interlocutors to be their audience. They also mark the ending of the story so that the audience can respond, for example, with other stories. In addition, one narrator may select another as the next narrator, attributing to him/her the right to tell. While narrator proposes a story suited to the audience and the context, the listeners contribute to its construction, interrupting, correcting and co-narrating. Narrating is always interactive, more or less polyphonic, but always the result of negotiation between the participants, since the listeners are also actively involved in the process. In fact, even when listeners are not co-narrators, they are co-authors who, through questions and comments, help determine the structure, trajectory and relevance of a narrative. In particular, listeners may produce observations, details and comments to the main story designed for sub-groups of listeners, and sometimes they may even interrupt narrator through negative evaluations of the story.

Co-narration is linked to the access to the events being narrated, so there is no need to negotiate the sharing of an experience, or to compete for the best story, although there may still be competition for the right to tell. Participants can become co-narrators using both supportive and antagonistic strategies. Although disagreement among co-narrators is possible due to differing expectations of what is relevant and worth telling, co-narration often affirms a group identity. In fact, two narrators may tell a shared story to the audience or a group of co-narrators can subordinate their personal identities to the success of the narration. This type of collaborative storytelling is reflected in the turn taking system and in overlapping turns (Norrick 2007).

Narratives can promote the production of interlaced stories: participants tell stories that hook on the current or to preceding stories resulting in a series of related narratives. Interlaced stories may establish a common experience, for example something that happened to several participants, or may compete with preceding stories, for example if a participant thinks he/she knows of a more significant event. Some stories show active listening, understanding and appreciation of previous stories and provide opportunities for participants to share their stories, expanding on a specific theme or recalling similar experiences. For example, after a third-person story, a new narrator may tell a story on the same theme or with the same protagonists, resulting in a series of thematically related stories. Moreover, two narrators may arrange to tell interlaced stories in sequence, with the second being a continuation of the first, with events and characters in common. Some contexts are particularly appropriate for interlaced stories, such as memories related to a particular significant event. interlaced stories are a useful and versatile communicative resource for interactive narrative production (Norrick 2007).

4.3.1 Interactive Production of Narratives

Interactive narrative production is a resource for promoting children's participation as both the facilitator and classmates can help enhancing disclosure and personal involvement. In this case, M1 starts from the description of a very special person (he's more like a big brother to me) to tell about the migration trajectories of different family members. This evolution of the story is possible thanks to the facilitation actions and the collaboration of the other children. This interactive form of storytelling affects not only the plot of the story but also the possibilities of expression (in terms of availability, accessibility and applicability). In other words, the boundaries of what can be told are widened and a trusting environment is created allowing even the most delicate and emotionally involving themes to be expressed. In this sense, it is interesting to note the child's question in turn 20, which gives the story a personal and intimate depth. The focus on the person rather than on the migrant in generic terms thus becomes prevalent.

Example 6 (Germany, SS2, second meeting)

1 M1:   The picture is important to me because he's not just my cousin, he's more like a big brother to me. Emm. ((looks for another picture))
2 FAC: Where was the picture taken, the first one I mean? I couldn't see it properly
3 M1:   The first one, you might as well pass it around
4 FAC: Ah alright, cool
5 M1:   This is the picture that we took a month ago. I was on holiday in (?)
6 FAC: Wait a second M1, I can't hear you right now
7 F1:   Okay, now
8 FAC: Okay, now
9 M1:   Err, the picture was taken about a month ago, I was in Austria during the school holidays and I visited him and my aunt. And yeah, so I would also like to have him here in Germany
10 FAC: Is he still in Iran?
11 M1:   Nope, he's in Austria now
12 FAC: Aha, yes I see. So basically he (.) you fl- fled to Germany and he fled to Austria
13 M1:   Yeah, about a year ago
14 FAC: Mm-hm. And how does he like it there?
15 M1:   Good because he lives with his other brother there and he's been there for quite a while too
16 FAC: Mm-hm. Alright, and when do you plan on, on seeing one another again?
17 M1:   Err, in the summer holidays
18 FAC: Mhm
19 M1:   F1
20 F1:   Erm, so, well. How did it feel for you to see your cousin or for you sort of big brother again after nine years?
21 M1:   I was actually really happy
((children talk at the same time))
22 M1:   And yeah, when I came back to Germany actually I came back with tears in my eyes because I knew that I wouldn't see him emm, see him for a long time again so yeah

4.3.2 Co-production of Narratives

Co-narration can be promoted by a facilitator to enhance the dialogue between the children, while allowing the construction of a group identity. It happens when two or more participants have access to a common event and present the same story to the audience. Example 7 is a co-production of a narrative of the beginning of the friendship between F5 and F14. The facilitator encourages the storytelling by asking the girls what they have in common (turn 1), if there was a conflict between them (turn 6) and to tell the story of the beginning of their friendship (turn 12). We can discern the cooperative nature of co-narration in some features of verbal and non-verbal communication: the girls look at each other before one of them takes the floor (turns 2 and 3, 36 and 37); the statements of one are accompanied by the comments or laughter of the other (turns 7 and 8); the talk often overlaps (turns 10 and 11, 19 and 20, 28 and 29, 54); the girls support each other by confirming information (turns 31 and 32), by aligning positions (turns 39 and 40) and by narrating the episode of the first interview in a supportive manner (turns 46, 47, 49 and 50).

Example 7 (Italy, SS2, third meeting)

1	FAC:	So it was a meeting: you have things in common
2	F5 e F14:	((look at each other))
3	F14:	Mh:
4	FAC:	Well you dressed like Indians,
5	F5:	Practically we haven't talked to each other for five years for all the primary school
6	FAC:	Did you dislike each other?
7	F14:	Yes [hh
8	F5:	[we thought hh
9	FAC:	Really!
10	F14:	[Hh
11	F5:	[We thought
12	FAC:	This thing is interesting and ho[w how: did this friendship arise?
13	Ins:	[Sh sh
14	FAC:	How did you realize that instead
15	F5:	Last year
16	FAC:	Isn't it a friendship?
17	F5:	No no last year we

18	FAC:	Yes but how trans– how did the transition happen? Do you remember?
19	F5:	We [met
20	F14:	[We happened to be in the same class
21	FAC:	So you disliked each other but you say we have to stay together let's try
22	F5:	H<u>h</u>
23	FAC:	Like that?
24	F5:	Yes
25	FAC:	But who is it that has approached the other? (.)
26	F5:	Both
27	FAC:	That is you have collided
28	F14:	[H<u>h</u>
29	F5:	[No<u>h</u>h
30	FAC:	How come on don't you remember how did it happen?
31	F5:	In the library maybe
32	F14:	Yes we went to the library together
33	FAC:	Ah
34	F14:	And
35	FAC:	No I like to understand the thought when (.) at a certain point you had a preconception one against other am I right?
36	F5:	((looks at F14))
37	F14:	Yes
38	FAC:	Eh and how did the change happen? That is
39	F5:	Eh learning to know her (.) because I thought I disliked her because she didn't speak to me and looked at me badly and therefore:
40	F14:	And the same for me
41	FAC:	Well then basically you were hostile to each other in defence (.) in the sense that you thought that the other didn't want [to: you and so
42	F5:	[Yes
43	FAC:	And and who was the first to speak?
44	F5:	Eh who remembers?
45	FAC:	It was you ((pointing to F5))
46	F5:	No! I don't know
47	F14:	No because it seems to me that we were sitting there ((points to a desk)), [at the beginning of the year
48	FAC:	[Here ah

49	F5:	Because	[we were in islands
50	F14:		[And yes we were in islands, and she and I were faced at some point we took out the pencil case it was the same and then we started laughing
51	FAC:	Ah: so a fortuitous episode	
52	F5:	Yes	
53	FAC:	But have you ever told each other when you disliked each other?	
54	F5 and F14:	Yes	

4.3.3 Interlaced Narratives

Interlaced narratives are multiple stories told by different participants in such a way that each one recalls one of the previous ones. This type of storytelling occurs especially when participants try to share their experiences and opinions on a certain topic. In these cases, the facilitator mainly takes on the task of promoting and empowering the stories that follow each other, as can be seen in Extract 8. In the first turn, the facilitator ratifies and closes the first story and in turns 3 and 5 remarks about the way recent and old memories come up when looking at a photograph. He then asks the other children to tell the stories that the same photograph reminds them of (turn 5). The facilitator repeatedly promotes F2's narrative with short actions of understanding and approval (turn 7), relevance of information (turn 9), formulations (turns 11 and 13). F2 shows that she welcomes this support, responding to the facilitator's solicitations and to the questions she is asked. The final comment and the question addressed to the other children allow the continuation of the story in an interlaced but not contradictory form (turns 13 and 15).

Example 8 (UK, PS2, second meeting)

1 FAC: So that reminded you of that memory
2 F1:   ((nods))
3 FAC: It's funny how memories just pop out sometimes out of nowhere (..) have you thought of that lately at all?
4 F1:   ((shakes head))
5 FAC: No? it's just popped out from the examples today (..) so your picture is bringing us loads of memories that we (..) er (..) some new memories and some very old ones (..) do you want to see if there are a couple of more memories before changing over pictures? Maybe from someone who's not had their hand up

6	F2:	My sister video'd me on her phone when I was little and I was in her room and I was in my mum's (?) and my mum video'd it (..) so I went down the (?) and the lift went down and then she asked where I was and then I came up and they made me laugh so much (..) and (..) and er (..) I've got another memory (..) when my cousin, when she was three years old and I was in nursery (..) she wanted her mum but she called my mum mum so she wanted her mum but her mum was at work (..) she called my mum her mum
7	FAC:	Ah
8	F2:	So my mum she wouldn't so she started crying for her mum
9	FAC:	Aww
10	F2:	And I gave her a cuddle and there's a really cute picture of me like hugging her and now we're like best friends after that
11	FAC:	Aww so she was a bit lonesome, she missed her mum
12	F2:	Yeah
	(..)	
13	FAC:	And she saw your mum and your mum kind of looked like her mum and then she looked like she kind of need a hug and you gave her a hug (..) so you kind of had a feeling that she needed a hug
14	F2:	((nods))
15	FAC:	Aww (..) and (..) and you're best of friends now? Do you still have a hug now and again?
16	F2:	Yeah ((nods))
17	FAC:	Sometimes you just need a hug from your friend, don't you or someone that's in your family just to feel alright (..) hugging's good (..) does anyone else like hugs?

4.4 Conclusion

The promotion of children's narratives is a complex and participatory activity. Children should not only be seen as subjects who need to be helped to express themselves but as active participants who can also play a co-facilitating role. In this perspective, each participant can help other participants to express themselves and thus support dialogue and shared narratives. If agency is consolidated by increasing the possibilities of expression and narration (in terms of availability, accessibility and applicability), the support and promotion of participation occur through appreciation rather than assessment of the expressions of individual participants. Activation also alerts the children that the adult cannot 'facilitate' without the children's collaboration and that only through everyone's contribution and responsibility is it possible to make interaction and dialogue work. Narratives of past events can evolve into narratives of children's lived experience, behind and beyond photographs. Consequently, not all the narratives can be considered as storytelling regarding past events (Norrick 2007, 2012). Any telling of past events can evolve in other types of narratives, starting from co-telling and listeners' comments. While memory may be encoded in the format of storytelling, the complex chain of telling, co-telling and comments enhances different narrative formats, e.g. when linked to previous stories. This complex articulation shows that narratives can be considered omnipresent in communication (Baraldi & Iervese 2017; Fisher 1987) and thus play a fundamental role in promoting children's participation also (but not only) in educational contexts. In this sense, narratives should therefore be seen as a re-elaboration of past experiences but also as a potential for further experiences, an opening for participation, confrontation, exchange and continuation of communication with others.

5

Meanings and Methods of Pedagogical Innovation

Federico Farini and Angela Scollan

5.1 Introduction

Based on rich data produced through the observation of SHARMED activities, this chapter discusses how children's authorship of narratives can be facilitated in practice, towards the construction of communities of dialogue in the classroom. The chapter is instrumental to the implementation of pedagogical innovation, providing examples and elements of reflection for teachers and educators who are interested in the methodology of facilitation. As a companion to the SHARMED training presented in Chapter 10, this chapter evaluates how an array of actions, such as questions, invitations to talk, minimal responses, reformulations of children's contributions and facilitators' personal initiatives can support children's voices in actual classroom practice of facilitation. Several video-recorded and transcribed examples from the three participating countries are used for this purpose. Before illustrating the results of the evaluation of facilitative activities, the reader is informed that Chapter 10 does not only present SHARMED training philosophy and methodology but it also directs to freely accessible SHARMED online trainings.

5.2 Promoting Narratives: Inviting Children to Talk

Inviting children to talk can be the starting point for the production of narratives and therefore it plays a crucial part in transforming the classroom into a community of dialogue. Invitations to talk are also addressed to bystanders who may want to link new narratives to an ongoing one or, more often in our data, to a just completed one. A third function of invitations is to promote questions from bystanders concerning an ongoing narrative. The common thread underpinning the three functions of invitations to talk consists in the extension of the area of active participation, making invitations to talk a pillar of facilitation.

In actual interactive practices, invitations to talk are mostly produced as questions, both open questions and focused questions. The choice of an open or a closed format for questions is associated with different intentions of the facilitators, as discussed in the chapter. The first type of invitation to talk to be discussed in the chapter are invitations to start a new narrative.

In our corpora of data, invitations to start a narrative are often constructed as focused yes/no questions. Focused questions invite affirmative answers (Clayman & Loeb 2018) whilst still keeping open the opportunity for children to make choices, including rejecting the invitation.

A second form of invitations to talk to start new narratives consists in open questions. Open questions have a higher potential to enhance children's agency because, differently from focused questions, they do not put the same level of constrain on children's actions.

In excerpt 1, the facilitator invites M12 to initiate a narrative about a photograph utilizing a focused yes/no question (turn 1). M12 shows that he understands the pragmatic function of the question because he does not answer the focused question which is duly understood to be meant to be an invitation to talk. In turn 4, M12 starts a narrative. In the course of the narrative, the facilitator supports M12 through a variety of actions that encourage continuation (turns 5–11). Among those supporting action it is possible to identify a focused question (turn 7).

Excerpt 1 Italy (PS1, 4A, second meeting)

```
01   FAC:   Can you you tell us about this photo?
02   Ins:   Sh
03   FAC:   I steal your seat
04   M12:   (I took:) photo photo: ID,
05   FAC:   Mh
06   M12:   E: for e: for the police,
07   FAC:   You too for the police?
08   M12:   Yes and then to take: the papers,
09   FAC:   The documents
10   M12:   Yes
11   FAC:   Ah
```

Invitations to expand narratives aim to extend the areas of active participation, involving more children. In particular, invitations to expand concern the production of new narratives stemming from a completed one. Excerpt 2 is connoted by a series of invitations to talk. In turn 1, the facilitator invites children to share a new narrative that could be linked to the newly completed one. The invitation is quickly taken up by F1, who narrates the sad circumstances of her cousin's death. In the continuation of the interaction, the facilitator systematically supports F1's narrative. When F1's narrative comes to a conclusion, the facilitator produces an invitation to expand with new narratives, asking a question to the cohort of children (turn 11). This second invitation to expand invites a series of contributions from children concerning the loss of loved ones. The interlacement of children's short narratives, 'initially' promoted by the focused questions in turn 11 is secured by more facilitator's focused questions in turns 15, 17 and 19.

Excerpt 2 Italy (SS1, 2A, first meeting)

01　FAC:　Does it remind you some photo that you have at home?
02　F1:　Yes that with my cousin that now is passed away
03　FAC:　Your cousin?
04　F1:　Yes
05　FAC:　Did he leave you?
06　F1:　E: when he was sixteen years old
07　FAC:　((nods)) did he have (.) an accident? [an illness?
08　F1:　　　　　　　　　　　　　　　　　　[((nods then pull head down with misty eyes))
09　FAC:　((nods)) so the the photo in this case could help you to to remember [eh?
10　F1:　　　　　　　　　　　　　　　　　　[((nods with tears in her eyes))
11　FAC:　To keep alive persons that that are gone do you have some photos that help you
12　M1:　Like my cousin (.) also my cousin
13　FAC:　That has has gone and that you remember because you see him him in photo
14　M1:　((we don't see if he nods))
15　FAC:　Or grandparents maybe someone grandparents (.) do you have grandparents that have passed away [because of their age:
16　M5:　　　　　　　　　　　　　　　　　　　　　　　　　　[I with my grandfather
17　FAC:　And that you remember looking at photos?
18　F5:　((nods))
19　FAC:　Or that you only know because you see him/her in photo

Invitation to ask is a sub-type of invitation to talk that is addressed to create opportunities for other children to expand an ongoing narrative, beyond being used as an invitation for children to ask questions to the current teller. In excerpt 3, turn 1, The invitation to talk succeeds in expanding the area of active participation, generating a series of comments and questions around the ongoing narrative (turns 4, 5, 7, 10, 11 and 13).

Excerpt 3 Germany (PS5, 3B, first meeting)

01	FAC:	Do you have a question about the picture?
02		((children put their hands up))
03	FAC:	((to F2)) Yes?
04	F2:	Here is- well I find this picture strange somehow
05	M8:	It's strange because it's a screen.
06	FAC:	Yes?
07	M9:	I wonder how he got on TV.
08	M5:	It was like this (.) there was a screen, behind it there was a dome. You could go in there and it would be transmitted automatically, but it wasn't really on TV. It was just a big TV where you go into it
09	FAC:	[oh great]
10	M8:	[oh cool]
11	M6:	In which year was that?
12	M5:	Mmh umm
13	M6:	Two thousand and- (4.0)
14	M5:	I don't know

In excerpt 4, the invitation to ask launched by the facilitator (turn 1) elevates F1 to the status of organizer of the interaction. F1 ask to the peer a question about an aspect of the ongoing narrative delivered (turn 2). The question succeeds in supporting an expansion of the ongoing narrative. The expanded narratives is the object of a second question, this time from the facilitator (turn 4), aimed to support the continuation of the narrative.

> **Excerpt 4 UK (PS1, 6A, meeting 1)**
>
> 01 FAC: Ok, so anyone else to ask any questions on that one (points) or shall we move on onto our last (…) is that (…)? (…) do you want to
> 02 F1: Um, what was your favourite part about the Ferrari World?
> 03 M2: Well, my favourite part was racing with my brother because whenever we did shared experience because he's older than me
> 04 FAC: Oh, he's older is he?
> 05 M2: Yeah
> 06 FAC: Yeah
> 07 M2: So once I beat him and when we went back, like after a few days (..) we had like a new house in Dubai so we set up everything in one week and then he kept on challenging me and we played outside and stuff then we had a few races

5.3 Asking Questions to Support Narratives

Asking questions is a crucial component of any conversation. Asking questions is of course a pivotal action for any pedagogical endeavour. Questions can fulfil a range of tasks beyond seeking for information. From a pragmatist point of view, asking questions can do many different things; in the context of facilitation questions can support authorship of narratives in conversations. Questions are therefore an important resource for facilitation. Section 5.2 highlights that there are different formats that questions can take; whilst all formats can successfully support active participation in conversation, there are differences of pedagogical relevance between focused questions and open questions: focused questions are effective in promoting participation, due to the pressure to provide an answer they exercise (Farini 2011); however, an issue concerns the quality of such participation, which is often limited to the minimal answer invited by the focused alternative (Keevallik 2010). Whilst still utilizing the interactional power of questions, open questions make relevant a wider range of actions as the reply, beyond the choice of a binary alternative. This appears to be more attuned with the principles of facilitation; nevertheless, open questions do not provide the same 'safe guidance' to children with regard to the expected the reaction to them; more possibilities for action entail more risk therefore a possibility that children choose to avoid the risk of a freer participation. For facilitators, choosing between the two formats of question is often a delicate choice that can be supported by considering the needs of the specific interaction: focused questions can help to kick-off a struggling conversation; open questions can work to further expand an already ongoing interaction.

However, an interest in the morphology of individual questions should not detract from the empirical reality of questioning in educational interactions, where pragmatic effects are achieved by sequences of questions rather than single questions. The support of children's narratives can be considered a possible pragmatic effect of questioning, and this section discusses how sequences of questions promote children's status as authors of narratives. In particular, the discussion will focus on two aspects related to questions in facilitation: (1) the insertion of questions in ongoing narratives; (2) the development of sequences of questions. Whilst Section 5.2 discusses invitations to talk, where individual questions are used to initiate new narrative or to invite expansion of narratives, in this section the focus shifts towards sequences of questions when the facilitators access the role of co-authors of narratives.

Expansions of narratives can be supported by open questions (henceforth OQ) that lend themselves as a tool to promote further developments. When used to support the expansion of narratives, OQs are often followed by series of focused questions (henceforth FQ) addressed to specific aspect of the expanded narrative. Excerpt 5 illustrates the effects of series of questions. It is presented in two parts.

In the first part (turns 1–19), an OQ in turn 1 explores the reasons for F7's choice of the photograph. F7's reply suggests some hesitation; in turn 3 the facilitator formulates a FQ addressed to a specific aspect of the ongoing narrative (presented in an earlier phase). As suggested, whilst OQs offer more opportunity for choice, FQs can be more effective in supporting action, albeit within a more limited range of options. Following F7's affirmative reply to the first FQ, a series of FQs is devoted to explore the child's feelings (turns 5, 9 and 14). The first part of the excerpt closes with a further FQ shifting the focus of the interaction towards presents for parents.

Excerpt 5 Italy (SP1, 4C, third meeting)

01   FAC: And how was that you chose to bring us just this picture=
02   F7:   E: because:

03	FAC:	I mean this picture gift that your uncle did to your aunt is one thing that you too liked?
04	F7:	Yes
05	FAC:	Because you like flowers?
06	F7:	((nods)) And (5.0) I took the picture because it was the day of Saint Valentine
07	FAC:	Which is the day of lovers
08	F7:	((nods))
09	FAC:	And are you in love?
10	F7:	[No
11	Some:	[Hh
12	FAC:	No?
13	F7:	No
14	FAC:	Well your parents (.) you have haven't you? A feeling of love for your parents
15	F7:	((nods)) Yes
16	FAC:	But you did not make any gift to them
17	F7:	Yes [e:
18	FAC:	[Did you make a gift to them?
19	F7:	((nods))

The second part of excerpt 5 (turns 20–36) is inaugurated by a new OQ concerning presents made by F7 to her parents. However, OQs do not pose the same strict restraint on the following action as FQs, leaving F7 room to choose to talk about a present to her aunt. The facilitator follows F7's line asking a series of FQs that link to specific aspects of the ongoing narrative (turns 24, 26, 28, 30 and 35). FQs can support expansion of the conversation in terms of its extension over time (Seuren & Huiskes 2017) with the caveat of limiting such expansion to the themes that they introduce.

20	FAC:	What gift did you make to them?
21	F7:	E: we bought some dresses
22	FAC:	Mh
23	F7:	And we wrote a big poster with written (…) m: we love you
24	FAC:	Ah but we love why? In- who did you and then?
25	F7:	E: my cousins
26	FAC	Your cousins?

```
27  F7:   ((nods))
28  FAC:  And are they children of this uncle and of your aunt
29  F7:   Yes
30  FAC:  Ah and do you live together?
31  F7:   ((nods)) Yes
32  FAC:  I understand
33  F7:   And I also live with my g- grandmother
34  FAC:  Who lives with you?
35  F7:   Yes, and (.) ((she shakes her head)) °that's it
```

Questions appear to be particularly effective in promoting children's narratives when OQs and FQs are combined: OQs offer children a wider range of options, as suggested by the sequence of turns 20–23, where F7 can choose to talk about her aunt's presents, rather than her parents' presents. FQs limit the range of choice for children but support children's action by reducing the demands of participation, as suggested by the effect of the switch from OQs to FQs in turns 1–3.

Besides the capabilities of OQs and FQs, a very important aspect for facilitation is the choice of the facilitator to follow F7 lead; this choice is particularly important from a pedagogical angle: if questions are used to control the flow of conversations and the facilitator does not follow the lead of children, a risk is to prioritize adults' agenda instead of supporting children's status as authors of narratives.

5.4 Minimal Feedback: Valuing Children's Narratives

Minimal responses are another common action in all types of conversations, including educational interactions (House 2013; Huq and Amir 2015). It is necessary to clarify that minimal responses do not refer to short replies to questions; rather, by 'minimal responses' this discussion means minimal actions undertaken by the facilitators as a form of feedback on children's actions. SHARMED data suggest that actions of minimal feedback can play a twofold role in facilitating children's access to the role of authors of valid knowledge: (1) supporting children's active participation and authorship of narratives; (2) acknowledging the importance of children's stories and comments

The first function, supporting children's authorship, is mainly accomplished by continuers. Continuers are very short actions that signal attention to the ongoing contribution (Gardner 2001). Continuers are minimal actions of feedback used to invite children to continue their narrations, reinforcing their status of legitimate tellers. Continuers include interrogative confirmations, short confirmations, paraverbal signals. Support can be accomplished also by another type of minimal action, that is, the repetition of words, or parts of sentences (Wong 2000). Continuers and repetitions display active listening (Voutilainen et al. 2019) of children's turns of talk. Repetitions display listening more explicitly than continuers.

The second function of minimal feedback, acknowledging the importance of children's stories and comments, is accomplished by acknowledgement tokens that display the understanding of the previous turn of talk, at the same time conveying interest, surprise, empathy (McCarthy 2003). Acknowledgement tokens provide a more explicit positive and supportive feedback than continuers do, but also a clearer feedback than repetitions.

As for questions (5.3) minimal responses will be presented in this chapter as part of longer sequences rather than abstracting them from their context. This choice is motivated by the intention to show how they fit into real, naturally occurring, educational interactions. In excerpt 6, a series of continuers support the ongoing narrative by confirming the status of F1 as legitimate narrator (turns 2, 4 and 6). In turn 6, the facilitator's continuer is expanded by a sentence that distils the meaning of F2's narrative (see Section 5.5).

Excerpt 6 UK (PS2, 5A, second meeting)

01   F2:   My sister video'd me on her phone when I was little and I was in her room and I was in my mum's (?) and my mum video'd it (..) so I went down the (cannot understand) and the lift went down and then she asked where I was and then I came up and they made me laugh so much (..) and er (..) I've got another memory (..) when my cousin, when she was three years old and I was in nursery (..) she wanted her mum but she called my mum mum so she wanted her mum but her mum was at work (..) she called my mum her mum

02   FAC: Ah ah

03   F2:   So my mum she wouldn't so she started crying for her mum

04   FAC: Aww

05   F2:   And I gave her a cuddle and there's a really cute picture of me like hugging her and now we're like best friends after that

06   FAC: Aww so she was a bit lonesome, she missed her mum

07   F2:   Yeah

Repetitions are a very simple type of minimal turn, echoing the previous turn, or at least part of it. Repetitions can be employed to display attention (active listening), as well as to encourage further talk.

Excerpt 7 UK (PS3, 5A, first meeting)

01 M1:   How long did it take to draw this?
02 F1:   I don't know. Five minutes. 10 minutes.
03 F1:   It takes me about an hour to draw.
04 FAC: About a hour.
05 M1:   How old are you?
06 F1:   Ten.

SHARMED data suggest that repetitions can be followed by questions in the same turn, these more complex turn working as an interactional device to promote children's contributions. Children's reaction may range from minimal answers which is the most common situation illustrated by excerpt 8, to longer narratives.

Excerpt 8 UK (PS1, 6A, second meeting)

01 FAC: Oh wow (..) was it a nice surprise?
02 M2:   Yup
03 FAC: And what were you chatting about, if you don't mind me asking
04 M2:   Stuff
05 FAC: Stuff ((laughs)) was it easy to chat to him when you hadn't seen him for so long?
06 M2:   Yeah

Acknowledgement tokens are a type of minimal feedback displaying recognition of the children's role as legitimate authors of valid knowledge. Whilst continuers and repetitions invite further talk, acknowledgement tokens are designed to display engagement in the conversation. In excerpt 9, the acknowledgement token 'wow' is followed by a second acknowledgement token ('ahi') to signal both engagement in the narrative and emotional alignment with the narrator stance on the memory of his grandmother's death. Acknowledgement tokens are minimal actions but they can play an important role because displaying attention and emotional involvement creates favourable conditions for personal expression.

Excerpt 9 Italy (SS1, 2A, second meeting)

01 M2:   And he sank with the whole submarine
02 FAC: Wow! And so the grandmothers remained alone
03 M2:   Yes
04 FAC: That however you didn't know
05 M2:   No no these ones are still there well my grandmother that of the one who died in the submarine died this year
06 FAC: Ahi
07 M2:   And instead the other one is d- I mean the other one is still alive

---

In the reality of pedagogical interactions, continuers and acknowledgements tokens can be combined to display active listening and engagement in important passages of a narrative, as shown by excerpt 10 that includes a continuer ('uh uh') and an acknowledgement token ('aaaah').

Excerpt 10 UK (PS1, 6A, first meeting)

01 M1:   So basically, this is my brother when he was younger
02 FAC: Uh huh
03 M1:   As like a seven month year old baby (..) yeah and his favourite colour's orange
04 FAC: Aaaah

5.5 Making the Point: Formulations

Formulations are a type of communicative action that distils the gist of previous turns of talk and presents it to their authors (Heritage & Watson 1979). Research suggests that formulations play an important role in educational conversations to check mutual understanding (Skarbø Solem & Skovholt 2019), to manage conflicts (Baraldi 2019b) and also to promote dialogue in the classroom (Baraldi 2014). Formulations are a more complex action than minimal feedback and can display facilitators' attention and engagement in children's narratives more emphatically. However, differently from minimal feedback, formulation are more intrusive actions that entail an interruption of the conversational flow therefore they should be utilized carefully. The analysis of empirical facilitation during SHARMED activities suggests that in the practice of interaction with children, facilitators used two variants of formulations: (1) explications to clarify the meaning of previous turns of talk (Chernyshova 2018); (2) developments of previous turns to present some possible implications (Peräkylä 2019).

Developments involve a more creative work from the facilitator; developments take a risk of expanding the conversation in directions that were not foreseen by the author of the summarized turns. The risk consists in the rejection of the formulation. However, such risk is not necessarily a problem for facilitation. This statement can be justified by reminding that, pedagogically, facilitation aims to support children's active participation, children's trust in the interaction as well as children's access to the role of authors of valid knowledge. If the facilitator's gist of previous turns is not accepted, still this provides children with opportunities for active participation, in the form of rejection, or correction, of the formulation.

In the practice of facilitation as observed in SHARMED activities, formulations more often refer to short individual turns, rather than summarizing longer turns or series of turns, although the latter situation could be observed in a minority of cases. In particular, SHARMED data suggest that in empirical interactions working with children formulations take place as the third turn that follows a facilitator's question/children's answer dyad. As the third turn after a question/answer dyad, formulations distil the gist of children's answers, triggered by facilitators' questions. Formulations can be standalone turns as well as part of longer turns, for instance as the middle part of a tripartite complex turn of the type: 'acknowledgement token, formulation of the acknowledged turn, facilitator's question', the latter utilised to expand the conversation.

With regard to the reception of formulations, children's turns of talk following formulations consist in minimal confirmations in most cases. However minimal, for instance nodding, children's confirmations are pivotal because they display that the gist presented by the facilitator has been accepted. Other possible children's reactions to facilitators' formulations may include longer expansions as well as rejections of the formulation, albeit this is a very rare instance in our data.

In excerpt 11, turn 7, the facilitator presents a possible gist of F7's previous turn of talk (turn 6); the formulation infers a possible meaning of sartorial choices at wedding celebrations. The formulation distils the gist of turn 6 by suggesting that F7 wanted to convey that the choice of identical dresses is a symbolic representation of familiar unity. As several formulations in our corpora of data, the formulation in turn 7 is anticipated in the turn by an acknowledgement token to suggest engagement in the ongoing narrative and receipt of F7's narrative. It may be noticed, with reference to Sections 5.3 and 5.4, that F7's narrative is supported across the sequence by questions and continuers.

Chapter 1 offers the theoretical tools to appreciate how formulations in excerpt 11 not only contribute to the co-construction of a narrative; they also contribute to the co-construction of the meanings of cultural identities through the narrative. F7 and the facilitator cooperate to contextualize the story of F7's family, transforming the interaction in a living, localized small culture (Holliday 1999). Cultural meanings of narrated experiences are not traced back to predefined cultural identities; rather, they are (co) constructed interactively (Baraldi 2015b).

Excerpt 11 Italy (SP2, 5A, second meeting)

01 FAC: But: for what reason was the photo taken? Because I see that you have the same special dresses what tell us what does it mean
02 F7:   Eh that: we are united, which is not true because that is not my father but my uncle,
03 FAC: Yes
04 F7:   E: (.) wearing dresses made of the same tissue,
05 FAC: Yes
06 F7:   It seems that we are one
07 FAC: Ah the idea that you have the same dress the same: tissue it's union
08 F7:   ((nods))

In excerpt 12, formulations work as developments. They are anticipated by display of active listening via acknowledgement token (turns 2 and 4). In turns 6 and 8, two formulations develop the narrative by distilling a gist of the previous turn and presenting possible implications of it towards further expansion. Both formulations as developments are confirmed with minimal actions by F2, the author of the narrative.

Excerpt 12 UK (PS2, 5A, second meeting)

01 F2:   My sister video'd me on her phone when I was little and I was in her room and I was in my mum's (?) and my mum video'd it (..) so I went down the (?) and the lift went down and then she asked where I was and then I came up and they made me laugh so much (..) and er (..) I've got another memory (..) when my cousin, when she was three years old and I was in nursery (..) she wanted her mum but she called my mum mum so she wanted her mum but her mum was at work (..) she called my mum her mum
02 FAC: Ah
03 F2:   So my mum she wouldn't so she started crying for her mum
04 FAC: Aww
05 F2:   And I gave her a cuddle and there's a really cute picture of me like hugging her and now we're like best friends after that
06 FAC: Aww so she was a bit lonesome, she missed her mum
07 F2:   Yeah
08 FAC: And she saw your mum and your mum kind of looked like her mum and then she looked like she kind of need a hug and you gave her a hug (..) so you kind of had a feeling that she needed a hug
09 F2:   ((nods))

In some instances, formulations are a way for facilitators to support the interactional production of narratives, accessing the role of co-tellers. This is a very important function of formulations. The co-construction of narratives based on formulations is particularly common with regard to explications rather than developments.

If compared with formulations as explications, formulations as developments can support more complex forms of children's participation. In turn 5 of excerpt 13, the facilitator distils the gist a series of turns advancing a possible implication of it. Based on F7's contributions, the facilitator infers that her parents' wedding was a proxy wedding. F7 confirms the development by nodding before further expanding the narrative by adding the information that someone else took the place of her father (turn 6). In turn 7, the facilitator summarizes the previous turns asking F7 to confirm that the uncle took the place of the father as a proxy. After F7's confirmation, the facilitator produces another development, suggesting a cultural meaning of the use of a proxy (turn 9). F7's further confirmation in turn 10 closes the development of the narrative, which was thoroughly prompted by formulations. It is important to notice that, as in excerpt 11, formulations contribute to the co-construction of the cultural meaning of narrated experiences.

Excerpt 13 Italy (SP2, 5A, second meeting)

01 FAC: And why did he came here? To search a job?
02 F7:   Yes
03 FAC: And do you know where did he live?
04 F7:   In ((city))
05 FAC: In ((city)) ok and the wedding between you dad and you mum took place without you dad,
06 F7:   ((nods)) but there was someone who took his place
07 FAC: So ((points at the photo)) e he took your father's place she didn't marry your uncle
08 F7:   No
09 FAC: They needed a male figure
10 F7:   ((nods))

In SHARMED data formulations as often found embedded in more complex turns that they cohabit with other conversational components, mostly questions. The turns of talk that include a formulation and a question are designed to promote a quick reaction from the child, based on the interactive power of the question that prompts a reaction from its recipient (5.3). Interestingly, in complex turns where a formulation is followed by a question, is the question, rather than the formulation, that projects the next speaker's reaction. For instance, questions can facilitate children's expansions of narratives. In excerpt 14, turn 5, the facilitator produces a formulation as an explication to distil the gist of F1's narrative; the formulation is followed in the same turn by a question to explore F1's feelings. The combination formulation, followed by a question, succeeds in supporting the expansion of the narrative.

> **Excerpt 14 UK (PS2, 4A, third meeting)**
>
> 01 FAC: Do you want to tell us about the picture?
> 02 F1:   So this one is when I was going to meet a meerkat
> 03 FAC: Uh huh
> 04 F1:   And there was a man who was telling us about them and he said if you put your back against the wall of the cage, they'll climb up you and use you (?) to look out (..) so that's one of them on my shoulders and
> 05 FAC: So he climbed up you (..) a meerkat climbed up your back like this ((indicates to the back of the students and makes an upwards hand motion)) and how did you feel about that?
> 06 F1:   Um (..) well actually I had to take my jumper off because it was wool and they kept on going behind it and inside it

5.6 Making It Real: Facilitators' Personal Contributions

SHARMED data include several types of facilitators' personal contributions; in this section the focus of attention is placed on two types of personal contributions that proved to be effective in promoting children's narratives in the context of empirical educational interactions: stories and displacements. The first type, stories, are produced to display facilitators' closeness to children as well as their interest in the narratives that children author. It is true that by telling personal stories, facilitators upgrade their role in the interaction, accessing the status of authors; however, this can be functional for facilitation when facilitators' stories are connected and not competitive with the ongoing narrative. By telling their personal stories, facilitators join the interaction expressing their persons and the contexts of their experiences (Mandelbaum 2012), displaying trust in children (Farini 2014) and suggesting their commitment to the relationship. By sharing their own stories, facilitator promotes expectations of personal expressions rather than role performances.

Personal stories can have the function of enhancing children's participation. In excerpt 15, the facilitator shares a personal story concerning a swimming trip to the seaside; the story includes references to her father's behaviour, to her lack of risk awareness and to her happiness when on her father's shoulders. Although this facilitator's personal story is loosely coupled to M3's one, still it successfully promotes the engagement of another child, M4, who shares a similar narrative concerning fear, swimming and relationship with the father.

Excerpt 15 UK (PS3, 5A, first meeting)

01 M3: I have a memory. So, I went to Dubai this waterpark is called (?) and there is like KFC and McDonald's, and they have this surfing place (?) over there. So, I just put my tummy on the ground. I didn't learn how to swim, and then there were trees like this and then I ate McDonald's.

02 FAC: You know when you put your belly on the ground, was it so that you could pretend to be swimming?

03 M3: Yeah.

04 FAC: Do you know what – you really remind me when I was a little girl, which was a really, really long time ago, my dad took me swimming to Brighton which is a seaside

05 ((Class all talk – talking about also visiting the same seaside as FAC))

06 FAC: And my dad, he couldn't swim but I didn't know he couldn't swim. And he put me on his shoulders when I was a little girl, probably about your size, and I was on his shoulders and he took me up. And I was wondering why my mum was getting really cross. She was standing on the side of the sea and she was going like this come in, like this. And my dad was laughing. And I think he was laughing because he was kind of joking with my mum because she knew he couldn't swim. And he took me out a little bit. And I thought my dad was the best swimmer in the whole wide world and I was safe, but really he was taking me out and he couldn't swim either. And I was on his back and then he had to come back in because my mum told him off, and you've really made me remember that.

07 M4: And my dad he took me to the deep end like 2 m and (?) and those boys over there (?) sometimes the wave comes, so what happened my dad said come here and then I went there, he picked me up and then he's like jump and I will catch you, and I was no – I'm scared and then he'd take me back.

The second type of facilitators' personal contributions, displacements, is a unique way of upgrading facilitators' contributions. Displacements enrich an ongoing narrative with side-stories or comments that aim to surprise and entertain children. Pedagogically, displacements have a double function: (1) creating a positive relationship between facilitators and children; (2) sustaining expectations of unpredictability and surprise, which represent a favourable context for personal expressions.

A unique feature of SHARMED activities, displacements have been overwhelmingly used by an Italian facilitator. In excerpt 16, the connection between displacement and unpredictability is made explicit by the facilitator. The sequence starts with a question about photographs taken at parents' weddings. F3 narrates about a photograph taken at parents' wedding. In turn 13, the facilitator asks what F3 was doing when the photograph was taken. This is an example of displacement that initially generates some disorientation in F3, who hesitates to answer. In turn 15, the facilitator provides the answer to his own question (turn 15: 'you were not there'), immediately followed by F3's confirmation. Although some children are laughing about the facilitator's displacing question, the displacement sequence is not over, as the facilitator suggests that maybe F3 was not at her parents' wedding because she was at another party (turn 19). The child rejects facilitator's hypothesis and protests that she was not born at that time (turn 22); at the same time, however, another child seems to join the facilitator's line by suggesting that F3 was not at the wedding because she was at a discotheque.

In response to F3's rejection, the facilitator acknowledges it but still continues in his displacing strategy by displaying surprise about the fact the F3 was not born when her parents got married (turn 24: 'a Ah: you were not yet born I see'). In turn 26, the facilitator asks the rest of the classroom if anyone was at her or his parents' wedding. M5 replies that this would be an impossible scenario. However, the facilitator rejects this statement, keeping open opportunities for the widest range of children's contributions: F4 takes this opportunity to share that she indeed was at her parents' wedding as she was born by then (turn 33). Connecting to F4, who is therefore valued as author of valid knowledge, the facilitator concludes the sequence by sharing his idea that many different scenarios and realities can be true at the same time, in this way also making a plea for the need to be prepared to unpredictability.

Excerpt 16 Italy (SP1, 4C, first meeting)

01   FAC: Some of you ((question to the whole class)) (..) has seen the pictures of you parents during the their wedding?
02   ((Some raise their hands))
03   FAC: Ah ah there are others (.) and what what what pictures are they? Who who who wants to tell the parents' pictures?
04   ((some lower their hands))

05	FAC:	Try to tell
06	F3:	A picture about when dad and mum were were entering the car (.)
07	FAC:	The day of their wedding or another day?
08	F3:	No, the day of their wedding
09	FAC:	Ah so (.) you don't have a picture (.) of of the ceremony but of the following moment
10	F3:	Yes
11	FAC:	When the ceremony was done and they were were greeting everywhere and leaving for the honeymoon
12	F3:	Yes
13	FAC:	And what were you doing?
14	F3:	I:
15	FAC:	You were not there
16	F3:	I was not there
17	FAC:	Eh hh
18	Some:	Hhh
19	FAC:	Because that day you were at a party elsewhere, weren't you?
20	?:	H
21	?:	No
22	F3:	No, because I was not yet [born
23	?:	[(??) to the disco
24	FAC:	A Ah: you were not yet born I see
25	?:	H
26	FAC:	And is there someone who was there (.) at their parents' wedding instead?
27	M5:	It's impossible
28	FAC:	No, it's not impossible [because [it can happen it can happen
29	M3:	[((says something to M5))
30	F4:	[((raises her hand))
31	M5:	[ah!
32	FAC:	Were you there?
33	F4:	Yes
34	FAC:	And why were you there?
35	F4:	Eh because I was already born
36	FAC:	You see ((to M5)) it is possible because things are possible in many ways (.) and and do you have a good impression of those pictures? I mean, did your parents talk of them to you ((he gesticulates)) showing emotions, enthusiasm, or did you find them (.) while looking for (.) family albums?

5.7 Conclusion

The promotion of children's agency sits at the very foundation of the transformation of the classroom in a community of dialogue. Facilitation can create favourable conditions for children's agency. Throughout this chapter different types of facilitative actions that proved successful in promote children's agency as authorship of knowledge have been discussed. The discussion was organized around the different functions that each type of facilitative action fulfils in the context of real, empirical exchanges in educational settings.

Some actions are particularly apt to initiate conversations as well as to expand the area of active participation to an ongoing conversation. We have grouped such action in the category 'invitations to talk'. Invitations to talk can take several forms, although in the practice of facilitation, the most common way to invite talk consists in questions. Whilst focused questions seem to be more effective in promoting participation, the kind of participation they promote can be sometimes limited, in form of a minimal response. Open questions allow for a wider range of actions from children; nevertheless, they do not have the same power of generating a reaction from the recipient of the question. A fine balance needs to be struck, and invitations to talk should be neither too generic nor too specific.

In actual facilitative practices questions are not used to invite children's contributions only; they can also be utilized to support an ongoing narrative, thus displaying recognition of the narrating child's status as author of valid knowledge. The implications of the use of open question and closed questions are similar to the ones related to initiation, with open questions offering children a wider range of options and focused questions reducing the demands of participation, facilitating a more diffused, albeit often more limited, participation. When questions are used to support ongoing narratives a note of caution is needed: questions have the power to orientate the flow of conversation, therefore the risk for facilitators can be to exert an excessive control, diminishing the status of children as authors of narratives.

A third type of facilitative actions that proved to be effective is a varied one: actions of feedback that aim to display acceptance and support of the role of children as authors of valid of knowledge. In the chapter a distinction was drawn between minimal actions of feedback and formulations. Minimal actions work well when the narrative is fluent so the important task of acknowledging the right of the child to present his or her stories can be fulfilled with minimal, non-disruptive actions. However, in some instances, more complex actions of feedback are required. Formulations are actions of feedback that not only recognize the narrator's role but also have the power to support and advance the narrative. It is very important in terms of pedagogical practice to highlight that facilitators should monitor children's reactions to a formulation, because it is not to be taken for granted that children will have a genuine interest in further expanding the narrative after a formulation that has either summarized the gist of the ongoing narrative or proposed possible implications of it. In SHARMED data, formulations are often combined with question in the same turn; whilst it is acknowledged that questions are important to monitor children's reaction to the formulation, it is also true that questions, particularly if focused, can restraint children's action, with the effect of limiting the scope of their agency.

The last type of facilitative action examined in the chapter relates to facilitators' personal expressions, in the form of stories and displacements. Personal expressions are a powerful action to display engagement in the interaction as well as the facilitator's availability to participate in the interaction as a person, rather than as standardized role, therefore promoting mutual closeness, surprise, sense of unpredictability. However, personal expressions are pervasive action that can effectively alter the course of an interaction; particular attention is needed in order to make sure that facilitators personal expressions are always relevant and connected to the ongoing narrative, in this way confirming children's status as the primary authors of knowledge. If such attention is not translated in facilitative practice, the consequence could be prioritising facilitators' agenda and belittling the status of children as legitimate authors of valid knowledge and equal participants in the interaction. In other words, a less than careful and measured use of personal stories or displacement can hinder the foundation of a community of dialogue.

This latter point advanced with regard to the risk of facilitator's personal expressions can be extended, of course in a more nuanced fashion, to all the facilitative actions discussed in this chapter: facilitation needs children to accept facilitators' actions; otherwise, facilitation is ineffective. However, children's alignment to facilitators' action should be based on their autonomous choices, rather than forced upon them by heavy-handed facilitative styles that abuse the power of actions such as questions, formulations and comments. It is pivotal to remind that the aim of facilitation is to extend the range of actions available for children's autonomous choices, which is the key aspect of agency and genuine dialogic pedagogy. When facilitation is successful, non-hierarchical interactions are created where facilitators waive the possibility to control interaction, as demanded by the support of children's agency. Facilitation transforms the classroom in an environment that enables children's autonomous decision-making, by upgrading their status as legitimate authors of valid knowledge (Allen et al. 2019; Scollan & Farini 2021). In these situations, children's personal initiatives become more probable, and their management becomes an important aspect of facilitation. Chapter 6 is dedicated to the discussion of that scenario.

Part Two

Managing a Community of Dialogue in the Classroom

6

Children's Initiatives in the Classroom

Claudio Baraldi

6.1 Introduction

Chapter 5 has shown that facilitation can enhance children's agency and communities of dialogue and Chapter 6 reveals that children's agency and communities of dialogue can also be based on children's autonomous and unpredictable initiatives during facilitation. This chapter shows another way in which children may exercise agency through facilitation and thus a community of dialogue can be constructed. The chapter analyses some ways in which facilitators can react to children's initiatives, by leaving the floor to children who ask for talking, leaving autonomous coordination to children and reacting to children who take initiatives while other children are narrating stories in conversation with facilitators.

6.2 Conditions of Children's Agency

The concept of agency is very important in sociological studies on childhood (see Chapter 1), including studies on early childhood (Farini & Scollan 2019; Kirova et al. 2019). However, children's agency may be interpreted in different ways (Larkins 2019; Morrison et al. 2019); for instance, it may be interpreted as competence, self-determination or practice (Stoecklin & Fattore 2017). Interpreting agency as *practice* means associating it with children's opportunities to choose ways of acting autonomously (James 2009). In this view, agency is visible through the choice between different courses of action, a choice which is important because it enhances changes of orientation in communication (Baraldi 2014a; Baraldi & Cockburn 2018). Thus, exercising agency means showing authority of accessing to and above all producing knowledge, i.e.

epistemic authority (Baraldi 2015a). However, concepts as autonomy, choice and epistemic authority are not sufficient to define agency, which is not an individual property. It is necessary to understand the social conditions of agency (Baraldi 2014a; Leonard 2016; Moosa-Mitha 2005).

According to some studies, children's exercise of agency is paradoxical since it is based on hierarchical structures, according to Alanen (2009) on a 'generational order'. Thus, children's actions are subordinated to adults' actions, in particular in education (Kirby 2020) and protection services (Morrison et al. 2019). Moreover, recognition of children's agency can be instrumental in institutions pretending to protect children (Baraldi 2019b). Subordination and instrumental recognition of agency depend on the dominant narrative of children's emotional and cognitive weakness. Paradoxical and instrumental interpretations make agency a controversial issue, above all in global society (Baraldi 2020).

Against this background, agency may be seen as having different meanings and degrees, for instance in the education system (Kirby 2020). Giddens (1984) talks of 'simple agency' for what concerns children, who are unable to enhance important social changes through their actions. This distinction between 'simple' agency and 'normal' (adult) agency reproduces the distinction between incompetent children and competent adults. Another distinction, more frequently used to explain children's different opportunities of participation in the 'global south', is between *thin* agency and *thick* agency (Klocker 2007; Muftee 2015).

The concept of thin agency explains children's minimal contributions, e.g. minimal responses to adults, where these contributions are not expected since conditions of interaction are strongly hierarchical. However, the empirical meaning and boundaries of thin agency are unclear. This concept leads to conceive agency as a general way of acting (Moran-Ellis 2013), since any action has an impact on the interaction (e.g. Goodwin & Heritage 1990; Heritage & Clayman 2010); any action is point of reference for further actions, which connect to it.

For instance, the student's answer to the teacher's question has certainly an impact on the following teacher's action. However, the student's answer is based on the teacher's authority to ask for it and is followed by action based on the teacher's right to evaluate it as appropriate or inappropriate (see Mehan 1979, and more recently, Margutti 2010). The student's answer is based on a hierarchical organization of the interaction, i.e. on teachers' rights to act and evaluate it.

What is defined thin agency is certainly active participation, but it does not display the child's autonomous choice which may activate a change of orientation of communication, thus ignoring the specific presuppositions of the concept of agency, i.e. *choice* of action and social *change*. The distinction is between exercise and lack of exercise of agency, rather than between thin and thick agency. Agency is visible only when an autonomous choice, which activates a change of orientation in communication, is visible. Choices of action and social change may be visible in different ways in different contexts.

Chapter 5 has shown that facilitation is indeed a paradoxical condition of children's agency (Baraldi 2014a), since children are expected to accept facilitator's action, collaborating with her/his intervention. This collaboration ensures that facilitation works. Children's collaboration is based on their autonomous choices since facilitators do not ask for predefined ways of acting. Facilitators' actions enhance children's autonomous actions and are designed to increase children's opportunities of choosing themes and ways of acting in the interaction. Although paradoxical, facilitation creates a non-hierarchical form of communication which allows children's exercise of agency and contribution to change social and cultural orientations.

This chapter aims to show that children can exercise agency through their autonomous and unpredictable initiatives in interactions with facilitators and classmates. In these cases, children do not take action to collaborate with facilitators; they take initiatives autonomously from facilitators' actions. Thus, comparison between Chapters 5 and 6 shows a distinction between children's agency as collaboration to facilitation and children's agency based on autonomous initiatives. On both sides, children's actions are unpredictable: children collaborate in unpredictable ways to facilitation and take unpredictable initiatives in the context of facilitation. The distinction is between (1) children's unpredictable actions enhanced (paradoxically) through facilitation and (2) children's unpredictable actions as autonomous consequence of facilitation. The distinction is also between different levels of unpredictability associated with children's different ways of exercising epistemic authority.

In case (1), agency is visible through children's actions that enhance facilitators' actions: facilitators may show listening or surprise, formulate the gist of what children say (Baraldi 2014a, 2014b), ask new questions, and so on (see Chapter 5); thus children's actions change orientation in the interaction, but facilitators always take initiative. In case (2), children's actions are not directly enhanced by facilitators' actions. Rather, children's unpredictable initiatives are challenging for facilitators' authority of coordinating the interaction.

The following sections show how facilitators react to this challenge, in particular leaving the floor to children, who ask for talking (Section 2), leaving autonomous coordination to children (Section 3) and reacting to children who take initiatives while other children are narrating stories in conversation with facilitators (Section 4). During SHARMED, asking for talking and autonomous coordination were more frequent in the German and Italian contexts than in the English one, while taking initiatives during conversations were more frequent in the Italian and English contexts. Probably, this is related to both the school system (in England children were used to teachers' systematic initiatives in the classroom and in Germany an ordered discussion was preferred), and the different forms of facilitation (see Chapter 9).

6.3 Leaving the Floor to Children Who Ask for Talking

In school classrooms, children are used to ask for teacher's permission to speak. Thus, children frequently asked for facilitators' permission to take initiatives and facilitators systematically authorized them to take the floor. In example 1, F asks to start a story (turn 1) and the facilitator leaves her the floor in a simple and direct way ('tell me'); then, he supports the narrative through a minimal response (turn 4) and some questions (turns 6, 8, 10 and 12). The narrative continues for a long time in the following conversation.

Example 1 (Italy, PS1, second meeting)

1	F:	I have something to tell
2	FAC:	Tell me
3	F:	About the previous picture of M2
4	FAC:	Yes
5	F:	E: I have a picture like that more or less too
6	FAC:	How would you de- define it?

In example 2, F takes the floor in overlap with the facilitator's turn (turn 2). The facilitator authorizes the child's initiative (turn 3), then he shows understanding (turn 6) and authorizes M2 (turn 8).

Example 2 (Italy, PS3, second meeting)

1	FAC:	Ah I understand (.) o[k
2	F:	[I want to say something too

3	FAC:	Let's hear
4	F:	That I agree with M5
5	M1:	There you are
6	FAC:	I see
7	M1:	(?)
8	FAC:	Yes and: what do you want to say?
9	M2:	I agree with M5 and M1 though

In extract 3, after the facilitator's appreciation of F's previous narrative (turn 1), the girl asks if the facilitator is interested in knowing her belts of judo, which is the sport she practices (turn 2). The facilitator turns the question to the children who are happy to approve (turn 4). In the following sequence, starting with turn 5, F tells about her belts.

Extract 3 (Germany, PS1, first meeting)

1	FAC:	Oh, that is really great. He apologised. Mm-hm. Okay.
2	F:	Should I tell you the belts?
3	FAC:	Do we want to hear the belts?
4	Children:	Yeeeees.
5	F:	Well, white, white-yellow, yellow, orange-green, no wait, orange, orange-green, green, blue, black, black, black, black, red, red-white.

6.4 Children's Autonomous Coordination

While asking for taking initiatives was frequent, children's autonomous coordination of production of narratives and dialogue showed children's agency very clearly. In these cases, facilitators left the floor to children's autonomous coordination. Facilitation was almost suspended, but occasionally facilitators supported children's contributions. Children could talk with each other, sometimes for a rather long time; sometimes one child coordinated the conversation. Children's coordination was particularly meaningful in showing children's interest in dialogue. We provide two examples here of this coordination, from the Italian and the German contexts.

In the long example 4, turn 1, M1 tells about his conflictual relations with his mother. The facilitator utters a formulation developing this narrative (turn 2), an open question (turn 4) and another formulation (turn 6). In turn 8, F1 takes the floor addressing M1 to 'contest' his negative attitude towards his mother. In the following sequence, until turn 21, the facilitator only provides minimal feedback and very short formulations, leaving the floor to F1. In turn 23, he supports M2's manifestation of interest in taking the floor. The conversation is based on children's autonomous coordination until turn 39, when the facilitator supports M1's contribution. Facilitators' turns 23 and 39 support children's initiatives, without interfering with their autonomous coordination.

Example 4 (Italy, SS1, second meeting)

1   M1:   E: so now I hate my mum a bit let's say I mean I can't bear her and above all because when he ((his grandfather)) was ill the night before he died, my mother went to the hospital to visit him and she knew she was pregnant of my brother and she didn't tell him
2   FAC: And so this thing annoyed you
3   M1:   Yes
4   FAC: But in your opinion for what reason did your mum do that?
5   M1:   Eh because she believed that he could survive
6   FAC: Ah I understand so she didn't think that he was (.) dying
7   M1:   Yes exactly and:
8   F1:   Yes but anyway M5 remember that at the end, I mean telling him or not she is always your mother, I mean you haven't to hate her because of this because this is a thing well I speaking about myself, in my opinion it is a small thing because look at some families
9   M2:   [At least she could
10 F1:   [There there are bigger problems problems where like children are abused and there you can say (.) I stand against my mother because she she uses a I mean but I don't think that you mum has never [abused you.
11 M2:   [she could have
12 F1:   For things that you did not do or other things I mean she used you (.) I mean she abused you in a few words [I mean there are
13 FAC: [Well no but If I understood well, he was
14 F1:   Eh no, okay I say ok he is upset because he is fond of his grandfather [and your mum

15	FAC:	[Of course
16	F1:	She didn't not tell she was pregnant of your brother but let's think of ot- I mean [a bit beyond this, I mean
17	FAC:	[the worst mh
18	F1:	In my view this is a small thing because listen e: to the news and the newspapers where you can read some time ago I read a newspaper where there were two parents who injected heroin to their children to make them fall asleep, I mean these are thing where you can say what mother I mean I hate her but not for a thing like that because at the end are you a believer? I am not a believer, I mean I don't think that there is an afterlife if your parents are believers. I mean in my view you grandfather is looking at you from heaven, do you understand? I mean your grandfather somehow knows that your brother exists like with mu mum when because my last brother ((name)) who now is six years old, I mean my grandfather, who is the father of my father, has never seen him but once my mum has, I mean before being pregnant and all things, she dreamt my grandfather who who had a child in his hand and then after a while my mum got pregnant so my mum was: I mean she believed in these th- [I mean she believes in these things
19	FAC:	[ah
20	F1:	So I mean she says even if didn't see him, he is not here physically ((gesticulates))
21	FAC:	But she [can can see him
22	F1:	[yes
23	FAC:	Would you like to add? ((to M1)) [do you want to answer or? ((to M5))
24	M2:	[Yes
25	M1:	No no no
26	M2:	I wanted to say that you could avoid hating your mum because (?) but somehow you are right a bit because he could have passed away with with happy?:
27		With a smile
28	M2:	Yes? With a smile?
29	M1:	((extends his hands))
30	M2:	Knowing that that his d- daughter's daughter was waiting a child, it se- isn't it? ((looking at F1 and M2)) [I think it's right
31	M3:	[no because after that he wanted to see him
32	M?:	[the daughter of his son

33	M3:	He said ah if you show it to him then yes he is happy if you tell him but he doesn't see it ((spreads his arms))
34	M2:	Yes but he is now looking at him from above
35	M3:	Ok yes bu- eh ((spreads his arms))
36	M2:	He could could pass away with with a smile like my nephew will have a child.
(..)		
37	?:	Another one
38	M2:	Eh okay [she will have another child
39	FAC:	[Would you like to add
40	M2:	That it is always nice, isn't it?
41	FAC:	Would [would
42	M1:	[at the beginning I believed that my mother telling him maybe he could try to survive but he had a lung cancer he could no more breathe because he had breathed asbestos for all his life because under: the roofs of the stables they were covered with asbestos and everything and but I have again two great-grandmothers I have all my grandparents and two are in Sardinia and those ones I don't know what they do ((smiles)) when they do it and where they do it then I have the other ones

In example 5, M1 describes the context of the photograph he has presented (turns 1 and 3), supported by the facilitator's appreciation (turn 2). In turn 4, F1 takes the floor asking a question, responded by M1. In turn 5, the facilitator stresses that there are other questions, and M1 starts coordinating and giving the floor to F2. In the following sequence, until turn 15, M1 coordinates the conversation, giving the floor to his classmates, answering to their questions, and also accepting a self-selected contribution (turn 14).

Example 5 (Germany PS1, first meeting)

1	M1:	Well, that was and that was four years ago. That was when we first were in Magdeburg. Well, we did travel from Berlin well, this day we travelled the firstest time to Magdeburg. And em, then first we were in the city centre and, this is here my brother ((points to picture)). And it is a long, for me it's a long time ago. Not so much memory.

2	FAC:	Mm-hm. Great.
3	M1:	And that's me here.
4	F1:	And who is that just adjacent?
5	M1:	That's my brother.
6	FAC:	I think there are quite a few questions, look.
7		((M1 points to F2))
8	F2:	How old were you then?
9	M1:	F3.
10	F3:	Did you get [on well with your] brother?
11	M1:	[just turn-,] just turned nine.
12	F3:	Did you get on well with your brother?
13	M1:	Emm, yes.
14	F4:	How old was your brother then?
15	M1:	My brother? About four.

6.5 Facilitation as a Way of Balancing Current Narratives and Initiatives

Children's initiatives may be problematic when they are provided while a narrative of another child is ongoing. This type of initiative enhances a dilemma for the facilitator, between the choice of continuing to enhance the ongoing narrative, and the choice of enhancing a new narrative based on the child's initiative. Both chosen actions are risky for the production of narratives since they reduce the exercise of agency of one child to enhance the agency of another one. Management of these situations is thus a delicate aspect of facilitation. The following examples show different ways of managing these initiatives.

First, management of children's initiatives may be based on clarification of their meanings, thus leaving the floor to them. In extract 6, M1 is explaining the photograph he has presented (turn 1). In turn 2, M2 comes into the conversation, recognizing his father in the photograph, which thus becomes personal also to M2. This initiative is developed into a narrative, supported and enhanced by the facilitator's questions (turns 3, 5 and 8), which contribute to clarify M2's initiative. In turns 10, 12 and 14, the facilitator asks questions to make sure that both children understand what is being asked, but also prompting to elicit further narratives. The example shows that, because of the recognition of another child's father in the picture, the development of a new narrative is allowed.

> **Example 6 (UK, SP2, third meeting)**
>
> 1 M1: Well, this one (..) well that's my uncle, that's my brother ((nome)) this is like a Palace legend called Speroni and this is me (..) I just look silly ((picks peers in the audience))
> 2 M2: I'm pretty sure that's my dad in the picture
> 3 FAC: Where's your dad?
> 4 M2: ((child comes up from his seat to point to picture)) There!
> 5 FAC: Behind him (..) behind him? How do you know that's your dad?
> 6 M2: Because I er (..) went there (..) a couple of (..) like one year ago
> 7 M1: It was the Palace-Burnley game (..) it was Palace-Burnley or it was Palace-Valencia
> 8 FAC: So were you there the same day?
> 9 M2: ((nods))
> (..)
> 10 FAC: So do you remember seeing each other?
> 11 M1: I think I did
> 12 FAC: Did you see each other (..) so you remember
> (..)
> 13 M2: Only when we were leaving
> 14 FAC: And you think that was your dad just behind him there?
> 15 M2: ((nods))

Children's initiatives can also be responded, rather than clarified. In extract 7, after F1's narrative (turns 1 and 3), three children take the floor (M1, M2 and F2). The facilitator has not time to react to M1 and M2 (whose contribution is not understandable) since F2 is very quick to take a new initiative. The facilitator's response to F2 is a formulation which explicates the gist of the girl's contribution (turn 7). Interpreting this formulation as a manifestation of interest, F2 continues her narrative and the facilitator shows listening through a minimal feedback (turn 11).

> **Example 7 (Italy, SS1, first meeting)**
>
> 1 F1: Then the other ones that come from ((city in the south)), e: they have: I see them and I have been more often recently because my father lost lost his job and: my parents split so he went to their home
> 2 FAC: I see so (.) they live here as well n[ow

3	F1:	[yes they live in ((place))
4	M1:	I care more about maternal grandparents though because basically I grew up with them everyday I go to their ho- home with them to eat, and: instead with the paternal ones that are d- e: they are both dead, that is my grandmother who died before I was born in two thousand one, and the grandfather died last summer in august
5	M2:	(?)
6	F2:	No I, on the other hand, had a closer relationship with my fathers' parents (.) because my mother's ones come from down there and I see them only when I go there on Christmas, Easter and: during summer holidays
7	FAC:	You have less opportunities to meet them
8	F2:	Yes while with my grandparents: who live here
9	M3:	Mum's side
10	F2:	I mean, I have lived most of my life with my grandparents but not s-not because: because of problem- some so- for a period because of family problems, arguments in the family, that is between my mum's family and my fathers' family and so I went to live for a while with my grandparents and my uncles and then we got separated for a while because of other problems then we get closer again but then my grandfather died of cancer
11	FAC:	Mh

In example 8, the facilitator's initial focused question (turn 1) enhances M1's short confirmation. In the following turns, the facilitator continues to ask questions, thus enhancing M1's narrative about siblings. In turn 7, M2 takes the floor with a long narrative about his old house in Greece. In turn 8, the facilitator comments, in short, what M2 said. This comment is not interpreted by M2 as an invitation to go on but, since the facilitator does not ask a question or provide a conclusion, she leaves the floor open for other initiatives, and M3 takes the floor to share another narrative (turn 9). In turn 10, the facilitator formulates this narrative, showing commonality between shared memories within the classroom, asking a new question, responded by the child non-verbally, and adding a concluding comment.

Example 8 (UK, PS2, second meeting)

1	FAC:	So was it a happy memory (..) because you're smiling, so was it a happy memory?
2	M1:	Yes ((nods))

3	FAC:	Oh that's good (..) so was it (..) was being in France a happy memory was the interaction a happy memory?
4	M1:	The interaction with my sister (..) I knew that if she pushed me off, my mum would've pushed her off to come and get me
5	FAC:	Ah, ok (..) so your mum was like protecting you then, yeah?
6	M1:	((nods))
7	M2:	Once in my old house in Greece there was a park it was technically the same as that place ((points to photo)) and it had a big fence and you could see all the children used to play inside of this and there was a place for little children that was like that high ((shows with hands)) and there was another place for big children where the water was that deep ((shows with hands)) and I used to play on the safe side and then once my sister she went to the other side because she was tall enough and she was playing (..) I wanted to go to the other side because I wanted to have fun (..) I knew how to swim and I went there and then when I went there, I felt because it was too big so I started crying and my sister saved me and she took me onto land and I started crying and crying and then I sneezed over my dad and then I went back to the pool
8	FAC:	It's nice to have a brother or sister so they can save you (..) that's nice, isn't it (..) so
9	M3:	Once (..) I think it was in the Isle of Wight or something yeah, I was in Isle of Wight (..) there was a beach right next to this river (..) this very long river and it had a kind of circle river and it had this part and thing that you go around (makes hand gesture) then when I was in the river, me and my brother had separate boats not boats but canoeing (..) canoeing (..) and then my mum and dad were got this boat they were rowing and I kept going really, really fast but it wasn't that safe and the things was I fell into the water and the boat turned upside down and then I came back and then (..) er (..) he came back and I kept on crashing into my brother and my brother kept shouting at me and then I banged into him again so he would fall into the water (..) and then when he fell (..) when he came up, his head hit my canoe and then I fell into the water and then when we were both upside down we hit each other's head and then we turned around and swam away and then once more I crashed into my brother and then I turned around and (cannot understand) and turned around and then I got back up and then I went to the beach and then in the beach there was right next to it (..) it was so long and when I got into the beach there were little (..) I think there

		were snails and there was so many there I ran screaming (..) and then I went to the next beach and it was a bit (?) and then I went too forward and the water was above my eyes and it was like so high and I got back
10	FAC:	So we have another beach story (..) quite a few people (?) (..) I wanted to ask something (..) you said you were rowing a canoe and you said rowing a (?) so do you think it's the same thing or is it similar, or is it ((M3 nods)) is it similar, you think (..) ok (..) I don't know (..) I've been a passenger on a boat but I've never driven one (..) so I think that's an interesting thing.

In the previous three examples, children's initiatives were clarified or responded. Sometimes, children's initiatives were not pursued by facilitators, who continued to focus on the ongoing narrative showing preference for its development. First facilitators provided very short feedback to children's initiatives, followed by support of the ongoing narrative. In extract 9, F1 tells the story of her relation with her boyfriend, starting from a photograph (turns 1–4). In turn 5, F2 takes the initiative providing a contextual information. The facilitator gives a short feedback, acknowledging the initiative ('ah okay') and asking a yes-no question of clarification (turn 6), then she continues to ask questions to F1.

Example 9 (Germany, SS2, second meeting)

1	F1:	Well, he is just important to me and he always stays at my house from Saturday to Sunday.
2	Children:	((laugh))
3	F1:	And em yeah, we just talk a lot all the time, it's always really fun with him. Emm ((laughs)) this weekend he stayed at my house again and we met up with F8 and what else. And ((name)) and ((name)). That was fun too because we messed about a bit. And, well yeah.
4	FAC:	Mhm.
5	F2:	Well, F11's boyfriend is in the army and then mostly when I'm at her house on a Saturday he's there too and then we do a lot of stupid things together. We chat together or sometimes he tells us about the army and then it's really interesting and funny.

6	FAC:	Ah, okay. So you get on well with him?
7	F2:	Yes.
8	FAC:	Was it important to you that he also gets on well with he- that he also gets on well with your friends?
9	F1:	I only ever see him at the weekends, yeah so, because he's in the army.

Second, in few cases, children's initiatives were not taken by facilitators. In example 10, the facilitator talks about keeping secrets first with M1, previously accused to violate secrets, but the boy does not respond, then with F2 who starts to tell her point of view. In turn 10, F3 takes the floor saying that she does not find difficult to keep secrets, but the facilitator ignores her and continues talking with F2. In turn 13, F3 insists in her initiative proposing an example, but once again she is ignored by the facilitator, who continues to solicit F2's narrative.

Example 10 (Italy, SP2, third meeting)

1	FAC:	Why don't you keep secrets?
2	M1:	[((expression of ignorance))
3	F1:	[(??)
4	F2:	Because it is hard
5	M2:	Because it's nice to say them
6	FAC:	Is it hard?
7	F2:	Yes
8	FAC:	You too lik- are
9	F2:	((nods))
10	F3:	No, to be honest [to be honest I keep them for me it's not difficult
11	FAC:	[Can't you keep secrets?
12	F2:	((shakes her head))
13	F3:	In the first year they told me a secret and I kept it until year five
14	FAC:	When was the last time you could not keep a secret?
15	F1:	This morning
16	Some:	[Hhh
17	FAC:	[No way
18	F2:	((says something to F2))
19	FAC:	What secret could not she keep this morning?
20	F1:	I won't say anything

In these cases, facilitators' decisions show their assessment of importance of narratives in the context of the classroom, in particular the importance of narratives based on children's autonomous initiatives. In extracts 6–8, children's initiatives introduce relevant narratives. In extract 6, child adds something personal to interpret the photograph. In extracts 7 and 8, children's initiatives develop series of narratives which are coherent with the topic of dialogue. On opposite, in extracts 9 and 10, the ongoing narratives seem to be more interesting in a dialogic view than the children's initiatives, which aim to get attention from facilitators replacing the current tellers.

6.6 Conclusion: Ways of Managing Children's Initiatives

Children's initiatives introduce unpredictability in communication, thus they challenge facilitation. These initiatives are both an important opportunity and a challenge for the function of enhancing agency and narratives, thus constructing a community of dialogue. Facilitators' actions may leave room for children's initiatives in different ways and with different outcomes. With decreasing effects on support of children's agency, facilitators may: (1) leave the coordination of the interaction to children; (2) clarify or respond children's initiatives; (3) give short feedback to children's initiatives and support the ongoing narrative; (4) ignore children's initiatives (very rarely, discourage them explicitly).

Children's initiatives are their most evident way of exercising agency; thus, they are particularly relevant for facilitation. Decision about the way of managing children's initiatives depends on facilitators' assessment of effects of their unpredictability for production of narratives and construction of dialogue, in particular when children's initiatives compete with other children's narratives and facilitators need to choose which contribution should be supported. This dilemma arises when support of agency (initiatives) and support of narratives diverge. Against this background, however, facilitation can include a methodology to manage unpredictable initiatives. While ignoring or discouraging children's initiatives may be a strategy to protect ongoing narratives, it cannot be systematic since it denies the most evident way of exercising agency, thus reducing children's motivation to exercise it.

In conclusion, facilitators should consider very carefully the meaning and importance of both one child's unpredictable initiative and another child's right of narrating. They should decide which action and narrative is more important to enhance in order to support a dialogic form of communication. Leaving the floor to children's autonomous coordination, on the one hand, and encouraging initiatives which introduce relevant narratives, on the other, are risky actions since they may randomize the effects of facilitation, but they also lower the impact of adult's coordination and strengthen children's trust in facilitation as a way of enhancing both agency and dialogue.

7

Dealing with 'Intercultural Issues'

Luisa Conti

7.1 Introduction

As described in Chapters 3–6, the analysis of SHARMED workshops focused not only upon the young participants and their contributions but also on the way in which the facilitators interacted with them. The project being intended to harness diverse underlying knowledge and thus increase agency among the youths, it was of particular interest to observe the manner in which adults' actions enabled or, indeed, hindered this. The contributions of young participants from first- and second-generation migration backgrounds were highlighted as an especially complex field in which the individuals were autonomous to put forth any aspect they found salient to their own experiences and identities. Although questions of migration came exclusively from this group of students, it permitted them to show more commonalities with their peers. In this manner, the children themselves drew attention to what is referred to as 'transdifference' (Breinig & Lösch 2002): difference cannot be understood as a clear, fixed boundary separating certain people from others. Difference, just like sameness, flows throughout identities without following binary logic. All class members are indeed different and this takes place on a variety of planes, as do their commonalities. This underpinned one key goal of SHARMED: not to pigeon-hole children with migrant backgrounds as 'other' but rather to draw attention to them as experienced complex individuals in their own right.

These pupils typically find themselves in social positions which are considered 'disadvantaged', a feature which is frequently projected onto their identities by others and can thus become part of their own identity construction. The classroom, however, could be a key space to counter this dynamic. All pupils participating in the project should experience themselves as valued contributors to their peers' social and intercultural awareness, and the particularly varied backgrounds of such pupils categorized as migrants provides an especially diverse field of knowledge which enriches the otherwise often narrow scope of information in educational institutions. Further to the benefits for the children listening to their stories, the exercise was wholeheartedly intended as empowering for such pupils. However, some facilitators' actions ran counter to the goals of facilitating agency or empowering the pupils. This chapter focuses upon successful actions and specific difficulties that facilitators showed in dealing with children who have themselves experienced migration or whose parents did. Which are the most important ways in which facilitation can enhance narratives of migrant children's personal cultural trajectories (Chapter 1)? Which pitfalls could have been avoided and how? This chapter aims to foster awareness of facilitation of intercultural communication and competences in order to allow pedagogues to facilitate participated learning processes in a more insightful way, reinforcing the second article of the Convention for the Rights of the Child: *children shall not experience discrimination*. In order to support the realization of this ideal, I shall share some theoretical reflections and subsequently formulate practical guidelines.

7.2 Theoretical Concepts and Reflections Brought Up by the Analysis

SHARMED project was carried out with a number of goals, one of the most significant being empowerment (see Chapters 1, 5 and 6). This empowerment is multifaceted. The children should be empowered to bring their own knowledge and experiences to the classroom and be treated not as subjects but rather as co-constructors of meanings in a reciprocal environment. They should also be empowered to learn from peers and thus diversify their cultural and social skill base. Empowerment is not just necessary for the processes themselves but also part of the outcome. The children are empowered by a more heterogeneous understanding of their own identities, as well as those of others. They can thus experience themselves as important actors and holders of cultural knowledge, characterized by true agency. From one act of empowerment, educators and facilitators can allow pupils in their care to thrive in the domino effect of their own increasing agency (Chapters 1 and 6). This self-determination is most clearly beneficial to pupils who may have been victims of discrimination due to identities which are interpreted as migrants. However, the empowerment intended and often achieved in the context of the SHARMED action research project creates self-confidence and mutual respect in all participants, growing steadily with time. Rather than being othered due to their diverse cultural heritage, such pupils can be considered valuable contributors to the dialogic intercultural communication and intercultural skills of their peers.

This conception of pupils of first- or second-generation immigrant status as self-determined agents shapes not just their perception by others but also their self-image. During (pre)adolescence, young people may find themselves at a challenging stage in identity formation (Fail et al. 2004). A dynamic and dialogic perception of identity processes on the part of educators can aid a more individual and constructivist self-image formation which breaks free from mutually exclusive collective, national or ethnic identities which otherwise dominate the discourse (Holliday 2011). Indeed, such essentialist cultural views are frequently evidenced in the behaviour of pedagogues towards children and youths with first- or second-hand experience of migration (Artamonova 2017). In this manner, a neo-racist ideology in which the taboo term 'race' is replaced with (ethnic) culture (Balibar & Wallerstein 1991) and a debasing subclassification of the Other can therefore be perpetuated under a more socially acceptable moniker. This form of essentialist discourse dictates that experiences of migration, even in later generations, are predominant in identity formation at the expense of other personal characteristics and may be supported by studies on intercultural education (e.g. Gay 2000; Mahon & Cushner 2012). Thus, although widely discredited in contemporary academic discourse in the field of cultural studies, it remains tenacious in politics, the media and thus also civil society (Bolten 2015: 102–3).

An example from Germany: the German Federal Statistic Office plays a role in perpetuating concepts of Germanness or otherness. Their framework classifies a 'migration background' as having at least one parent who was born with non-German nationality (DESTATIS 2020). Parents who have been in Germany since early childhood, were perhaps even naturalized as German citizens, therefore nonetheless pass on their label to their offspring. In this manner, the concepts of origin and ethnicity can be politically legitimated as placeholders for race. Essentialist neo-racist discourse is thereby also validated in the mass media and trickles down to institutions such as schools, even if the German education authorities (the Standing Conference of the Ministers of Education and Cultural Affairs, the KMK) claim to reject this ideology. Indeed, they advocate for a host of open-minded and intercultural skills to be acquired in schools. These include the following: mutual responsibility for equal access and participation on personal, education and societal levels; deliberate countering of discrimination and racism in both communication and cooperation; overcoming sociocultural, linguistic or interest-driven barriers; settling conflicts peacefully with respectful safeguarding of various interests; appreciating cultures as dynamic collective points of reference; reflecting upon one's own cultural influence or interpretation, mutual social classification and stereotypes; developing an openness towards others and other cultural interpretation; learning tolerance for contradicting cultural interpretations when communicating with others (KMK 2013: 4, translation by Luisa Conti). The SHARMED action research project could provide a useful tool to further these skills.

SHARMED aimed to promote a constructivist and thereby more interculturally aware conception of identity (Byrd-Clark & Dervin 2014; Dervin & Liddicoat 2013; Grant & Portera 2011; Holliday & Amadasi 2020; Kramsch & Uryu 2012) through the negotiation of culture in small groups (Holliday 2011). The children decided on their own terms what pictures to bring and thereby dictated what should be considered a key part of their identities – or not, for that matter. For the most part, the approach could indeed empower children to attain a constructivist understanding of identities, a key aspect of intercultural communication and competence, helping them to appreciate and value their classmates' specific and cultural knowledge. By challenging the standard direction of information flow from adult to child, the newfound intercultural competence is thus not classically hierarchical but rather *dialogic intercultural competence*. The examples presented in this chapter focus upon a specific form of intercultural awareness, which includes both general aspects, such as awareness regarding personal cultural trajectories, and more specific skills, such as techniques for supporting children's narratives, including narratives of second-language speakers. The examples and analysis show that this form of intercultural awareness and communication can lead to a highly effective dialogic intercultural competence, to be applied in all contexts.

7.3 Guidelines for Facilitators

Each of the workshop facilitators in the UK, Italy and Germany were selected and hired based upon their enthusiasm for non-hierarchical dialogic communication as well as highly relevant experience. The eight facilitators involved all had experience in working with school groups, yet the original contexts were quite diverse. For example, the German SHARMED project included: an intercultural trainer, a qualified outdoor adventure educator, a museum pedagogue and an intercultural mediator. All facilitators were trained on the project through a face-to-face training or an online MOOC on the concept of dialogue and of agency, on the use of pictures to foster dialogue, and on cultural identity. Although the training across the countries was almost identical, a great deal of variation was seen between the individual facilitation styles and thus also their degrees of success (empowerment) or, indeed, failure (disempowerment). Central areas of action will be summarized below under six headings and illustrated by several examples. The six areas of action concern the support of narratives of personal cultural trajectories and include (1) understanding diversity and fostering inclusion, (2) letting children decide their own field of experience, (3) creating conditions of curiosity and trust, (4) recognizing when removing from the exchange, (5) dealing with delicate issues and (6) creating awareness about prejudices.

7.3.1 Understanding Diversity and Fostering Inclusion

The method of the SHARMED action research project was based upon a constructivist understanding of identity formation, which was variously interpreted by the facilitators.

In excerpt 1, the facilitator asks questions about place of origin (turn 3) and identity (turn 5) to F2. The child's answer highlights her multiple identities (turn 6: 'I'm German, British and African'), although she clarifies that she only speaks English. This explicit disconnection between identity and language(s) spoken enhances the facilitator's question about the relation between language and culture (turn 7). F2 rejects any relation between language and identity (turns 8 and 10), and this rejection is recognized by the facilitator through an explication (turn 11), which is then developed by F2 through a reference to 'blood' as the basis of identity. In turn 13, the facilitator agrees with F2 and adds a personal story about her multiple identities. Then, in turn 15 she asks another question about the social conditions of the child's construction of identity. In turn 16, F2 rejects any specific classification of her identity, asserting that she is from all places. Thus, F2 stresses her multiple identities.

Excerpt 1 (UK, fifth grade)

01 FAC Ok (..) and it's interesting (..) because you've got your birth certificate and you were born in Germany?
02 F2   Yeah

03	FAC	ah (..) so would you say that you're German (..) what's your culture, who are you (..) what's your first name, M.?
04	F2	M. (..) My first name's S.
05	FAC	Your first name's S. (..) so S., how would you describe yourself? You're living in England but you've got a German birth certificate and maybe your family are from other places in the world so how would you describe yourself? Who are you? (..) What's your (..) yeah, who are you?
06	F2	Um, I'm German, British, and African (..) um so I'd say I do not speak the languages but I speak English
07	FAC	so do you think speaking the language makes you from that country, or?
08	F2	No
09	FAC	So what is it then, what do you think?
10	F2	I think it's the way (..) I think it's if you know that you're from there either you can't speak it or not
11	FAC	yeah, so it's not the language that you speak, it's that you know that you were born here or that you've lived there or that your family were like this because of where they're from
12	F2	Yeah (..) It's from your blood that's where you come from
13	FAC	From your blood? Yeah (..) I er (..) I think I agree with you actually because I was born here I was born in England but my family are Irish so someone said to me but you're English and I said well I was born in England but my family are all Irish so I think like you said my blood is Irish but I was born in England so it's a bit of a tricky ((does hand movement)) kind of thing to explain, isn't it?
14	F2	Yeah ((nods))
15	FAC	Yeah (..) does anyone ever ask you these things or is it just your own thinking?
16	F2	Yeah because some people say that you're born in Germany but your name's English, you talk in English and you sound like an English person but I'm not and then they say you're not from Germany because um, my name is pretty English as well, so I am from all places

The four facilitators in Germany appeared more stricken by the fear of essentializing identities of ethnicity or nationality. This often led to them missing the opportunity to empower children: even when children told stories or made comments related to their past in another country, the facilitators tended to act rashly to shut down the space to develop this narrative. Immediately after M6 has finished presenting his picture, he is given the possibility to specify where it was taken (by M8, another pupil). However, the facilitator fails to notice this positive reaction from M6, happy to tell that it was taken in Syria (turns 2 and 4). Instead of supporting him to develop a narrative around his 'memory of Syria', she insists upon inviting the other children to ask new questions (turns 3 and 5).

Excerpt 2 (GER, sixth grade)

01 M8: Emm, was it in Germany or in Syria?
02 M6: No, it was in Syria ((smiles)).
03 FAC: Okay, are there any more questions about the picture, has everyone seen it? Maybe also about why it was important for you to bring it in?
04 M6: Emm, it was my memory of Syria.
05 FAC: To share it. Exactly. Do you *plural* maybe have any questions.

7.3.2 Letting Children Decide Their Own Fields of Expertise

The basis of the SHARMED workshops were the photographs contributed by the pupils themselves. They were given only brief instructions (see Chapter 1) and were otherwise autonomous in their chosen contributions. These pictures can be considered a form of identity declaration: the youths clearly selected the images as most representative of them or their 'worlds'. Facilitation supported the narratives of personal cultural trajectories starting from the chosen photographs.

Excerpt 3 presents the narrative's co-construction by the facilitator's focused questions inviting the child to explain the contents of the photograph (turn 1) and focuses on the identities of the people depicted (turns 3 and 5). The facilitator asks questions such as when and where the photograph was taken (turn 7, 9 and 11), and the facilitator's repetition in turn 13 confirms the reception of the child's answers. The facilitator's open question (turn 15) opens a narrative about the clothes in the photograph that links family relationships through the symbolic meaning of clothes for the child's family (turns 16–22). The facilitator produces two minimal feedbacks (turns 17 and 19) as active listening and encouragement for the child to continue talking, without changing the narrative's content. Active listening is followed by a formulation that makes the relevance of the child's utterances explicit (turn 21). In turn 23, the facilitator's open question directly refers to the child's memory of photographic circumstances. In turn 26, M1 asks if the child's mother married her father, probably suggested by the fact that F has only talked of her mother. M1's question (turn 26) is fundamental for understanding the description of the photograph and to open a new course to the girl's narrative, which changes the context of events and their possible meanings for her. F's surprising answer in turn 28 is followed by the facilitator's formulation making this answer explicit (turn 29), thus stressing the new information. Using the pronoun 'we', the facilitator then invites the child to explain the situation, and suggests the expectation that he and the other children have different experiences (turn 32) to stress F's story as relevant in the context of the workshop, and indirectly invite F's classmates to pay attention. The facilitator reviews the marriage narrative, making the unusual situation explicit (turns 53 and 55), and developing the perceived meaning of marriage between the child's mother and her uncle (turn 57).

Excerpt 3 (IT, Italy, fifth grade)

01 FAC: It's a photo in which you are dressed: explain this photo to me (..) first of all, do you think there are some similarities with those that we have already looked at? ((pointing at the photos on the desks))
02 F: ((looks at the photos)) no
03 FAC: No? who are those two people? ((pointing at the photo))
04 F: My mother and my and my uncle
05 FAC: Your mother, your uncle and that one there is you?
06 F: ((nods))
07 FAC: Let's see if I find a photo that looks like this eh? ((browses through the photos on the desk)) you're right there aren't any (.) but when was this photo taken?
08 F: When I was: five years old
09 FAC: Were you five years old?
10 F: Yes
11 FAC: And why were you in that situation? What is this, a tent? A: What was that, what place is this?
12 F: Nigeria
13 FAC: It's in Nigeria

14	F:	((nods))
15	FAC:	But: for what reason was the photo taken? Because I see that you have the same special dresses: what are you telling us, what does it mean
16	F:	eh that: we are united, although that is not true because that is not my father but my uncle
17	FAC:	yes
18	F:e:	eh (.) wearing clothes made from the same fabric
19	FAC:	Yes
20	F:	It seems that we are one
21	FAC:	Ah the idea that you have the same clothing the same fabric, it's union
22	F:	((nods))
23	FAC:	And, and what do you remember about this photo?
24	F:	That it was my mother's wedding
25	FAC:	My mum's wedding
26	M1:	With your fa[ther?
27	FAC:	[who is
28	F:	With my uncle
29	FAC:	Who married your uncle
30	F:	yeshh
31	M2:	So [with her brother with her brother
32	FAC:	[explain it to us because we are not used to this and so we don't understand it very well
33	Some:	((comments))
34	T:	s[h::
35	F:	[my mother married my uncle but my uncle, who is my father's brother, took my father's place
36	M3:	[why, is he ((meaning F's father)) dead?
37	FAC:	[Why is: [what happened?
38	F:	[because he could not come to the ceremony
39	FAC:	ok
40	F:	Because he could not pay for the journey
41	FAC:	Yes, because where was your dad?
42	F:	In Italy
43	FAC:	Ah, um, you didn't tell us you were still in Nige- Niger or Nigeria?
44	F:	Nigeria
45	FAC:	in Nigeria
46	F:	((nods))
47	FAC:	And your dad had already come to Italy
48	F:	((nods))

49	FAC:	And why did he come here? To look for work?	
50	F:	Yes	
51	FAC:	And do you know where he lived?	
52	F:	In ((city))	
53	FAC:	In ((city)) ok and the wedding between your dad and your mum took place without your dad being there	
54	F:	((nods)) but there was someone who took his place	
55	FAC:	So ((points at the photo)) um, he took your father's place, it wasn't that she married your uncle	
56	F:	No	
57	FAC:	They needed a male figure	
58	F:	((nods))	

7.3.3 Being Curious and Having Trust

By inviting pupils to describe their pictures and tell their stories, the process of communication starts (see Chapter 4). By inviting the presenters to add details or the others to comment or ask questions it continues. The facilitators were tasked with embracing their own curiosity for personal cultural trajectories by retaining a situation-appropriate balance between open and focused questions and formulations (Chapter 5). The migrant students could then feel listened to and being a source of interest for their fellow workshop members, child and adult alike. Particularly effective facilitators employed a variety of information-seeking techniques in short succession.

In excerpt 4, F1 tells of her cousin, who, unlike her, is not considered Indian, but Scottish and English. F1 regrets that the place of living is more important than the place of origin. After asking for confirmation of the child's view, the facilitator develops the child's narrative through a formulation regarding her cousin's multiple identities (turn 4), then she stresses that labelling leads to missing part of someone's identity (turn 6). In turn 8, the facilitator investigates the child's interpretation of lack of recognition of multiple identities. F1 asserts that skin colour leads people to ignore the Indian part of her cousin's identity. In turn 12, the facilitator stresses 'all of the bits' of personal identity, thus showing her appreciation for the child's view on multiple identities. In this case, the facilitator is very active in developing the narrative of multiple identities.

Excerpt 4 (UK, fifth grade)

01	F1	um (..) people (..) because my cousin's dad is Scottish um and her mum is half-Indian, people say that she's not Indian, she's Scottish and English but she is
02	FAC	She is?
03	F1	Yeah
04	FAC	So, she's Scottish, English and Indian
05	F1	Yeah
06	FAC	because she couldn't be just half and half and then miss a bit out
07	F1	Yeah ((nods))
08	FAC	so why do you think that happens? Why do you think we all miss out a bit of somebody?
09	F1	Because (..)
10	FAC	It's tricky, isn't it?
11	F1	because she's got a different skin colour and we're cousins and people don't really think we're cousins and think we are not Indians
12	FAC	yeah (..) and I think all of the bits that we have that make us, us are all lovely and wonderful and it's good to know about them (..) yeah
13	F1	((nods))

Enabling agency is more challenging if the children do not yet master the classroom language, as the pitfall of facilitators' using closed questions and speaking *for* them is difficult to avoid. Furthermore, it is easier to divert or ignore content related to unknown cultures or experiences, especially if the content seems uninteresting or too delicate. This is demonstrated in the following excerpt, involving pupil from Aleppo who brought pre- and post-war pictures of her hometown. The girl invited discussion into her experience of war and the trauma of leaving her home, compressing eight different elements of information into one sentence (turn 1). Yet the workshop facilitator, who until that moment has shown brilliant competence in constructively facilitating the other students in speaking about their more positive associations with war, ignored these cues (turn 2). Instead, she asked for information about her online image search process (turn 2 and 6) before noting the tense atmosphere in the room and deciding that they would move onto the next picture (turn 8).

> **Excerpt 5 (GER, fifth grade)**
>
> 01 F6: well, I come from Syria and I live in Aleppo and I searched for this photo on the internet and I saw em, a war there and and the bo- bomb how they fall down and of course I am scared and that's really not good, that we must to flee Syria and I wish against the war, well, away, and err Syria is good again.
> 02 FAC: mm-hm. Thank you very much. Is it true that it's a before and after picture?
> 03 F6: emm, yes.
> 04 FAC: yes.
> 05 F6: that is.
> 06 FAC: so well spotted by all of you, yeah, mm-hm. Would you *plural* like to ask any more questions? Do you have any questions about the picture? Did you spend a long time searching the internet or had you found that picture before? Or what did you type into the search engine to find that picture?
> 07 F6: em, I wrote, em, photos of Aleppo. In those war and after- and er, before the war and then I found.
> 08 FAC: ah I see, that it was important to you wasn't it, that you that erm yeah. Mm-hm. Great. I notice the atmosphere now. I can see that we're all a bit uptight here now. It's that kind of feeling of, er, just like you already said, yeah you wouldn't like to go there on holiday, that's not a nice feeling, when you look at the picture, thanks very much to you for looking out that picture for us and sharing the memory with us. Okay.

7.3.4 Being a Co-pilot … from the Back Seat

The pupils showed a remarkable capacity to determine and guide the process of memory sharing once given the platform to do so and once they had understood and practised the new SHARMED dynamic. While the facilitator was key to negotiating complex interchanges, one of the most challenging facilitation skills to master was recognizing when to remove themselves from the exchange. Examples of simple yet effective tactics were the mix of open-ended and closed-ended questions and minimal feedback, in which the facilitator merely acquiesced in a signal of active listening and appreciation, repeated the wordings or verbally reflected the feelings shown by the children. This often promoted a continued presentation and truly empowered the students: they were being listened to, appreciated and the chance to display agency was given to them.

Excerpt 6 shows the child's construction of uncertain identity based on a narrative of loose connections with her mother's choice. The facilitator's question about the child's interest in her country of origin follows a long narrative about holidays in Romania. The facilitator's questions elicit the narrative of F1's grandparents' life in Romania, which is supported by the facilitator's minimal responses (turns 1–17). The facilitator's question in turn 18 enhances the child's narrative of uncertainty. F1 shows uncertainty about the choice between a traditional way of life in the town in which her grandparents live, on the one hand, and city life in Italy on the other (turns 19–23). This narrative of uncertainty is supported by a minimal response (turn 20) and it is developed through a very short formulation (turn 22). In turn 24, the facilitator asks if F1 would like to return to Romania and she confirms this possibility. In the last part of the sequence, the facilitator asks what F1's mother says about this possible return (turn 31). F1 says that her mother will certainly return to Romania, but she will leave F1 free to choose what to do. Thus, facilitation supports the narrative of the child's future choice as undetermined.

Excerpt 6 (Italy, seventh grade)

01	FAC	And: what do your grandparents do there?
		(..)
02	F1	e: they live in a village, [where
03	FAC	[Small?
04	F1	Yes yes
05	FAC	Mh
06	F1	where there are no cars,
07	FAC	Why?
08	F1	Eh because it's still a small village that is ((backward hand gesture))
09	FAC	They use: traditional me[thods
10	F1	[Yes
11	FAC	For example there are carts
12	F1	Yes ((nods))
13	FAC	I understand
14	M	Horses
15	FAC	Horses
16	M	[Yes
17	F1	[((nods))

18	FAC	And would you like to live: in a place like this? (..)
19	F1	yes and no (.) that is on one hand yes because well it seems better [except for:
20	FAC	[really?
21	F1	((nods)) but now I got used to the city
22	FAC	Did you? So you miss things you have in the city
23	F1	Yes
24	FAC	But did you ever get the idea to go back to Roma- to go to live in Romania?
25	F1	Yes
26	FAC	Really?
27	F1	((nods))
28	M	Nice
29	FAC	And your: who is Romanian? Your mum?
30	F1	Yes
31	FAC	What does your mum tell you?
32	F1	That: well she tells me: she lets me choose (.) she tells me that: when I grow up she will go to live there [and if I want to g-
33	FAC	[ah will she go to live there?
34	F1	Yes if I want to go with her I will go if I don't I will stay here

During the SHARMED workshops, dialogic culture was able to spread in the class: as the following excerpt shows, the children themselves began to successfully facilitate, expressing sincere curiosity and interest as well as contributing astute observation and moderation skills. This example is particularly interesting as their brilliant facilitation allowed them to get to the real memory hidden in the picture, which itself was key for discovering the uncertainty characterizing the reality for many migrant children – being at the mercy of institutions.

M7 brought a picture of himself and his brother in front of a fountain, explaining that they were in that city for the first time. F7 observes their serious expression in the picture and queries whether they were happy in that moment (turn 5). F7, F9 and F10 join the facilitators in posing interested questions until, twenty-five turns later, M7 reveals the fact that at that very moment they were awaiting the decision of the judge about a possible deportation. The dialogue continues in the same participatory manner and leads to further discoveries.

Excerpt 7 (GER, 4th grade)

01 F7:   Emm, were you *plural* happy, because in the photo it doesn't look, well, so-
02 F6:   Looks strange.
03 F7:   Yeah, like, smiling and stiff.
04   ((individual children go into the middle again))
05 F7:   Well, were you *plural* happy?
06 M7:   Yes. We were firstest time in ((city)), we didn't even know. Well so.
07 FAC: From where you *plural* come from, I see.
08   ((M7 chooses F10 to speak))
09 F10: Who took the photo?
10 M7:   Emm, my uncle.
11 F10: We-were you *plural* with your uncle or with your parents?
12 M7:   Emm, with parents and uncle.
13 FAC: Where did you *plural* come from if you were in ((city))for the first time?
14 M7:   Emm, er, well we- I mean, in ((city))for the first time, when arrived, first we were here in Stendal and then it was our first time in ((city)). And well we come from, from, well I'm not from Germany, I come from the Chechnya. That's the federal state in Russia. And, we were, well in ((city)) the firstest time here.
15 F7:   And er, do you know where exactly that was?
16 M7:   Umm, that was somewhere in the city centre, I don't remember very well.
17 F7:   Okay.
18 FAC: Mm-hm. And how
19 F9:   Was it nice that day?
20   ((M7 laughs))
21 F7:   I already just asked that though.
22 F9:   Was it fun in ((city)) then? You hadn't been there before.
23   ((M7 nods))
24 F?:   What did you *plural* do there?
25 M7:   Em, we were, em, we were in court, well in court if we will stay here in Germany or have to go back and err we will stay here in Germany.

7.3.5 Taking a Chance on Delicate Issues

As explained in Chapter 8, facilitation of narratives of conflicts and management of interactional conflicts required very long interactions, including tentative forms of mediation.

Furthermore, narratives about personal cultural trajectories were challenging when they included delicate issues or taboos, which are usually not allowed in communication, especially in educational contexts.

Excerpt 5 shows how difficult it is to handle topics such as war, indicating that educators ought to trust and support students in their decisions to discuss their related personal experiences. Excerpt 8, on the other hand, provides an insight into successful facilitation on delicate issues. The following dialogue regards eating habits that may be disapproved of or negatively evaluated in Western culture. F7 tells that her uncle ate his dead monkey; then she further explains that in Nigeria, where her relatives live, they eat animals such as mice and cats (turns 1–10). The facilitator promotes a contextualization of this habit in poor countries, but F7 rejects it and claims that this food is good, receiving the facilitator's confirmation (turns 1–16) without any judgement. Facilitation avoided an essentialist assessment of a delicate issue from the perspective of Western culture.

Excerpt 8 (IT, fifth grade)

01 FAC: Mh (.) what did you want to add?
02 F7:   The same thing happened to my uncles my uncle who is the owner of the monkey,
03 FAC: Yes
04 F7:   Right after the monkey died he said let's cook it and have it ((shrugs and raises an arm))
05 FAC: And they had it
06 F7:   Yes but they eat mice as well
07 FAC: Mice as well?
08 F7:   Yes and the ca- cats too
09 FAC: And when
10 F7:   And many other animals
11 FAC: And do you think this is because they are starving
12 F7:   ((shrugs nodding))

13	FAC:	Much poverty or [because
14	F7:	[no because they are yummy
15	FAC:	They are yummy
16	F7:	Yes ((smiles))

7.3.6 Being Aware of Prejudices

Facilitation can create the opportunity to deal with prejudices when they are identified in the migrant children's narratives. This requires much attention to what the children tell. For instance, in excerpt 4 the child suggests the existence of a prejudice concerning her cousin, 'because she's got a different skin colour and we're cousins and people don't really think we're cousins and think we are not Indians' (turn 11). The facilitator is able to find in this story the roots of a prejudice; thus, she comments on the importance of overcoming prejudices, respecting personal identities and avoiding categorisation: 'I think all of the bits that we have that make us, us are all lovely and wonderful and it's good to know about them'.

Particularly challenging is the situation in which a participant expresses a prejudice as a response to the picture or story told by someone else. That gives to the facilitator the task of protecting the person potentially hurt, while simultaneously allowing the other to reflect about the words they have used. This balance is hard to strike, as the following excerpt shows. The adults (FAC and T1) thus reclaimed their positions as responsible adults and called back into question the role of pupils as equal contributors, often for the sake of protecting pupils from culturally insensitive comments (turns 7 and 77). The opportunities to explore underlying prejudices and thereby work towards stronger mutual understanding and a constructivist conception of identity were therefore lost. Instead, the children were reminded that they were precisely that and the adults were in control of who may speak and decide what may be said, or not. Furthermore, this dialogue gives the opportunity to highlight the importance for pedagogues themselves to reflect about their own prejudices, as they might unconsciously flow into their behaviour. The picture was supposed to be presented by three pupils, yet T1 only directly invited the sole student without a migrant background (turn 1) to speak instead of giving all the same chance to start and play their part.

> **Excerpt 9 (GER, sixth grade)**
>
> 01 T1:   M10, please say something.
> 02 M10 ((holds the picture in their hands so that everyone can see it; legs are shaking)) Um: we have, we think that this is a lovely old house. Like, (?) because it really looks a bit older than the ones that people build these days. (?) But my theory was a bit different, it made me think more, (3) more of (?) ((laughing)) hiding place for terrorists.
> 03 M9   [((covers his face behind the page with his notes and laughs))]
> 04 M3   [((covers his face with one hand, giggles, and covering his mouth, says something quietly to M9))]
> 05   [((Some of the children laugh))]
> 06 M?: [Oh M10, eh!]
> 07 FAC: [I want to, I want to ask you, umm, it's about the stories and memories that each one of you has, and each memory is different
> 08   [((Some of the children laugh))]
> 09 F1: Shh! People!
> 10 FAC: So:::
>   […]
> 77 T1: I've got a question for M10. Right, seriously, what was … what do you say about your thoughts that you had, now that it has been cleared up?
> 78   ((M9 laughs briefly))
> 79 M10: Well, that I umm really underestimated it, that it's really a house, because it really doesn't look 100% like a normal house does.
> 80 F4: Maybe for him, because he has different fantasies than we do
> 81   ((Pupils laugh))
> 82 F4: [Well when I see the picture, (?) I thought straight away, who lives in there (?)]
> 83   [((Pupils talk at once))]
> 84 T1: [I actually] thought, that it's someone who comes from another country and I didn't know that it was F10's house, and I think that it's quite a nice house.

7.4 Conclusion

One of the most important outcomes of SHARMED is the fulfilment of the goals regarding intercultural communication and competence. SHARMED aimed to extend these goals to include all pedagogical staff involved in the schooling system in embracing dialogic intercultural communication and fostering peer-to-peer learning. Non-hierarchical communication provides an ideal platform for true intercultural exchange and social learning which benefits pupils, staff, the school community and the community at large.

Lessons live and breathe from the contributions of the distinctive pupils and the SHARMED workshop format reinforces this in a cross-disciplinary context. Each pupil provided a unique insight which was distinct to that of the other participants and frequently broached issues unfamiliar to her peers or teaching staff, a fact especially true for youths whose diverse identities included a variety of personal cultural trajectories. Appropriate facilitation of such content can aid students to develop dialogic intercultural competence. Several examples show that facilitators enhanced the understanding of diversity, fostered inclusion, supported children's decisions about their own fields of expertise, enhanced curiosity and trust, recognized when to removing themselves from the exchange, dealt with delicate issues and prejudices. Facilitation can enhance a variety of narratives, which lead to different types of small cultures formation (Holliday 1999). The interactional construction of narratives may concern personal cultural trajectories of migration, which lead to children's identity construction. The analysis shows facilitators' actions leading to co-construct children's identity, such as questions, which may be both focused and open, formulations that elicit children's narratives by explicating or developing them, comments and personal stories inspired by children's narratives. All these actions support narratives concerning children's personal experiences, feelings and views. The analysis of facilitated interactions shows that the interactional construction of identity depends on children's personal experiences.

This analysis leads to four important lessons concerning the facilitated interactional construction of migrant children's identity. First, facilitation of narratives is an important way of constructing the meaning of cultural identity. Second, facilitation can support either explicit narratives of identity or narratives of personal experiences suggesting identity. Third, facilitation highlights that the contingently constructed forms of identity are based on children's personal cultural trajectories, rather than on their belonging to cultural groups. Fourth, facilitation encourages different ways of constructing children's identity, leading to different types of small culture formation.

However, the analysis also revealed occasions upon which the pupils could or would have liked to share their expertise but were not given this opportunity. As such, the analysis also revealed some *dis*empowering situations. This shows that dialogic competence is not enough: intercultural competence is needed. The mere employment of a mutual contribution format is thus not sufficient, but those carrying it out must be specifically and extensively trained to be able to implement it in a way most likely for it to be successful and meet its objectives.

The six critical fields in which the results of the analysis have been clustered represent the areas in which pedagogues ought to be trained. Pedagogues should develop intercultural competence, becoming aware of their prejudices, being continuously conscious of the multifaceted identity of all children and critically reflecting upon their own behaviour towards them, as well as developing more specific skills in dealing with multilingualism, where relevant, in a fair and enriching way for all.

8

Conflicts in the Classroom

Claudio Baraldi

8.1 Introduction

When children's initiatives (Chapter 6) fuel classroom conflicts, challenges for facilitation and the construction of a community of dialogue increase. Classroom conflicts may be interpreted as communication systems which arise through a participant's rejection of communication and continue through mutual rejections between participants (Luhmann 1995). SHARMED revealed that conflicts arise occasionally in communication with high frequency; they become important when participants interpret them as symptoms of crisis in a communication system. Analysis in this chapter shows that conflict mediation may be based on invitations to reflect on different social constructions of accusations, deconstructing negative identities and proposals of alternative narratives. In particular, this chapter examines formulations, 'circularity' in questioning and facilitators' personal stories and explores how these may be useful for conflict mediation.

8.2 Narratives and Management of Conflicts

Conflicts become important through three phases: amplification, reproduction and stabilization (Tilly & Tarrow 2007). Amplification is based on dissemination of conflictive positions, convergence of conflictive positions and coordination which transforms this convergence into shared intents. Reproduction may be based on several factors, such as importance of topic, establishment of boundaries (e.g. between Us and Them or between Us and an individual), negative labelling. Some types of action, for example enquiring and pressing questions (Maoz 2001), defensive statements (Stewart & Maxwell 2006), assertive explanations (Ramsbotham 2010), interruptions (Zupnik 2000) and attribution of negative responsibilities to participants are important for conflict reproduction. Stabilization is based on accumulation of problems, and stable conflicts may continue through phases of escalation and de-escalation.

Conflictive communication produces opposite narratives which describe and explain the meaning of conflicts. Conflictive narratives are based on accusations, defences, explanations, justifications and negative attributions to participants (Ramsbotham 2010; Stewart & Maxwell 2006). Through these narratives, 'truth' is narrated as unique though it is always partial. Narratives include constructions of positive and negative identity and allow the stabilization of conflicts, in particular when they deal with negative responsibility of actions and incompatible interests or values. Conflictive communication may also produce the distinction between dominant narratives and counter-narratives.

Conflicts allow the reproduction of communication, but they also introduce problems and uncertainty in this reproduction (Luhmann 1995). Thus, conflicts highlight that it is necessary to pay attention to communication problems and open the possibility to change communication systems. However, if conflicts continue for a long time, they can have destructive effects in communication systems, and lead to violence.

These characteristics of conflicts may be observed in the classroom during facilitation. Thus, the first important problem in facilitation is identifying conflict dynamics, i.e. the conditions of their amplification, reproduction and stabilization. This requires attention to the ways in which conflicts are narrated and to ways in which these narratives establish negative responsibilities and identities. This means using facilitation to manage conflicts in the classroom (Winslade & Williams 2012).

In classrooms, conflict management is frequently based on right/wrong distinction which enhances monologues. Monologue means that participants in the interaction: (1) give more value to their own action than to their interlocutors' understanding, (2) show certainty of their own understanding, attributing errors to their interlocutors' actions, (3) show indifference towards the consequences of their own actions on their interlocutors, (4) do not pay any attention towards their interlocutors' expressions of feelings and thoughts. In contrast, mediation may be considered an effective method to manage conflicts (Picard et al. 2015), which does not establish a distinction between right and wrong positions; rather it aims to lead all participants to take advantage from the reduction of destructive effects of conflicts and from the establishment of dialogue.

Conflict mediation shares with facilitation a method of enhancing personal expressions and trajectories and, most importantly, positive responsibilities, thus reducing or eliminating attributions of negative responsibilities and identities. Moreover, conflict mediation may integrate facilitation and production of narratives. For instance, the method of transformative mediation includes facilitation of recognition and empowerment of participants' views and actions (Bush & Folger 1994). The method of narrative mediation includes facilitation of production of participants' personal narratives and new narratives of collaboration (Winslade & Monk 2008; Winslade & Williams 2012). Thus, mediation may use facilitation to transform 'the adversarial narrative into an emergent, co-created, collaborative narrative' (Stewart & Maxwell 2010, p. 77). An interesting method of facilitation in narrative mediation, suggested by Winslade and Monk (2008), is double listening: mediators listen to participants' adversarial narratives on the one hand, and elaborate and propose alternative narratives, based on collaboration, on the other. Thus, facilitation is not a form of conflict management, since it aims to enhance collaboration, but it may be used to mediate conflicts (Baraldi 2019a; Baraldi & Iervese 2010).

8.3 Facilitation as Tentative Mediation of Conflicts between Children

Children's initiatives may enhance conflicts that are amplified, reproduced and stabilized in classroom communication. The following examples show tentative conflict mediation, based on narratives of conflict, during facilitated meetings in the SHARMED project. Conflicts were almost non-existent in England and frequently avoided in Germany. Thus, the following examples are from the Italian context; they are partial transcriptions of long interactions. They show how facilitation may lead to enhance narratives of conflict, empower participants' actions and recognize different positions. Mediation aims to reduce labelling and attribution of negative responsibilities and identities, discouraging reproduction and stabilization of conflicts.

The following examples concern action of one facilitator working in classrooms where conflict narratives arose occasionally, starting from children's initiatives, but indicating existing and important conflicts in the classroom. These examples stress limits and possibilities of conflict management through facilitation, in particular based on double listening. They also highlight the importance of the mediator's 'personal qualities' (Bowling & Hoffman 2003).

8.3.1 Alternation of Narratives and Alternative Narratives

In example 1, the conflict narrative is based on a video in which a child (M1) describes the photograph of a red flower. M1 declares that red is his favourite flower and the facilitator asks him the reason of this preference. In turn 1, the child provides his answer ('the blood (.) the blood') and the facilitator asks if he intends that life is in blood or if he likes blood, suggesting the possibility of a 'deviant' answer, which is provided by the child in turn 3 ('I like to hit'). Thus, the narrative of conflict is based on M1's unpredictable initiative, as choice of the photograph and explanation of its meaning. The facilitator repeats the child's statement confirming understanding; then he asks classmates if someone has been beaten up by M1. With this move, the facilitator avoids closing the conflict or engaging a conversation only with M1, and involves the class into the narrative. Moreover, he does not judge or label M1's position, avoiding to assign him a negative responsibility which could influence his construction of identity.

Example 1 (Italy, SS1, third meeting)

1 M1: Blood (.) blood
2 FAC: Ah the blood is there life in blood eh? Or is it because you like blood?
3 M1: No I like to hit
4 FAC: You like to beat up ok is there anyone who got beaten up by him?

The facilitator's question enhances a general confirmation of M1's behaviour (turn 8), and thus a collective narrative which amplifies the conflict, creating convergence and coordination of conflictive positions in the classroom and enhancing the negative responsibility of M1. In particular, M2 claims for his own identity as a victim (turns 10 and 12). M1 takes a new conflictive initiative saying the names of those who have never been victim of his violent actions (turn 13), stressing again his negative identity and challenging his classmates. Thus, a boundary is arising between the two positions. The facilitator ignores M1's action and addresses again M2 asking his opinion about M1's behaviour (turn 17). With this question, the facilitator moves the attention from M1's negative identity to the way in which this identity is constructed in classroom communication, then to the way in which the boundary between M1 and the rest of the classroom was fixed. The facilitator's following question aims to understand how the conflict is produced (turn 19). M2's answer ('those times') stresses the repetition of M1's violent action and then the stabilization of the conflict, based on the narrative of M1's negative identity. M1 takes another initiative to confirm his negative identity through the reference to an apparently well-known episode (turn 24). Once again, the facilitator ignores M1's initiative and continues to ask questions to understand M1's motives from M2's point of view. Eventually, M2 attributes a humoral behaviour to M1, who rejects this attribution which weakens his self-constructed identity (turn 29).

5	Some:	Yes
6	FAC:	Eh?
7	M2:	((rises his hand))
8	M?:	Everybody
9	FAC:	Did you get you beaten up?
10	M2:	((nods))
11	FAC:	And you never reacted?
12	M2:	((shakes his head))
13	M1:	Well, (names)) never got beaten up
14	M3:	(?)
15	FAC:	But why do you think he likes to hit people?
16	M2:	I don't know
17	FAC:	You don't know
18	M2:	no
19	FAC:	You've never asked yourself you but you didn't react- would you like to tell us about that time, would you?
20	M2:	But those: [those times
21	M?:	[those times
22	FAC:	Ah more than once
23	M2:	Yes (?)
24	M1:	They were two, one and two ((indicates))
25	FAC:	Do you think he does enjoy it like that [or
26	M2:	[yes he wakes up and says I go to school and I hit someone
27	FAC:	Ah
28	M9:	(?)
29	M1:	No! It's not like that

The facilitator turns to M1 to investigate his rejection (turn 30). Now, M1 seems more uncertain in assigning a meaning to his own actions, and the facilitator explores this uncertainty through a formulation (turn 33, 'that is, you don't') and an open question (turn 35). Since M1 does not react properly, the facilitator attempts a development, suggesting an interpretation (turn 37, 'when you are most nervous'). M1 continues to avoid reactions while M2 insists on interpreting his behaviour as oscillating between aggression and friendship (turns 45 and 47) and thus on defining M1's identity as unstable. This interpretation leads M1 to a reaction, which is however blocked by a hostile objection (turn 49), which re-establishes the boundary and the negative identity. In the following turns (51–54), the facilitator actively co-constructs the narrative of M1's necessity of unloading by beating up, through a formulation which suggests that M1's behaviour is something normal, thus reducing his negative identity.

30 FAC: It's not like that?
31 M2: I [think it is so then
32 M1: [no, for boh I dont' know (.) I mean I don't I mean I don't wake up and say ah today I am going to beat someone up for instance ((he looks around))
33 FAC: So, you don't
34 M1: E: (.) well
35 FAC: But is there something that makes you to behave like that?
36 M1: Eh boh well
37 FAC: F[or instance when you are more unsettled
38 M1: [when
39 FAC: Or when
40 M1: [I mean when
41 M2: [well sometimes
42 M1: Go ahead go ahead
43 M2: Go ahead go ahead
44 M1: Go ahead
45 M2: Sometimes I mean there are days when (.) boh he com- he comes to your desk and other days when
46 M1: Well [you what
47 M2:   [he is a good friend of yours
48 M1: Wait you what (?)
49 M8: But you just told him to speak, let him
50 M2: He is very friendly like he comes close to you, he gives you some snack, he chats ((spreads his arms)) and [sometimes
51 FAC: [but there are moments when he needs to:
52 M2: Let off steam
53 FAC: To let off steam physically I mean instead of listening to some music and relax he lets off steam by beating people up
54 M2: Yes

Later, the same day, in a second meeting the facilitator resumes the different narratives, in particular the narrative of M1's oscillating behaviour. M1 confirms the facilitator's summary through minimal responses. The facilitator attempts to enhance the narrative of the causes of the conflict, but without success, while M1 continues to show uncertainty, in this phase renouncing to affirm his negative identity. In the shown sequence, the facilitator tries again to involve M1 (turn 1), but unsuccessfully. In turn 7, however, M1 takes the initiative of attributing a negative responsibility to his classmates ('some here provoke'), thus redefining the boundary between him and his classmates. The facilitator emphasizes this new narrative, and M1 takes this opportunity to reopen the conflict, confirming his negative identity. Although the facilitator insists on explicating M1's interpretation with an interrogative tone (turn 11), M1's action is successful in fuelling the conflict with M2. He is immediately interrupted by the facilitator who insists on interpreting M1's position, through two questions (turns 15 and 17). The facilitator is finally able to enhance M1's interpretation of his own way of acting (turn 20: 'one tells me you're a loser') and identification of a classmate (M6) as instigator. Against this background, the facilitator is able to suggest an alternative narrative of the conflictive position towards M1 ('I don't know, he's angry with you') to lead him to consider more complex explanations of the conflict.

```
1    FAC:   Eh? But do you like to talk about this?
           (..)
2    M1:    Yes
3    FAC:   Eh? (..) but do you think that this can change your behaviour or not?
4    M1:    E: boh
5    FAC:   You don't know
6    M1:    ((clicks his tongue)) (..) Also, I mean, some here wind me up
7    FAC:   Wind [me up
8    M?:         [mh:
9    M1:    For instance you
10   FAC:   So, there are things that wind [you up, right?
11   M1:                                    [(S.)
12   M2:    Not all the times
13   M1:    I am not saying all the times [sometimes
14   FAC:                                  [may I: what's that what are the
           things that wind you up?
```

15	M1:	Well, boh, that is for instance (.) so
16	FAC:	so, is there something that annoys you when you react?
17	M1:	That one tells me you're a loser
18	FAC:	Ah
19	M1:	For instance M6 [e:
20	FAC:	[Well maybe one tells you that you a loser because he wants
21	M1:	((nods looking at M6))
22	FAC:	I don't know he is angry [with you

M6 rejects the negative identity and this opens a new conflict with M1 (turns 44–49). This short conflict amplifies the risk of reproducing classroom conflict, fuelled by combination of negative labelling of M1 and his attempt to identify his classmates' negative responsibilities. The facilitator continues in his attempt to develop the narrative of conflict, stressing the divergent interpretations of the conflict. Then, he introduces an alternative narrative, paying attention to avoid the reproduction of negative identities (turn 53: 'he probably has a sensitivity that allows him to see things as provocative that maybe you didn't want to provoke him'). In the following turn, the facilitator suggests dialogue as solution of the conflict (turn 55: 'but if he perceives it like this or you talk about it or if not it becomes difficult right?'). He concludes the tentative mediation with a question about M1's reaction to his own possible incitement, which leads M1 to abandon a conflictive position.

23		[excuse me so on Saturday when you kicked and punch me when we were leaving, tell me why
24	M1:	(?)
25	M6:	Did I do anything? [((name)) (name and ((name)) they were with me
26	M1:	[(??)
27	M6:	You [suddenly started
28	M1:	[no no no you winded me up
29	FAC:	So from his point of view there were [provocations (.) probably he
30	M8:	[°(?)° ((to M6))
31	M6:	[not at all, I didn't abuse him, do you remember last Saturday` ((to M8))
32	FAC:	Yes no, he is delicate probably and this makes him feel to be provoked when maybe you didn't want to provoke him

```
33  M6:   But I didn't say anything at all [that time
34  FAC:                                   [eh but if he feels like that either
                you talk about it or it gets messy, right? (.) because if I wind you
                up you what do you do?
35  M1:   Eh: me?
36  FAC:  What do you do?
37  M1:   I don't do anything to adults
38  FAC:  Ah here hh
```

Much later, M1 affirms that he attends a group of boy-scouts and that he does not behave in a provocative and violent way in this group. The facilitator resumes briefly the previous narrative suggesting a link between behaviours and social contexts. Although he does not explicitly suggest the link between M1's negative identity and the context of the classroom, this link was implicit in the way in which the facilitator mediated the conflict.

Example 2 shows a form of mediation which is similar to that shown in example 1. In the previous conversation, F3 talked about her peaceful friendship with F4, but she also referred to M15 as a person who should stop opening conflicts. This accusation enhances a narrative of conflict, since the facilitator asks for the meaning of F3's statement, suggesting that M1 might like conflicts (turn 1). After F4's confirmation, the facilitator asks her how would be possible to tell those who like conflicts to keep them from fighting (turn 3). This question moves from the construction of M15's negative identity to the way of managing conflict. F4 says that she does not know and the facilitator asks her why she does not like conflicts. This question leads to observe conflict as destroying interpersonal relations. The following facilitative action (turn 9) is complex: it includes first an interrogative explication both emphasizing this topic and suggesting that it is an interpretation rather than a 'fact' ('because you think that'), then a development that links this interpretation to the interpersonal relation between F3 and F4. Attention paid to F3 is useful to co-construct her narrative of negative responsibility and to focus on the way of managing it, while questioning the 'negative' side of conflict. An unpredictable effect of this conversation is that M15 takes the floor to express his point of view that a relationship without conflicts does not exist since affect needs conflicts.

Example 2 (Italy, SS2, third meeting)

1	FAC:	Eh? That is, what would you tell him to make him stop fighting? because he is one who likes a fight
2	F4:	Eh I know hh
3	FAC:	And so what do you do? If one who likes a fight, how do you make him stop?
		(..)
4	F4:	I don't know
5	FAC:	You don't like fighting, why?
		(..)
6	F4:	Boh maybe not to damage a relationship
7	FAC:	Because you think arguing ruins things (.) in a few words
8	F4:	Yes
9	FAC:	((nods)) And instead she is one who gets offended
10	F4:	((looks at F3))
11	F3:	((smiles))
12	FAC:	[Because I think
13	M15:	[In my opinion without arguing a relationship doesn't exist I mean if you like a person you argue

This unpredictable initiative changes the trajectory of the interaction introducing the point of view of the accused person. The facilitator develops the gist of this initiative with a formulation which resumes the pleasure of conflict (turn 14). However, M15 rejects any generalization about pleasure of conflicts insisting on the importance of conflicts in interpersonal relations. The facilitator proposes a new development concerning the absence of limitations in personal expressions (turns 18 and 20). A new unpredictable initiative is taken by F3 who opens a conflict with M15, inviting him to consider that personal expressions do not necessarily imply conflicts (turn 23). The following gaze at the facilitator may be interpreted as a way of asking for his approval. However, the facilitator avoids any judgement, asking her point of view about M15's expression (turn 27), then he explicates her answer stressing its wisdom, but also reaffirming the difference between the two positions (turns 29 and 31). This positioning enhances a de-escalation, shown by the participants' smiles. The facilitator takes this opportunity to invite M15 to reflect on the ways of managing conflicts (turn 36) and concludes the interaction stressing again the different ways of interpreting interpersonal relations (turn 38).

14	FAC:	You like arguing
15	M15:	no [it's that
16	F4:	[yeshhh
17	M15:	It's not that it's that in my opinion if you really love someone well you argue [I mean (?)
18	FAC:	[let everything out
19	M15:	((nods with a light smile))
20	FAC:	Without without without (.) holding anything back
21	M15:	((seems to shrug his shoulders a bit))
22	F3:	Yes but you can let it all out e without arguing (.) [I mean you talk and the you put:
23	M15:	[it's not true, I mean if you Never argue that means that you don't care about that person at all
24	F3 and F4:	((look at him showing disagreement then they look at FAC))
25	FAC:	Don't you agree?
26	F3:	No ((smiling))
27	FAC:	What do you think?
28	F3:	well if two th- I mean if one thinks one thing and the other thinks differently (.) they argue but they don't start to fight then a they find an agreement
29	FAC:	They must be reasonable
30	F3:	Yes
31	FAC:	And then the find an agreement
32	F3:	Yes
33	FAC:	While he says we argue I while you find an agreement
34	F3, F4 and M15:	((smile))
35	F4:	Hh
36	FAC:	And then, because we love each other, we shake hands, right? Is that it?
37	M15:	((seems to nod lightly while he curves his lips not completely convinced))
38	FAC:	Two different ways
39	F4:	((nods))

Examples 1 and 2 show that facilitation can first disclose the features of a conflict, then its motives, and finally suggest an alternative and more complex narrative. Facilitation stresses the importance of different ways of narrating conflicts and interpersonal relations, leading to recognition and empowerment of different legitimate positions. In example 2, in particular, recognition and empowerment concern different metanarratives (Somers 1994) which give negative or positive meaning to the conflict in interpersonal relations, moving the focus on an alternative narrative.

While a complete and effective conflict mediation was not possible in the context of facilitation during the SHARMED project, it is interesting to observe that facilitation can include this mediation, avoiding that conflicts become destructive in the classroom and suggesting alternative narratives of conflicts, through double listening. The production of alternative narratives contrasts the production of judgements, i.e. the distinction between right and wrong positions, and the construction of negative identities.

The facilitator's conflict mediation was based on the alternation of different narratives, avoiding the construction of the dominant narrative and enhancing different and alternated contributions. This way of acting enhances the explanation of conflicts from different points of view, reducing the risk of constructing predefined negative identities. In examples 1 and 2, conflict mediation is certainly incomplete, but these examples show that it is possible to include conflict mediation in facilitation.

8.3.2 Rules and Personal Story

The last example concerns a football game in the school courtyard which originated a conflict. The conflict arose because the referee expelled M2. In turn 1, M2 is telling his version of this conflict, but the facilitator interrupts him to ask him why he is angry. M2's answer is not clear in the recording but it seems that he is constructing a positive identity. The facilitator reassures M2 with a joke about his ability (turn 4: 'obviously you are too good'), but M2 claims that he is more interested in justice than in his ability. The facilitator focuses on the version of the referee (F3), who tries to explain the reason of the expulsion. This move is used by the facilitator to understand M2's point of view about rules, thus looking for a different way of constructing the child's positive identity.

Example 3 (Italy, PS1, third meeting)

1   M2: The-then they got together to tell me you are out and I got angry and I told them no you cannot [sunt-
2   FAC: [excuse me why did you get angry?
3   M2: Eh because (?) sent- [(?)
4   FAC: [obviously you are too good so

5	M2:	But no no! I am nothing because M1 was playing with M4 and I was on my own doing nothing
6	FAC:	The referee wants to share her opinion eh ((F3 raised her hand)) let's hear to – what the referee says
7	F3:	That we told him you are out [he didn't
8	FAC:	[but was there a reason to tell him he's out
9	F3:	Yes because each e: the first time that I told him that was a foul, he said who cares so I told him look it's foul and then it's foul (?) f[oul
10	FAC:	[ah
11	F3:	He says I don't [care
12	M2:	[well but
13	F3:	So I told him e: go go to ask to M1 how to play [foul if you don't know and the e: he turned against me
14	M2:	[how-
15	FAC:	[however in your opinion
16	M2:	Eh
17	FAC:	Accepting rules (?) (.) you don't like it ?
18	M2:	No

This move is successful since M2 affirms his positive attitude towards rules. The following move concerns the referee's authority in establishing rules and the consequences of rejecting them (turn 20). M2 seems to understand that he has no valid reason (see Fisher 1987); therefore, he changes topic saying that it is important to discharge the energy accumulated during the school time. In this way, the child continues to construct a positive identity. When the facilitator develops this topic, stressing that discharging energy requires playing rather than being expelled (turn 22), M2 claims again his innocence and his sense of justice. The facilitator recalls the importance of rules (the referee makes decisions) and stresses the problem of the way of acting ('so what? How do we do it?'). This enhances M2's difficulty in putting together respect of rules and sense of justice. The facilitator does not show the intention of stressing M2's wrong position, but to show that M2's conflictive action has damaged him and to suggest an alternative action based on dialogue ('but maybe you were right, weren't you? But (.) One says okay but now the referee decides and then later when we are in class we talk about it and I explain my reasons'). Finally, in turn 32, the facilitator mitigates the meaning of the conflict saying that reflecting in that situation ('there and then') is not easy.

20	FAC:	E: to accept the rules as you were saying right? And who enforces the rules on the pitch?
21	M2:	The referee
22	FAC:	And so if you don't listen what happens
23	M2:	No but because because all children are are always energetic because they spend two hours sitting to study and then they recharge their energy and I (?) for example I have very much of it usually I do many things at home so I have lots of it
24	FAC:	However (.) I understand that you needed to play it was important for you to play even if you did a:
25	M2:	I didn't do nothing really [to
26	FAC:	[but is it important what you really did or what the referee saw?
27	M2:	What the referee did
28	FAC:	Eh so? How [do we do this?
29	M2:	[eh yes but (?) actually this happened for (?)
31	FAC:	No, but maybe you were right, weren't you? But (.) One says I get it now the referee makes the calls and then later when we are back in the classroom we talk about it and I explain my reasons
31	M2:	Eh yes [(?)
32	FAC:	[is it possible to do that?
33	M2:	Yes but
34	FAC:	It's not easy on the spot

Later, the facilitator recalls the mitigation, insisting on it (turns 64–70). This action enhances M2's alternative narrative blaming aggressive behaviours in football games, which is coherent with his construction of positive identity. This new narrative is followed by the introduction of the facilitator's personal story, which allows a final reflection on the conflict. The facilitator introduces his story by creating the expectation of an exceptional case (turns 74–81) and attracting the children's attention. In turns 83–103, the facilitator tells the story of his expulsion from a football game and the following suspension from football games for one year. The facilitator concludes that his behaviour was wrong (turn 108), suggesting that it was based on a negative identity. This story, which seems to be very interesting for the children, is a testimony of the damages of inadequate interpretation of the meaning of football.

64	FAC:	Eh football is anyway very physical it's difficult then to stay calm [then
65	M?:	[but
66	FAC:	No?
67	M2:	(?)
68	FAC:	Is it not difficult?
69	M4:	Difficult
70	FAC:	It's difficult
71	M2:	Have you ever watch games where someone gets angry? Because
72	FAC:	Y[es
73	M2:	[it makes me thing of terrorism
74	FAC:	Now I am going to tell you one thing but then (.) will you forget about straightaway? If I tell you?
75	Some:	Yes, no
76	FAC:	Are you sure?
77	F10:	Tell anyway
78	FAC:	Sure you'll forget about it?
79	F10:	[no?:
80	?:	[yes
81	FAC:	And that you won't tell that around?
82	Some:	Yes
83	FAC:	So when I was (.) fourteen (…) I was playing football and I was a little nervous maybe a little bit: ((pointing to M2)) I too had a lot of (.) energy to spend, right? And I was playing in defence (.) Then a forward dribbles me, and I tackle him and I fouled him? Then the referee came to me and show me and: show the red card [and me
84	M14:	[what? Yellow yellow
85	FAC:	No, direct red
86	M14:	Red?
87	FAC:	((nods))
88	?:	(for?)
89	M3:	Yes [it can be it can be
90	FAC:	[as it was a foul that I shouldn't have done do he thought
91	?:	(?)
92	FAC:	And guess what I did
93	M2:	[You kicked the referee
94	F3:	[Boh you were angry
95	FAC:	((points to M2)) I did like he did him I got angry with the referee

```
 96  ?:      (?)
 97  M3:     Like Higuain
 98  FAC:    And do you know what the referee did?
 99  F3:     What did he?
100  FAC:    He wrote in his booklet that I had reacted and they suspended
             me for a year
101  Some:   Ah: !
102  F10:    What does it mean?
103  FAC:    That for a year I couldn't play football
104  M2:     [When they explode you from school
105  M3:     [But what did he write?
106  FAC:    Mh?
107  M3:     But
108  FAC:    After that I understood that in conclusion
```

Example 3 shows once again that facilitation can enhance an alternation of narratives, avoiding the construction of negative identities, stressing the different positions and suggesting alternative narratives. In this case, it is interesting that the alternative narrative is pursued through the facilitator's personal story. Moreover, example 3 shows the strategic use of a narrative of rules to mediate the conflict. Thus, facilitation first enhances acceptance of a dialogic form of communication, then mitigation of negative identities and finally a telling about negative effects of constructing a negative identity.

8.4 Conclusion

The aim of this chapter was highlighting the conflictive consequences of children's initiatives and the ways of managing them by enhancing children's agency and communities of dialogue. Facilitators' decisions about conflict management depend on their assessment of the impact of conflicts on exercise of agency and production of narratives. While managing children's unpredictable initiatives is a difficult task of facilitation (Chapter 6), this task is much more difficult when these initiatives initiate conflicts.

Effective conflict management implies conflict mediation. Facilitation cannot be transformed into professional conflict management since it has a different function, which limits its possibility to conclude an accurate conflict mediation. However, facilitation can be used for conflict mediation because it includes some methods of this mediation. The SHARMED experience showed that some actions that can be useful to mediate conflicts are: (1) invitations to reflect on different social constructions of accusations and identities, avoiding judgements and proposing a deconstruction of negative identities; (2) activation of double listening and proposal of alternative narratives. In conflict mediation, formulations are often very important (Baraldi 2019a) since they may reframe existing narratives and enhance alternative narratives. The analysis in this chapter has shown that 'circularity' in questioning is also important, since it allows the co-construction of more complex narratives and, above all, it avoids isolation of 'guilty' children in the classroom and the corresponding construction of negative identities. Finally, the analysis shows that facilitators' personal stories may also be important in conflict management as testimonies of relevant experiences (see also Baraldi & Iervese 2010).

While avoiding or ignoring children's conflictive initiatives may sometimes prevent the destruction of communities of dialogue, this cannot be a general practice in facilitation since it would mean limiting or repressing children's agency and leaving conflicts unheard. Thus, it is important to understand the ways in which classroom conflicts are reproduced and stabilized to evaluate if conflict mediation is useful or necessary. While conflict mediation will probably be incomplete and insufficient in facilitated meetings, it can make narratives and practices of conflicts evident and show that negative identities and forms of delegitimization produce negative effects in classroom communication.

Part Three

SHARMED Evaluation and Outcomes

9

Improving Pedagogical Work: Evaluation

Claudio Baraldi and Chiara Ballestri

9.1 Introduction

This chapter includes reflections on the ways in which SHARMED could enhance educational innovation and communities of dialogue in multicultural classrooms. SHARMED showed that children appreciated activities and social relations with classmates and facilitators, and this chapter explores how teachers were not only able to identify the innovative aspects of classroom activities, but also to suggest interesting improvements. These reflections are based on the final evaluation of SHARMED regarding the following aspects: variety of ways in which facilitation was applied (Section 2); relevant results according to teachers and children (Section 3); final outcomes which can support the construction of communities of dialogue (Section 4). Chapters 10 and 11 will provide further reflections on two of these outcomes, i.e. training and archiving.

9.2 Ways of Applying Facilitation

SHARMED proposed a method of facilitation which can be adapted to different social and cultural contexts, while enhancement of narratives, agency and dialogue are always relevant. Local adaptation of facilitation is based on: (1) different ways of combining facilitative actions (such as invitations, questions, minimal feedback, formulations, comments, appreciations), which enhance and support children's narratives and agency and (2) children's unpredictable actions, both enhanced by facilitators' invitations and suggestions, and as autonomous initiatives.

The analysis of SHARMED meetings highlights three forms of facilitation, associated with three different social and cultural contexts, respectively in Germany, Italy and England. The influence of these contexts depends on differences among school systems and facilitators' training and styles. The following three examples show the three different forms of facilitation, although in a schematic way, based on the types of actions which have been described in the previous chapters.

9.2.1 Combining Several Types of Turns of Talk

The first form of facilitation is based on a variety of supporting and enhancing actions, which are provided in different turns of talk. In particular, it is based on the combination of frequent questions and formulations, enriched through minimal feedback and few comments. Narratives are co-constructed through the interlaced contributions of facilitators and children. Facilitators' actions, co-constructing narratives, are perceived by children as forms of personalized participation: thus, these actions enhance children's agency, even when it contradicts the facilitator's view. This form of facilitation was more frequent in Italy.

Example 1 shows the facilitator's enhancement and support of an emotionally intense narrative, through a combination of questions, formulations and few continuers. Before this sequence, M2 told of his parents' separation and revealed that his father has a new fiancée, who is not appreciated by the child. In turn 1, the facilitator asks a focused question about the child's possible dislike of his fathers' new fiancée, which is confirmed by the child. In turn 5, the hypothetical nature of this question is developed through a formulation (Chapter 5) inferencing that M2 does not know the woman (turn 5). This formulation is rejected by the child and the facilitator repairs the misunderstanding through another formulation as an explication (turn 7). M2 confirms and adds information about his parents. In the next phase, the facilitator supports the narrative through a two-part development (turns 9 and 11), a continuer (turn 13) and another development (turn 15). The story becomes very intimate and emotional, as it is also stressed by F3's exclamation (turn 17). The facilitator continues to enhance the narrative through other developments (turns 19 and 21), which both invite M2 to continue to tell and show the facilitator's action as a co-teller. In turn 21, a new development leads to a change of topic, from the child's parents to the photograph. The facilitator investigates if M2's mother is aware of the child's use of the photograph, through a focused question (turn 25), which prepares two further developments concerning M2's mother attitude (turn 27 and 31). Both these developments are rejected by M2. These rejections are followed by the facilitator's active listening (turns 33 and 35). In turn 37, the facilitator proposes an interrogative development. This action leads M2 to a contradictory statement about her mother's feelings (turns 36 and 38), repaired by the facilitator's final development (turn 39) about his mother's positive feeling for his father, which is confirmed by M2.

Example 1

1	FAC:	Because you may not like her?
2	M2:	Mh ((shaking his head))
3	?:	H
4	M2:	I and my brother don't like her at all [a
5	FAC:	[but you don't know her yet
6	M2:	Eh: actually I know her
7	FAC:	Ah so you know who she is
8	M2:	Y:es that: that ac- that actually they were g- they were alright together only that: sometimes when my father was taking was losing control because he to- he was taking lots of medicines for something that I don't [know
9	FAC:	[and they make him strange
10	M2:	Eh? [he, my mother
11	FAC:	[Those medicines
12	M2:	Once she threw the medicines out
13	FAC:	Ah
14	M2:	And: he m: one day in the following days after he started shouting at her, beating [her,
15	FAC:	[Because he could not find the medicines
16	M2	[Eh
17	F3:	[Oh my god
18	M2:	Yes and then and my bro- and my father no I mean my mother a: she was: ((makes an horizontal gesture with the hands)) she was going
19	FAC:	I mean she didn't agree with this behaviour
20	M2:	No
21	FAC:	Mh so you keep this photo (..)
22	M2:	I ke- [I: kept it in my mother kept it in a red box with glitters
23	FAC:	[Or or yes
24	M2:	And: th- then I took it because it reminds my of that
25	FAC:	But your mum gave it to – does she know that you were bringing this photo?

26	M2:	Yes ((nods))
27	FAC:	And so your mum cares about this photo
28	M2:	E: actually not ((shakes head))
29	FAC:	No?
30	M2:	No be- because she can't stand my father anymore and so she: she just – in fact she put it away in my drawers
31	FAC:	She took it off from from the album
32	M2:	Y:es no it's not an album it was a photo frame
33	FAC:	Eh
34	M2:	It's not an album a photo frame the: I don't know the name
35	FAC:	Yes yes a photo frame
36	M2:	And then and then she put it away in one of my drawers in my bedroom
37	FAC:	But then did she want you to keep it?
38	M2:	She didn't want to throw it away but she wanted to keep it because it's because mum says that l- she is not in love with dad but she loves him very much
39	FAC:	Because after all [they hav- have did some important things [in their life together
40	M2:	[((nods)) [together yes ((nods))

9.2.2 Combining Different Actions in the Same Turn of Talk

The second form of facilitation is based on a variety of supporting and enhancing actions, in particular formulations, comments, personals stories and appreciations, frequently combined in single turns of talk. Comments and appreciations are much more frequent than in the first form, showing facilitators' warm involvement, which is important to enhance children's stories even when facilitators' turns are long and articulated. This form of facilitation enhances children's agency by connecting different narratives (interlacements). This form of facilitation is more frequent in England.

In example 2, the facilitator acknowledges M2's story about meeting his cousins at a wedding, showing her interest, then she comments providing a possible interpretation of his cousin's nasty behaviours (turn 2). M2 continues to tell his story and the facilitator checks a detail of it through a focused question (turn 4) followed by an open question on the child's feelings (turn 6). These questions enhance M2's disclosure. Then the facilitator provides a formulation as explication and asks a second question focusing on M2's feelings (turn 8). In turn 10, she also tells a short personal story which enhances the continuation of the child's narrative. In turn 12, the facilitator asks a third focused question on the child's feelings; then she provides a comment and invites the other children to add stories (turn 14). Following this invitation, F2 takes the floor and the facilitator, after a comment, tells another short personal story showing that she shares her feelings with children (turn 16). In turn 17, M3 tells another story and the facilitator provides an explication (turn 18), followed by the child's further detail. Responding to the invitation of the facilitator (turn 20), M4 and M5 self-select and tell other stories (turns 21 and 22). In turn 23, the facilitator comments on memories, asks a question and adds a new personal story. At the end of this turn, she starts to change topic, but F3 takes the floor to add her story (turn 24). The facilitator makes a final comment, promising to resume the topic next time and adding a general appreciation for children's contributions, repeated thanks and a final question about the will of bringing new pictures next time (turn 25). Finally, she greets the children and thanks again. This example shows a series of six interlaced narratives, some of them autonomously provided (by M3, M5, F3). This series shows that the facilitator's long turns work as connectors among different stories, through open invitations and indirect ways of opening the floor.

Example 2

1	M2:	On that day, I met one of my cousins (?) and he came to the wedding. He didn't like me that much but like whenever I got closer he'd scratch me on my face
2	FAC:	Oh wow, some cousins might do that sometimes when they're younger
3	M2:	And there was (..) I can remember that my oldest cousin he used to play cricket, he made this rumour that he met one of the famous players, a cricket famous player and then I got into him and he made me do stuff, like he made me do stuff that I didn't want to do, like go to the shops (?) and he would show me a picture of when I was a baby and it made me feel embarrassed
4	FAC:	Were you very small?
5	M2:	Yeah
6	FAC:	And what do you (..) when you look back at this picture how does it make you kind of feel, like to think of the time together with family, generations?

7	M2:	We're apart now, we're in different countries. My other cousin (?) like sometimes I cry about it because I never met them. I meet my grandparents every five years. When I met them this year, last year, I was so emotional and I kept sort of like following them and slept with them, but when I was leaving they cried their hearts out
8	FAC:	They didn't want to leave you, yes. Can I ask why you slept with them – was it to feel close to them and to get in with them?
9	M2:	Yeah
10	FAC:	I used to sleep with my grandma when I was little
11	M2:	My grandma she's (..) well, when I was in Afghanistan, we have this house, my cousin told me it was haunted and in one of the [unclear] they put their hands (?) in one of the pictures and told me like there's a ghost and a hand appeared
12	FAC:	So, you want to sleep with your grandma to be safe?
13	M2:	((Gesticulates with hands)) (?) in the new house we had (…) my brother even told me as a child stories, scary stories that because they had like plastic bags covering their balcony (?) and she told me that, she told me they were covering that up because the ghost doesn't like coming through the balcony
14	FAC:	So, lots of scary stories about ghosts. Did anybody else get told stories about ghosts from their grandparents or siblings or their cousins?
15	F2:	((standing up, hands of chair of girl in front)) My cousin, my cousin told me when I was in my Nan's house, and all of my cousins were there, and at night when we were all sleeping my eldest cousin told us this scary story and then when we went to sleep I just couldn't stop thinking about it
16	FAC:	Yeah, it gets quite scary doesn't it when you hear (…) especially at night time, things get a bit scary at nighttime when the lights off, doesn't it. I know I get a bit scared sometimes. I have to put a cheeky light on to make me feel a bit safer, so I can see what's going on
17	M3:	When I was at my cousin's house, he told my brother because he lived opposite a forest, and he told my brother that there was a man called the Bear Man in the forest, when he was like little. So, then when he went outside and it was dark he started crying. And there was this other time, it was like maybe a month ago. My sister she hates Michael Jackson because the rumour of everything that he did, and then he was sitting next to the window when it was dark outside and my cousin he put the music on and he screamed, and he said like it was Michael Jackson behind her and she got so scared
18	FAC:	So, she was really freaked out

19	M3:	Yes and she's like 13, so
20	FAC:	So, some more scary stories
21	M4:	So, basically when I was about five or six when I was sleeping in my bed and they said to me there's a man underneath your bed. There was a phone, it was ringing and I just jumped and ran to my mum and said mummy, mummy there's a man under my bed. And then I had to sleep with my mum because I was scared and then when I was asleep and she took me in the bed (?)
22	M5:	((smiles)) So, when I was really young my dad used to make up these, not scary ones, but about the snake who used to come to our house, he said that it was going to come for me, so I stayed next to him every single time and as I grew up I didn't really believe him at the time
23	FAC:	Yeah, isn't it funny how we get these memories and these fears and you don't know whether to believe them or not, it's a bit scary. Did anybody ever think there was somebody in their wardrobe? Sometimes, when I was a little girl, I used to look in my wardrobe to make sure there was nobody in there, there was never anybody in there but I used to get scared sometimes. I'll come back and see you next week, if that's okay
24	F3:	When I was little, my auntie, because I had like these two wardrobes next to my bed either side, it had murals on it, so my auntie said it was (?). So, when I was sleeping I used to leave the cupboards open, they faced me. So, when I go to bed I used to look at the mirrors and I would scream and go under the duvet and get my torch out and see if there's anything there and go back to bed (?) see it again (...) my duvet
25	FAC:	Do you know what I think a lot of people do that sometimes, get a little bit jeebie when the light goes off. I think we can talk about this next time I come back, this is a huge area that you're sharing, all of these kind of haunted stories, all from this picture. How did we know that we were going to start talking about hauntings and ghost stories all from a picture like this. Your memories are just so vast and the emotion of your picture that you began to tell us really shared lots of things. So, thank you so much and if you would like to bring in some pictures for next week and if you've taken a picture that would be great to bring that in, okay. So, thank you so much and shall we say thank you very much for sharing today, thank you, well done guys, thank you, thank you and thank you for the videotaping ((applause)) So, who would like to bring in some pictures next week?
26	M?:	Me
27	FAC:	Bring them all in then, I'll look forward to seeing them, thank you

9.2.3 Listening and Inviting

The third form of facilitation is based on linear exchanges between the facilitator and one child at time, followed by invitation to classmates to contribute and ask questions. This scheme is repeated for each photograph. This form of facilitation is based on minimal feedbacks, such as continuers, repetitions and acknowledgement tokens, few direct questions and formulations and several invitations to talk. Children's autonomous participation is the primary focus of facilitators, who are less active than in the other two forms. Moreover, facilitators show their appreciation for children's contributions at the end of all conversations about specific photographs. This form of facilitation was more frequent in Germany.

Example 3 shows the combination of questions and minimal responses (continuers, repetition and acknowledgements), followed by children's self-management of conversations. The facilitator asks an open question to M4 on the content of the child's photograph (turn 1), followed by continuers (turn 3), a second focused question about the way of taking the photograph (turn 5) and a final acknowledgement (turn 7), which is confirmed by the child. In turn 9, the facilitator changes the topic of conversation through an open question on the animal that M4 prefers, followed by a focused question (turn 11) which repairs the possible difficulty of answering to the first question. Then, the facilitator repeats the child's answer (turn 13), showing understanding, and asks about classmates participation (turn 15), inviting M4 to coordinate the conversation (turn 16), thus enhancing children's self-management of the interaction.

Example 3

1	FAC:	So what's the photo of?
2	M4:	Umm. Many animal (.) Elephant and stuff
3	FAC:	Mh. (.) ok
4	M4:	And also (?)
5	FAC:	And did you take them with your mobile phone or what did you use to take the photos?
6	M4:	Yes
7	Fac:	Okay (.) all right
8	M4:	Yes
9	FAC:	And which animals did you like the best?
10	M4:	Best?
11	FAC:	Were there any?

12	M4:	Yes (.) Elephant
13	FAC:	Elephant
14	M4:	Yes
15	FAC:	I see (.) Were you at the zoo too?
16	several:	Yes
17	M4:	M3
18	M3:	Emm, well we were at the zoo (?) Elephants, they were going like this the whole time ((gestures the movement)) and walked against the wall
19	M5:	((laughs))
20	M10:	One walked against the wall
21	F2:	He took a run at it and did ((gestures the movement))

9.2.4 Comparing Forms of Facilitation

The first two forms of facilitation are based on facilitators' intense activity of co-construction of narratives. The difference is between contingency of turn-by-turn co-construction (first form) and ordered sequence of more complex turns and narratives (second form). The more 'classical' third form of facilitation is based on questions and active listening through minimal feedback, aiming to enhance the autonomous voice of children with reduced personal involvement and collaboration of the facilitator.

The first form of facilitation is most effective in enhancing expansions of personal stories, thus promoting a community of dialogue based on a great number of narratives, often linked to the same photograph and developing contingently. This form is most effective in promoting dialogue between children on the same photograph or topic and in encouraging unexpected contributions. The second form of facilitation is most effective in enhancing a community of dialogue through interlacements, based on children's stories produced in one or more turns, and in enhancing ordered sequences of children's contributions, which follow facilitator's long and personal contributions. The third form of facilitation is most effective in enhancing a community of dialogue based on children's autonomous contributions, without facilitators' coordination and separation of stories through ordered presentations of photographs.

Examples 1–3 are very far from representing the complexity of facilitation. However, they show that facilitation may take different forms and may be adapted locally, to school systems, class composition, ways of communicating in the classroom context. They also show the importance of facilitators' specific training and style. Forms of facilitation are different in different situations and it can be expected that facilitators' construction of communities of dialogue will be based on facilitators' personal style and social and cultural contexts in which they work.

Different forms of facilitation have different effects on the enhancement of children's agency. Whilst the third form was more effective than the others in enhancing children's autonomous contributions through facilitators' minimal feedback, it was challenged by children's reluctance towards active participation (see also Chapter 7). The first and second forms of facilitation supported narratives related to children's personal experiences, including feelings, views and choices. In the first and second forms, facilitation enhanced the negotiation of children's narratives about conditions, events and changes relating to personal experiences, including experiences of migration and children's personal cultural trajectories. These two forms of facilitation co-constructed children's narratives in different ways: several questions and formulations in the first form, extended personal comments in the second form. However, the difference did not concern the enhancement of children's agency, which was effective in both cases; rather, it concerned the way of enhancing it.

In Germany and Italy, where both grades of education were included in the project, children's active participation appeared higher in primary schools than in secondary schools. However, the most important variable for children's active participation was the form of facilitation rather than the grade of education. With regard to the different effects of the same form of facilitation, this was related to contextual conditions of communication in the classroom.

9.3 What Can We Learn from Evaluation of Facilitation?

Local contexts can influence the form of facilitation and the constitution of a community of dialogue for two aspects: (1) school system, teachers' expectations and ways of teaching; (2) children's interests, migration fluxes and cultural *mélange*. For what concerns the first aspect, schools and teachers can consider innovative proposals as problematic in school routine (this may happen, for instance in England), or they can be convinced that what is already done in schools is very innovative (this may happen for example in Italy). Against this potentially problematic background, the lessons learnt by teachers and children in the case of SHARMED make clear what are the advantages of introducing facilitation in the school system.

9.3.1 Lessons Learnt from Teachers

The interviews with forty teachers in the three countries showed that SHARMED had important effects on expectations in schools. Teachers recognized several positive outcomes, including (1) facilitators' competence in involving children, (2) effective use of photography to encourage, motivate and involve children, (3) opportunities to improve mutual knowledge and understanding among children, (4) enhancement of children's personal and affective expressions through narratives and (5) opportunities for improving teachers' perspectives on children.

Facilitative methods were appreciated by teachers, who praised facilitators' interest for children, construction of trust and respect in the classroom, and ability in enhancing children's participation and cooperation, avoiding directive actions, involving them and creating affective relations. Teachers also declared that they learnt a lot about children's experiences and points of view. Finally, teachers recognized several positive outcomes for children, including:

1. Learning dialogue.
2. Overcoming problems of expression (e.g. language barriers, shyness).
3. Being listened by classmates.
4. Exceptional opportunities of understanding new things.
5. Better knowledge of classmates and their cultural experiences.
6. Development of affective relations and empathy.
7. Recognition and discussion of similar experiences in different cultural and family contexts, thus learning to accept diversity.
8. Enthusiastic participation and appreciation of activities leading to ask for repeating the experience and to talk about it for a long time after the end of the activities.

Teachers recognized the importance of spending time for facilitation, production of narratives, exploration of emotional experiences and conflict management, to ensure long-standing communities of dialogue. At the same time, teachers recognized the necessity to reflect on the ways facilitation and production of narratives can be connected to school curricula and the ways in which children's unpredictable actions enhanced by facilitation can be handled. This reflection led several teachers to implement innovative activities and facilitation in their classrooms. These initiatives included:

1. Use of produced narratives and production of new narratives for classroom reflection.

2. Planning of new activities, for instance taking photographs of the school to teach geography.
3. Use of photographs to welcome and include newly arrived migrant children.
4. Replacement of directive actions with facilitative actions in routine teaching.
5. Better understanding of children's personal trajectories, in particular for what concerns delicate and potentially problematic aspects.
6. Work on children's interpersonal relations, showing improvement of children's communicative competence, openness, mutual help and dialogue.

These types of feedback show that the use of photograph and the enhancement of narratives were understood and subsequentially applied as tools to stimulate children's active participation. From a pedagogical perspective, children's personal photographs offered an easy, visual way of collecting their personal memories and describing and explaining experiences, emotions, points of view that connected the past to the present situation of the classroom. The choice of a narrative form allowed a vivid experience of sharing that enabled a pedagogy of orality focused not on the quality of the oral production but on personalized contents that invited classmates' attention, offering opportunities to activate dialogue. The combination of photographs and narratives stimulated knowledge of the variety of children's personal cultural trajectories. This led to a complex understanding of how childhood may be lived in different ways while still being childhood, in a shared community of dialogue.

9.3.2 Lessons Learnt from Children

Children who participated in the SHARMED activities evaluated the project filling questionnaires and participating in final focus groups, making clear what lessons they learned from the project. This evaluation involved 981 children. The difference between Italy and Germany, where the project was applied in primary and secondary schools, and England, where it was only applied in primary schools, could impact on assessment, since facilitation was more welcomed in primary schools (see also Chapter 2). In this section, we present some important data from this evaluation process.

Enjoyment of activities (Table 9.1).

1. All activities were enjoyed by the majority of children in England and Italy, but not in Germany.

2. The most frequently enjoyed activities were being the audience for classmates' stories and pictures, and showing the high value assigned to listening and looking.
3. More engaging forms of participation were less appreciated: activities implying active participation, such as presenting pictures, telling stories and exchanging ideas, were less frequently enjoyed.
4. Producing pictures was much more frequently enjoyed in Italy than in England and Germany.
5. Telling stories was more frequently enjoyed in England than in Italy and Germany.

Table 9.1 How much did you enjoy (% very much)

	Italy	England	Germany
Looking at the pictures of your classmates	83.0	86.1	60.7
Listening to the stories of your classmates	77.7	85.8	61.4
Producing a picture	71.0	58.3	48.6
Choosing a picture	69.2	68.0	60.6
Presenting your picture	60.7	59.1	41.5
Telling your stories	59.3	66.7	47.5
Exchanging ideas and information with your classmates	56.4	60.8	47.0

Outcomes of activities (Table 9.2).

1. Data suggest the values of SHARMED for learning: the large majority of children had fun, discovered new things about their classmates, did something new and learned new things.
2. In almost all cases, positive assessments increased from Germany (lower frequency) to Italy and to England (higher frequency).
3. In England, very frequent positive assessment concerned feeling respect, appreciation and personal value.
4. In Germany, while children felt respected very frequently, only less than half of them felt appreciated and important.
5. The large majority of children, above all in England, but lower in Germany, found easy to get involved in the project.
6. The majority of children had much to share with their classmates, above all in Italy and England.

7. In England, supporting young children in discovering something about themselves became a lived experience for a solid majority of respondents.
8. In Germany and above all in Italy, children less frequently felt important during the activities and discovered new things about themselves.
9. Expression of feelings, which is very rare in ordinary classroom environments, was less frequent than other variables, but relevant, above all in England.

Table 9.2 During the activities (%)

	Italy	England	Germany
I had fun	92.9	94.3	88.9
I discovered new things about others	91.1	93.5	79.9
I did something new	87.6	82.5	80.5
I learned new things	82.4	89.3	75.3
It was easy to get involved	70.4	81.2	65.0
I felt respected	69.5	84.3	77.5
I felt that I have much to share with others	69.4	69.4	58.1
I felt appreciated	62.9	84.1	49.5
I felt important	41.0	68.9	48.6
I discovered new things about myself	38.0	57.7	50.9

Assessment of relations with classmates.

1. The large majority of children (from 83.9% in England to 73.5% in Italy) assessed relations with classmates positively.
2. Very few children assessed these relations negatively (from 5.4% in Italy to 2.5% in England).
3. The large majority felt that they were believed by classmates (from 75.5% in Italy to 63.4% in Germany).
4. Few children felt judged by classmates (12/14%).
5. Children appreciated expression of different opinions very frequently in England (84%) and Italy (71.2%), less frequently in Germany (54.8%).
6. In England many children did not perceive different opinions (39.8%, against 25.8% in Germany and 19.7% in Italy) or considered them as source of conflict (39% against 9% in Italy).

7. Video-recordings confirm that explicit difference of opinions was less frequent in England, but shows that conflicts have been more frequent in Italy than in England (see Chapter 8).

Relations with facilitators (Table 9.3)

1. The large majority of children felt comfortable or very comfortable with facilitators and very few children felt uncomfortable in all contexts.
2. In Italy, children felt very comfortable very frequently and few children expressed an ambivalent or negative assessment.
3. The most frequent ambivalent assessments were in Germany.
4. Focus groups showed strong appreciation of action and coordination of facilitators. In particular, in Italy children's contributions also showed understanding of facilitative methods.

Table 9.3 How did you feel with facilitator (%)

	Italy	England	Germany
Very comfortable	68.7	46.0	48.0
Comfortable	20.4	35.5	29.1
Neither comfortable nor uncomfortable	8.6	14.3	21.3
Uncomfortable and very uncomfortable	2.1	4.2	1.6

Definitions of facilitators (Table 9.4)

1. A majority of children in Italy and a large minority in England and Germany described facilitators as persons open to children's feelings and interests, which is an important ingredient of facilitation.
2. In England, another frequent description of facilitators was 'friend', stressing interpersonal relations.
3. In general, but above all in Italy, the definition of facilitators as authoritative persons was very infrequent.
4. A small minority, but larger in Germany and England, defined facilitators as teachers.
5. In Germany, about 22% of children chose definitions like teacher and authoritative person, and 6% did not find any definition, which show some problems of interpretation of facilitation.

Table 9.4 How would you define the facilitator (%)

	Italy	England	Germany
A person who is open to children's interests and feelings	50.8	42.0	41.0
A friend	20.1	29.7	18.0
A teacher	11.8	14.5	16.4
A moderator	9.0	0.7	9.0
I cannot find a definition	3.7	2.9	6.1
I would define her/him in another way	3.7	4.3	3.7
An authoritative person	0.9	5.1	5.7

Understanding of facilitators' actions (Table 9.5)

1. In Italy, almost all children appreciated facilitators' enhancement of interest, trust, respect and understanding, while a lower majority appreciated support of positive relations with classmates.
2. Few children felt judged by facilitators, very few in Italy (where focus groups revealed that judgement was frequently considered as a positive attitude).
3. Helping to get along with classmates was less frequently perceived, but still by a majority of children, more frequently in England. Video-recordings of activities confirmed that, with some exceptions, facilitators enhanced much more frequently children's agency and narratives than relations between children.
4. Assessment was less positive in England and, above all in Germany, where children felt much more frequently judged.

Table 9.5 During the activities the facilitator (% very much)

	Italy	England	Germany
Was interested in what I was telling	90.4	78.2	68.8
Believed me	89.9	70.9	71.5
Respected my opinions	89.8	81.5	72.5
Tried to understand me	87.5	78.0	74.2
Helped me to talk about what I am interested in	80.6	68.4	62.9
Helped me to talk about my memories	80.3	67.6	64.7
Helped me to get along with my classmates	59.9	64.7	56.6
Judged me	12.0	23.7	19.6

General Experience of facilitation

1. A very large majority of children had a positive experience of facilitation (from 83.7% in Italy to 82.1% in Germany).
2. Very few children had a negative experience (4.8% in Italy and Germany, 2.5% in England).

To sum up, several data show that facilitation was very successful, for what concerns enjoyment of activities, fun, discovering new things, doing and learning something new, feeling others' understanding, respect, trust, appreciation and involvement, expressing opinions and feelings, considering classmates as supportive, appreciating different opinions, feeling comfortable with facilitators and considering them open and interested persons or friends, appreciating facilitation as a positive experience.

Although children assessed positively facilitation everywhere, some differences between social and cultural contexts were important and can provide some useful reflections. First, differences may depend on different school contexts. Children may find more difficult to enjoy unusual activities, for instance implying active participation. However, enthusiasm for the activities may be very high in contexts in which regular teaching is strongly oriented to test and assess role performances (such as in England). In some contexts there may be low social cohesion (as in some German classes). Sensitivity for conflicts may be different in different contexts (e.g. higher in England and Germany than in Italy). Where conflicts are infrequent, all discussions may be considered conflictive.

Second, differences among contexts may depend on different forms of facilitation (see Section 2). In Italy, children understood and appreciated facilitators' intense activity of co-construction of narratives as open to children's interests and feelings. Facilitation was effective in avoiding a normative and judgemental appearance, in providing some mediation of conflicts and in enhancing agency. In Germany, facilitation was not always effective in enhancing children's agency and narratives and sometimes included normative orientations. In England, facilitation worked very well in enhancing new narratives and interlacements between narratives, but facilitators' appreciations and comments might be interpreted by some children as judgements.

Another interesting aspect based on research results is that children's assessments were infrequently associated with language (and cultural) differences and gender differences.

In Italy and Germany, some difficulties of expression depended on language barriers and migrant-background children less frequently assessed positively relations with classmates. However, migrant-background children also declared that they learnt new things and assessed facilitation positively more frequently. Video-recordings confirmed the strong involvement of migrant-background children, above all in Italy. This shows that where difficulties of expression are higher, facilitation may be more appreciated and effective facilitation may be more frequently appreciated by migrant-background children.

In England, cultural differences were never relevant. These data confirm that inclusion of children with recent migration experiences is important for both language barriers and competences, and motivation to participate, while where shared language and cultural mélange are relevant, as in London, communication is simpler and more fluid. In these cases, there is no difference in appreciation of facilitation.

For what concerns gender, girls assessed a bit more frequently activities and relations in a positive way. In England, in particular, girls were more frequently comfortable with facilitators, defining them as persons open to feelings and interests. In Germany, girls perceived more frequently trust, understanding and respect, and less frequently judging. They also perceived more frequently different opinions as a way to find shared solutions. Gender differences, however, were not very strong. This shows that facilitation may reduce gender differences: video-recordings confirmed that both girls and boys participated actively in the activities.

9.4 From Lessons Learnt to Outcomes

SHARMED research and evaluation lead to suggest ways of innovating education in 'multicultural' contexts in Europe by creating communities of dialogue. In particular, SHARMED provided some outcomes for this purpose, which are now available on the SHARMED website (www.sharmed.eu). The most important outcomes are a plan of training, an archive and a learning platform, which will be described in the next two chapters. Here, we briefly introduce some outcomes which are directly interlaced with the themes of this chapter: guidelines for facilitation, evaluation of facilitation and an e-book including photographs and transcriptions of children's descriptions of photographs. These outcomes may enhance the adaptation of facilitation to the specific contexts of application.

Guidelines are addressed to teachers and educators who are interested in applying facilitative methods. They include the description of methodology of facilitation and its dissemination, supported by a synthesis of basic concepts, description of potential addressees, suggestions about the planning and the organization of activities, description of the training programme and materials for training. Guidelines for evaluation of facilitation include a range of possible tools for evaluative research and suggestions and resources for their use. Combining guidelines for facilitation and its evaluation, users can achieve and evaluate innovative activities of facilitation in classrooms.

The e-book, which has also been printed, is an experimentation of a new way of disseminating outcomes of a project in which images (photographs) are very relevant. The e-book gives particular values to the photographs which were provided by children and used in the classroom and to children's narratives associated with these photographs, which were transcribed from the meetings. The e-book aims to represent the complexity of SHARMED from the point of view of children, and it is a way of stressing the meaning of a community of dialogue.

These tools highlight the operational character of the SHARMED project and stress innovative ways of doing applied research. Researchers are enhancers of innovation, while fully respecting teachers and facilitators' competences. This particular meaning of applied research is particularly evident in teachers' training and archiving of materials, which will be described in the next two chapters.

10

SHARMED Training: Design and Practice

Angela Scollan and Erica Joslyn

10.1 Introduction

One of the objectives of the SHARMED project was the development of a comprehensive training programme to support the use of facilitation in educational settings. In this chapter we explain the methodological foundations that underpin SHARMED training and describe the range of training resources developed from the evidence provided by the research activities in the classrooms. The SHARMED training model was designed to promote the understanding and use of facilitation as an active form of dialogic pedagogy, enabling trainees to support children's participation in interactions from the position of authors of narratives and legitimized sources of knowledge.

Crucially, this chapter illustrates how the SHARMED training model is a training programme *for* and *with* participants throughout all of its phases, framed around a continuous process of self-evaluation and self-reflection. By enabling continuous evaluation, SHARMED training encourages teachers and practitioners to challenge themselves through reflection and experimentation. This model of training uses a practice-based format, not least because, if traditional teaching practice is to be enhanced by the practice of facilitation, then training should provoke change that is understood and owned by those seeking to make that change.

10.2 The SHARMED Philosophy as a Focus for the Development of Training

The SHARMED project was based on the idea that visual materials selected and produced by children could serve as a trigger for the construction of narratives in the classroom. Sharing and co-constructing narratives based on similarities or differences across personal and cultural memories could help children build awareness of 'the other', learning about, with and from others. Key to the SHARMED project is the promotion of the production of narratives, which assigns a very important role to the adult(s) as facilitators of narratives and interactions in the classroom. The analysis of interactions discussed in the previous chapters suggests that facilitative actions can successfully prompt the production of narratives while prioritizing children's agency and self-determination.

The design of SHARMED training was therefore committed to provide trainees with the tools (Figure 10.1) to trigger participants' narratives of personal or family memories, encouraging the authorship of stories and the dialogic exchange of knowledge between children. The training programme focuses on the presentation of the facilitative actions that, based on the results of the research, proved to be effective in promoting children's agency as authors of narratives, as producers of knowledge.

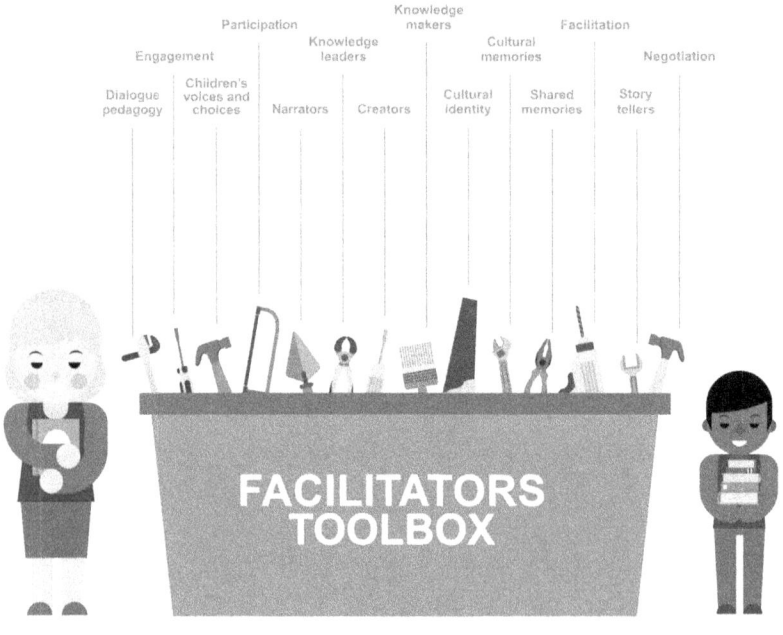

Figure 10.1 Facilitator toolbox.

The philosophy of SHARMED training recognizes that learners engage with learning in unique ways moving between a combination of preferred learning styles, experiences and perceptions. The facilitator's toolbox identifies the combination of pedagogical concepts that underpin SHARMED training and which is delivered via multimodal activities and resources. This philosophy is in effect driven by the acceptance of the value of combining visual, auditory and kinaesthetic (VAK) methodologies together. In particular, the VAK philosophy is designed to enhance cognitive, tactile and sensory learning styles (Coffield et al. 2004; Pashler et al. 2008).

SHARMED training seeks to provide a wide range of learning opportunities through experiential learning, as well as meeting a varied range of learning abilities. The VAK methodology was deemed as coherent with the SHARMED project because it exposes participants to different ways of learning and most importantly recognize that learning may often be a result of a combination of VAK learning styles. The VAK methodology aims to enable participants to both respect and value the different learning paths taken by other participants. It empowers participants to learn empathically and structurally through contributions of others as narrators, irrespective of the learning style of either the listeners or the narrators.

The application of VAK methodology throughout the training programme is designed around notions of repetition, reiteration and reformulation. The SHARMED training programme combines VAK learning styles through frequent and repeated use of, for example, photographs and videos, alongside the use of written materials designed to support visual learners in understanding of key interactions. This approach helps to aid *visual* learning opportunities and to also support the development of different types of memory aids, such as, taking notes, drawings, reflecting through quizzes, the use of collaborating groups, ultimately encouraging participants to engage through the use of any, or all VAK methods.

The centrality of narrations for the SHARMED project is reflected by the VAK methodology's commitment to *auditory* learning methods. In the training programme this includes the importance for learning of both internal (lips moving soundlessly) and external forms of dialogue. The training programme design recognizes the importance of tone and rhythm as well as content in auditory learning styles and ensures access to auditory learning through pace and structure of all forms of communications. The needs of auditory learners are also met through focused interactions, collaborating discussions and question and answer synthesis linked to and making other forms of VAK learning methods more accessible.

Finally, kinaesthetic forms of learning are implemented through conditions and environments that enable movement around and in unison with others as well as the opportunity to learn through an individual approach or hands-on experience. By planning kinaesthetic opportunities, the training programme aims to ensure that 'touch learning' was accessible – recognizing its value as an aid to improving concentration and information retention. Ultimately, the VAK methodology provides a creative although well-structured programme of training, enabling visual-spatial, auditory-percussive and kinaesthetic-channel forms of learning to coexist in non-linear approaches for constructing learning and interactions.

As indicated throughout this volume, facilitation is a form of communication that aims to change the hierarchical distribution of epistemic authority in adult-children interactions. Facilitation aims to enhance children's agency and children's actions that display their agency. It also enhances and promotes dialogue, as a specific form of communication in which adults' actions support children's self-expression, take children's views into account, involve them in decision-making processes, and share power and responsibility with them. The SHARMED project was designed to focus on this perspective of facilitation as a feature of classroom practice and the research findings presented in this volume emphasize significant differences between the role of facilitation and the traditional role of teaching.

Facilitation as the focus of the SHARMED training programme is designed to be the antithesis to the traditional style of teaching. Traditional teaching undertaken within educational structures and systems aim to transmit knowledge that guides the student towards a goal (Bantock 1970; Sternhouse 1983; Kitchen 2014). In traditional classrooms, authority and power are structured into classroom interactions with 'teaching' as the prerogative of the teacher. Bantock (1970: 19) argues that the student/learner 'has no authority outside of himself'. In his work 'Authority and the Teacher', Kitchen (2014) argues that the authority of a teacher should be absolute in education. He suggests that this is necessary for success given that the mission of teaching is to spread knowledge across generations. For Kitchen, traditional approaches to teaching focus on the need to learn and in his perspective the motivation for a child's participation is based on the authority of the teacher and the pleasure to be gained from learning. In order to secure learning, teachers must invite acknowledgement of their authority (based on knowledge and expertise) and stimulate learners' pleasure in learning (based on effective communication style and pedagogical skills) (Kitchen 2014).

By contrast, research findings from the SHARMED project demonstrate the importance of the role of facilitation in classroom practice and signals that facilitative interactions between adults and children in classrooms are very different from traditional interactions commonly used in teacher-centred approaches. While traditional teaching aims to impart specific knowledge so that learning can be achieved, tested and used for specific goals (James & James 2004; Wyness 1999), classroom facilitation aims to create an environment where all participants share knowledge and experience and build personal and collaborative narratives. Participants are knowledge holders and respected as equal partners during facilitation (Baraldi 2014a, 2014b; Baraldi & Iervese 2017; Hendry 2009; Wyness 2013). Facilitation evolves and unfolds powerfully when 'real' listening, respect and 'want' underpin interactions. It is within this process of engagement, negotiation, emerging awareness and *emergent listening* (Davies 2014) within peer interactions that SHARMED facilitation is positioned.

Teaching and facilitation share some goals but their pedagogical foundations and the very concept of the child underpinning them differ widely. Facilitation is not used to teach but rather to learn together, to listen, interact, marvel, empathize, find out, ask and be with children. In SHARMED training, facilitation is about creating a community of dialogue, by talking *between,* rather than talking *with* or even *to* each other. Thus, facilitation aims to promote the participation of children who are seen as autonomous and expert storytellers, narrators of their own life story, experiences and identity.

In the SHARMED training programme the image of learners and learning relationships do not pertain only to children but also to adult participants. Adult participants are considered as autonomous and experts in their own professional field, and recognized as legitimate authors of valid knowledge. They are therefore expected to be more than recipients of trainers' knowledge; they are expected to be active participants and contributors to the training. These expectations enable a transformation of participants' knowledge and experiences as an asset for training, and a resource for reflective learning (Gibbs 2015).

The philosophical underpinnings of the reflective design of the training are inextricably connected with the active participation of trainees as shown by the constant invitation presented to participants to explore and share their professional position and their ideas regarding facilitation. This invitation is accompanied by the promotion of discussions between trainers and trainees concerning the position of children in educational contexts. Choosing to use facilitation implies a vision of children as autonomous and expert storytellers, 'narrators' of their own life story, experiences and identity. This requires robust conceptual processing and transcendence from participants during training, as they are supported in exploring their position in the context of intergenerational relationships and how this intersects with the practice of facilitation (Gibbs 2015). This exploration takes place at the level of interactions (Alanen 2009; Qvortrup et al. 2005; Farini 2011; Baraldi 2012; Baraldi & Corsi 2017) and across several themes:

1. communication, facilitation, children's narratives;
2. critical evaluation of the position of children, teachers and facilitators, considering the influence of curricula and teaching routines;
3. how the actions of adults can open or close spaces for the active participation of children;
4. translating facilitation into practice;
5. critical reflection on the use of facilitation within educational contexts that influence the way children's voices and narratives are supported, or not.

The SHARMED training model promotes facilitation as the soft skills, such as listening, engaging, questioning, comparing and reflecting during peer-to-peer interactions designed to open up dialogic discussions that invite children to share personal stories or create shared memories with each other. In this context, facilitation aims to stimulate inclusive participation and sharing, even when carried out among children who do not share the use of a language.

10.3 The Methodological Foundations of SHARMED Training

The SHARMED training programme is designed to be flexible with all participants contributing as co-authors in line with the philosophical and methodological foundations of facilitation across the SHARMED project. There are six methodological foundations of SHARMED training:

1. Promoting facilitation as a 'community of dialogue';
2. Setting classroom conditions that promote facilitation;
3. Using a practice-based format;
4. Enabling reflection as 'a priori' to practice;
5. Focus on building collaborative relationships;
6. Using evaluation as a means to maintain momentum.

In addition, the training programme adopts the project's methodology in its use of photography and invites participants to use photographs and photography in innovative and creative ways as tools for promoting individual and collective memories.

Facilitation as a 'Community of Dialogue'

The SHARMED training programme aims to break down the concept of facilitation into manageable areas. The programme enables participants to explore the concept of facilitation in classroom practice and to critique and evaluate ways in which they already provide educational interactions that would, for example, invest in inclusive relationships across a diverse group of children. This training programme models facilitation through its opportunities to reflect *in* and *on* action to achieve greater flexibility and adaptability throughout the training process. This modelling of facilitation enables the training programme to operate in conditions of diverse interactions, increasingly complex interactions and to be able to transform the area and scope of participation to ensure inclusion. Facilitation within educational contexts is continually explored during the modules that make up the training for teachers, considering the ability and impact of facilitation to promote voices, expression, role and spaces belonging to children.

Setting Classroom Conditions That Promote Facilitation

SHARMED training emphasizes the importance of the classroom challenge by, for example, recognizing that the skills and relationships needed to be a facilitator within a teaching environment require a change of role and a change in the traditional expectations underpinning teacher–student interactions. From the point of view of classroom relationships, the use of facilitation implies a gradual process in which the role of the teacher (charged with authority linked to responsibility in the school context) changes into the role of facilitator and demands instead authority and responsibility to produce knowledge is shared by all those who participate.

This can be an exhausting process and sometimes a confusing one for both teachers and students and therefore building the conditions to support resilience in the classroom is a key feature of facilitative pedagogical practice (Joslyn 2017). For example, in the context of a classroom where communication is usually guided by a traditional teaching style, a change of mode and pace to facilitative pedagogical styles can provide a more supportive environment that promotes confidence and educational resilience. The management of alternating speakers and conditions of limited resources are just some examples of the complexities to be considered at the 'interior of scholastic classes' as they move between traditional teaching approaches and facilitation.

In order for the practice of facilitation to remain consistent with its own assumptions and to be effective in promoting the active participation of children, the facilitator must develop skills that enable them to transition from traditional classroom teaching styles to facilitation practice in classrooms, for example:

- To know how to activate the facilitation;
- To know how to respond and interact during facilitation;
- To know how to promote or instigate dialogue and spaces that enable and respond to children;
- To know how to follow children's initiatives;
- To know how to interact with complexities presented in the classroom;
- To develop conflict management strategies;
- To incorporate intercultural communication through interactions and dialogue initiatives.

All these aspects are an integral part of the modules that make up the SHARMED training.

Using Practice-based Formats

SHARMED training promotes an active role for participants using discussions and critiques and relies, in part, on participants recognizing that the skill to transform modes of interaction requires personal flexibility, resilience, emotional investment and a willingness to challenge well-established practices (Gibbs 2015; Allen et al. 2019). To bring about change within practice and to challenge habitual practice will always require emotional labour of the individual (Hoschild 1983; Williams 2002; Allen et al. 2019). For instance, all SHARMED training activities encourage reflection, self-assessment and discussion so that personal and professional reactions in relation to teaching and facilitation could be shared. SHARMED training recognizes and promotes the contributions of the participants, considered holders of knowledge and experiences that can enrich the meanings of the training itself. As trainees interact not only with the contents but also with the communicative style of the SHARMED training, participants gain direct and personal experience of facilitation. Such direct experience of facilitation nurtures learning that will be useful when participants will assume the role of educators for others. Throughout the training, participants are involved in practical exercises and so are able to draw on personal experience as well as their knowledge of the concept of facilitation, its aims and the educational practices that can derive from it.

Enabling Reflection as 'a Priori' to Practice

SHARMED training supports participants to foster sustainable conditions that would assist them to maintain and build the skills of facilitation and employ independent reflections on the theory and practice of facilitation. The SHARMED project emphasizes reflection *in* and *on* action (Schön 1987) and, cognate to that, the training model supports participants to evaluate what can be changed in real time (in action) and what could be changed in the future. Participants are enabled to reflect on prior objectives alongside the implementation of interventions whilst reflecting on cultural presuppositions (on action) that may frame these objectives and actions. Reflective practice is recognized as critical in providing regular opportunities to discuss, learn and change practice and cultural assumptions, what Schön (1987) elegantly defines as *professional artistic ability*.

Using Evaluation as a Means to Maintain Momentum

SHARMED training is not only based on the results of the evaluation of facilitation in action but is also based on continuous self-evaluation, undertaken through the different stages. Self-evaluation throughout SHARMED training is provoked using reflective engagement and SWOT (strengths, weaknesses, opportunities and threats) analyses. SWOT analyses are used to aid evaluation of the progress of facilitative actions and these were regularly discussed as a feature of training activities.

SWOT analysis is commonly used in a business context to enable organizations to undertake strategic planning to enhance productivity, deployment of resources and management responsibilities (Learned et al. 1969). SWOT analysis is also a respected strategic tool to support personal, professional and academic reflection and change making opportunities (Glaister & Falshaw; 1999; Helms & Nixon 2010; Allen et al. 2019). When used within education, SWOT analysis enables exploration of daily practice to be probed, celebrated and/or changed.

In the context of SHARMED training, SWOT events are used to provoke in-depth analyses of complex practice environments and to consider favourable and unfavourable challenges that either prevent or enhance goals and priorities. SWOT analyses are undertaken at macro levels to strategically plan and manage training goals and, at micro levels to analyse facilitation leadership and professional responsibilities in practice (Hofer & Schendel 1978; McDonald 1999; Kotler 2000). SWOT analyses are an important tool for evaluation throughout SHARMED training and every SWOT event enables examination of the complex layers that impact on the practice of facilitation in the classroom.

SWOT analysis can be also helpful as a tool for reflection on the realities of participant's teaching practices and on the eventualities of employing facilitation in the classroom. SHARMED training modules provide further opportunities for reflection on the use of facilitation in educational settings and were designed to encourage reflections on existing and new skills, existing and new risks and short-term and medium-term opportunities. In effect, participants were encouraged to assess their personal and professional strengths, risks and opportunities in relation to change in their own practice.

10.4 A Multi-phased Training

As part of the project, SHARMED training was experimented in two phases – positioned at the beginning and at the end of the project. The first phase was delivered before any planned classroom activities and included initial face-to-face training of teachers and practitioners of participating schools, directed to introduce the project aims and the underpinning concepts. A second component of phase 1 was the development of a Phase 1 Massive Open Online Course (MOOC), focused on the theoretical foundations of the project, in order to secure teachers' understanding of the scope of the activities in the classrooms. For the project, training via a MOOC was designed to take advantage of the absence of time constraints and to develop tools for self-learning, reflection and evaluation. The Phase 1 MOOC was designed for the participating teachers but opened to the general public through the e-learning platform EduOpen.

As with the first phase of training, the second phase was delivered both face-to-face and via a redeveloped Phase 2 MOOC. The second phase was delivered after the end of classroom activities and was designed to support educational professionals in the use of facilitation as a form of innovative pedagogy. An additional aim of the second phase of training was the delivery of guidelines to support trainees who wish to train others, securing the sustainability of the project.

Phase 1 of SHARMED Training

The first phase of training was provided at the beginning of the project and before the implementation of SHARMED activities in classrooms. This initial training was first delivered face-to-face either in schools or at agreed venues, supplemented by the Phase 1 MOOC designed as continuous professional development (CPD). This initial phase of the training was designed to introduce teachers and school staff to the SHARMED project, to its underlying philosophy, aims and its VAK methodologies. Face-to-face training ensured partner schools and staff had opportunity to engage with material and trainers whilst MOOC training and resources provided support to a wider audience. The main aim of this phase was to provide the opportunity for participants to engage with the facilitative methodology and with the concepts and principles that underpin the SHARMED project. Both face-to-face and online training used visual, auditory and kinaesthetic learning.

Phase 1 training modules addressed the following areas:

1. Interactions at school;
2. Facilitation and dialogue;
3. Intercultural communication;
4. Narratives and memory;
5. The use of photography;
6. The use of visual materials;
7. Memory and story telling;
8. The use of new technologies.

In this initial training, visual materials and in particular photographs were promoted as the key artefact to be used to encourage and capture the narratives of children. Photographs were introduced as the preferred mechanism for enabling children to share their life experiences by triggering personal or family memories. It was also stressed that other physical artefacts were not to be excluded if children choose to present or talk about something different. More detailed explorations of the underpinning concepts of the SHARMED project were a fundamental feature of the Phase 1 MOOC – providing opportunity and guidelines to engage with the concepts relating to facilitation. The development of the facilitative pedagogy and associated project activities were strengthened through the use of a multimedia archive with photographs, videos and texts, to promote exchanges among the classrooms and dissemination in European countries.

The phase 1 MOOC was published on the e-learning platform EDUOPEN (https://learn.eduopen.org/eduopen/course_details.php?courseid=112).

Phase 2 of SHARMED Training

The second phase of the training was designed to provide participants with the most effective tools to support children's agency as authorship of narratives. The contents of the training were underpinned by the evaluation of the SHARMED activities that enabled to identify the most effective facilitative actions as well as possible problems related to the use of facilitation. This second phase of training emphasized sustainability and dissemination of facilitation as an innovative form of dialogical pedagogy. Phase 2 comprised:

1. Development of a Phase 2 training package (following on from Phase 1)
2. Phase 2 training package – implemented as a pilot to inform the final project MOOC
3. Development of a final project MOOC Programme for Continuing Professional Development
4. Production of 'train the trainers' guidelines

The development of the Phase 2 training package was based on data collected through the observation of facilitation and interactions which took place empirically in the classroom. The second phase of training was developed as a modular training package to examine the most important aspects of the practice of facilitation.

Importantly, the Phase 2 modular training was piloted and tested during face-to-face training delivered to a selected number of teachers and participating schools. The pilot training was implemented in the form of face-to-face delivery for teachers with the primary purpose of allowing the collection of feedback useful for developing the final project's MOOC and for the development of the guidelines to frame training of trainers'. The pilot training took place in the schools involved in the research and was offered flexibly, depending on the needs of each school as well as on the specificities of the national contexts. Organized in a modular form, and using VAK principles, the face-to-face pilot training tested the effectiveness of different modules intended to be part of the final project MOOC programme.

Based on the feedback received and evaluation of observations from the Phase 2 training pilot package, a final MOOC was developed and is offered via a trilingual MOOC, aimed at:

1. Spreading innovation pedagogy produced by the project at European level;
2. Promoting Personal Learning Networks (PLN) adapted to the needs and interests of each individual participant.

On completion of the MOOC training programme, participants have the opportunity to assess their own learning experience using an online quiz leading to the possibility of a certificate for continuous professional development (CPD). The final MOOC is modularly structured. Each module is organized as follows:

- presentation of key concepts;
- discussion by the trainer of exemplary transcripts and video examples;
- self-assessment of learning.

Consistent with the needs of distance learning, the final project MOOC provides educational flexibility and on completion of all modules and a self-assessment exercise is designed to issue a completion CPD certificate that can be printed by the participant. The final project MOOC is accessible at https://www.sharmed.eu/uk-international/learning-platform/mooc.

The final stage of Phase 2 training was the production of guidelines for 'training the trainer' activities, designed as a handbook to support facilitators to train peers who wish to use facilitative pedagogy within their classrooms. The guidelines can be used independently from the MOOC and represent an agile manual that can be printed and kept at the disposal of teachers and practitioners irrespective of the educational context. Alternatively, these guidelines can be used as a complement to online training and consulted to support all modes of training. The 'train the trainers' guidelines are therefore very useful to leaders and stakeholders who are interested in accessing online resources that can support training that enhances inclusion and promotes diversity and multiculturalism. These guidelines allow facilitators to take an active role not only in their own learning, but also to develop the skills to support the learning of others in challenging learning environments. The full SHARMED guidelines for 'training the trainers' can be accessed at https://www.sharmed.eu/uk-international/guidelines/guidelines-for-sharmed-like-projects.

10.5 The Contents of Training

The topics of the final version of SHARMED training cover the fundamental aspects of the SHARMED project and concern the practical use of facilitation in the classroom as a form of innovative dialogical pedagogy. The contents of SHARMED training are articulated in its modular organization as follows:

Module 1 introduces the SHARMED project and explores the meaning of key concepts such as facilitation, narratives, identities. This module also includes a discussion on the use of photography to promote narratives related to individual or family memories. Module 2 introduces the characteristics and traits of the facilitative actions included under the 'activation' label. The concept of activation can be explained as part of the facilitation process and as a concept in its own right. This module explores, among other features, the skills and knowledge needed to activate children's narratives and the environmental conditions that support facilitation and the needs of children in these contexts.

Module 3 discusses reflection and feedback actions. In in module 3, for example, the notion of minimal action is considered as a frequent way to provide feedback to facilitators' actions and, in the SHARMED perspective, of great importance for facilitation. SHARMED facilitation is an example, where minimal responses (i) support children's active participation and storytelling and (ii) recognize the importance of stories and comments of children. Module 3 also recognizes that sometimes the action of feedback has to take more elaborate forms.

Module 4 is about the personal contributions of facilitators. The actions of facilitators are obviously not limited to activation (Module 2) or feedback (Module 3). This module discusses how facilitators can provide other forms of contribution to support ongoing narratives, to make them more complex, to extend the area of participation.

While modules 2, 3 and 4 are focused on facilitators' initiatives, facilitation training would not be complete without considering another pivotal aspect, namely the reaction to children's initiatives that are not solicited by the facilitators. Module 5 further develops the focus on children's initiatives by discussing the management of children's action that not only are not prompted by facilitator's action but also represents unexpected variations. The module focuses on the switch from traditional teaching to facilitative support to develop skills for when children act unpredictably. These issues were shown to be some of the most important within the training programme. This question is also very important within the SHARMED perspective where facilitation aims to promote action and acting most particularly in response to children's initiatives. This module discusses two broad categories of reactions to children's initiatives: coordinating children's initiatives and managing the situation when children interrupt the ongoing conversation to ask questions or make comments. Through modules 1–5, the training covers the major actions through which participants can develop a deeper understanding of facilitation. These modules also seek to demonstrate how several facilitating actions are intertwined in a number of interactions, rather than taking place in isolation.

Module 6 is designed to give participants an understanding of the complexity of facilitation in relation to the combination of its most recurrent actions, that is, invitations, questions, minimal feedback, formulations, personal stories, personal comments and appreciations in complex, longer, sequences of interaction. Module 7 deals with the topic of conflict management and other challenges for facilitation. This module discusses how facilitation actions can be used both to empower children as conflict managers and to promote healthier relationships by sharing narratives towards better mutual understanding. The module also addresses the risk of mistakes in promoting the active participation of children, in particular not supporting them effectively in the production of interactions/narratives, pointing to certain types of sequences that foreground the probability of failure in the facilitation.

Module 8 explores how facilitation can support narratives which, in turn, can allow for the representation of cultural issues, leading to the social construction of difference and identity. This module considers how intercultural narratives promoted by facilitation are examples of small cultures, because they are a product of contingent interactions rather than being essential components of children's personalities.

10.6 A Reflective Training

The SHARMED training model mirrors the SHARMED project in that it is designed around the premise that memory, individual and collective, is a fundamental human asset and can be the cornerstone of shared experiences. This model, as a mechanism for professional development, is designed as a genuine social process (Moyles 2006; Cable & Miller 2011; Nutbrown 2012; Siraj-Blatchford & Hallet 2014; DfE 2017) crafted around individual and collective engagement that respects the importance of history and memory. The momentum built into the model rests with the actions and reactions of participants involved in social exchanges which in turn create the influence that drives the passion and collaboration of social interactions as these evolve (Dewey 1966; Bolton 2010; Colwell 2015; Lindon & Trodd 2016). The momentum for social collaboration is both fuelled and sustained by the levels of actions and reactions within a structured, but not contrived, space.

Reflectivity was promoted throughout all stages of SHARMED training using a variety of VAK activities. For instance, SWOT analysis, development plans, reflective questioning and discussion enabled examples of facilitation to be analysed. Video examples of facilitation in action offered opportunity to observe and compare facilitation/facilitator tools and strategies. Video footage captured insight into how facilitation is (i) introduced, (ii) engaged with (iii) and evolves. Observation and discussion activities offer space to reflect on teacher–child interaction and communication; responses; engagement and participation. Space to explore and evaluate teaching styles can enable habitual practice to become visible through the act and art of self-reflection and translation of outcomes (Allen et al. 2019; Gibbs 2015).

The RARA Key model (Scollan 2009) in Figure 10.2 illustrates how professionals modify or focus their thinking during reflective practice to make

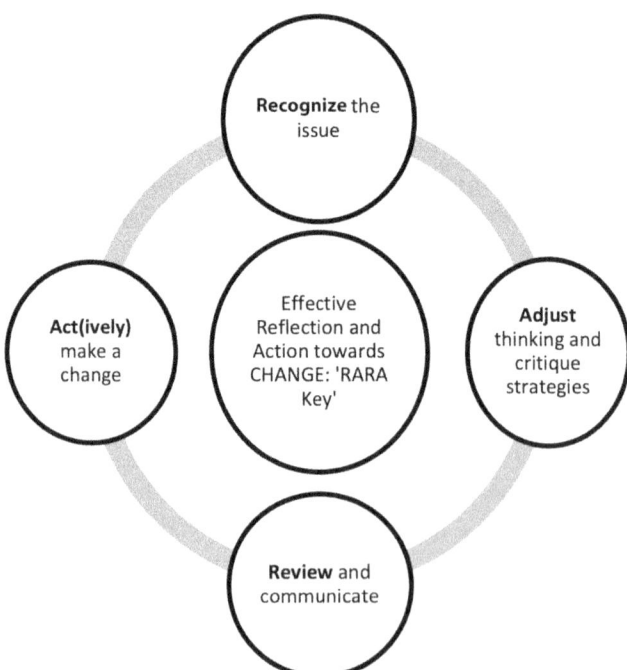

Figure 10.2 The RARA Model of reflection (Scollan 2009).

changes when introducing facilitation. The model developed from research with early childhood professionals, systematizing data collected through interviews and reviews of professionals' reflective journals (Farini & Scollan 2019). The RARA Key model describes four stages of reflection for professionals working with and for children: (1) Recognize, (2) Adjust, (3) Review and (4) Act and can be applied to SHARMED training as it provokes participants to consider how and why facilitation differs from traditional teacher-centred approaches and how the value of different kinds of relationships can be harnessed within the school and classroom environments (Table 10.1). Participants are encouraged to embrace reflective dialogue, encourage authorship of personal narratives and use critical self-evaluation of all stakeholders throughout the various stages of the programme. At all stages within this model, participants are invited to critically and continuously analyse the structure and process of facilitation and provoked into series of reflections on how classroom interactions relate to their aims for facilitation in their practice.

Table 10.1 Example of initial reflections

	If facilitation is introduced into the classroom environment what might be done differently and why?	Reflect and self-audit communication and engagement styles
Recognize	Recognize aspects of interactions used to engage children that may need to adjust or change when introducing facilitation. (self-assessment and reflective stage)	**Example:** How does the adult invite or engage children to communicate or talk about their knowledge or personal experiences during facilitation? How might this differ to traditional teaching?
Adjust	What action(s) or teaching approach might need to adjust if facilitation is to be engaged with? Why? (planning to adjust stage)	**Example:** Adjust expectations or interpretation about (i) children's knowledge and capability (ii) classroom routines or boundaries during facilitation to indicate difference between teaching/facilitation activities or outcomes.

	If facilitation is introduced into the classroom environment what might be done differently and why?	Reflect and self-audit communication and engagement styles
Review	Change needs to happen (although if change is not possible or is not working, there is a need to explore why?) Evidence or an example from practice is helpful to evaluate. (critical thinking stage)	**Example:** Facilitation did not work the way I expected. Children were not participating, they seemed to be waiting for the usual 'hands up' to engage during the activity … how do I work with children to promote and evolve facilitation? What do I need to do differently? Or Maybe, I didn't change what I usually do in the classroom, so how should I signal a change of approach? What non verbal cues or communication style can be used to signal a change in approach?
Action	Change is happening or has happened … but how did change actually happen and how did facilitation evolve? Reflect in action (during the activity) or on action (after the activity) (Schon 1987). Discuss changes with children and colleagues. For example, share reflections and views about how facilitation was experienced (evaluate, listen and do stage).	**Example:** Gauge reactions to facilitation. Encourage children to share their reactions about the use of facilitation. Teachers/facilitators reflect and share reaction towards classroom change and outcomes. For instance, focus on classroom dynamics, connections and relationships.

10.7 Conclusion

The training for the use of facilitation offers a vision of the complexities of the facilitation itself. However, SHARMED training offers something more, that is, a vision of what happens when children are recognized as equal rights holders and participants with high epistemic status in educational interactions. The SHARMED activities and research outcomes that underpin training have captured the voices, the fun but also the leadership of children during the facilitation activities. Developed from research data, the training is built to support teachers to reflect on the implications of facilitation for their professional practice, as well as to support them in using facilitation as a form of communication capable of generating learning whilst at the same time elevating children to the role of co-authors of valid and important knowledge through their contributions during educational interactions. Mirrors the training content.

These are important objectives that can lead to significant pedagogical innovation and it is for this reason that much attention was paid to the development of the training resources presented in this chapter, both those to support face-to-face training and those in support of distance education. SHARMED training in all its components intends to represent the realities of current-day teaching shifts and needs. Training can be engaged with in situ, via MOOC for distance training and interacting with guidelines for trainers. Options are available to all those interested in using facilitation as an educational practice, but also to all those interested in becoming trainers of trainers, to change education towards pedagogies centred in, and on, children's rights.

11

The SHARMED Participatory Digital Archive

Luisa Conti

11.1 Introduction

Intimacy with the unknown. Wildly unknown corners of the world in the palms of our hands. All-encompassing knowledge, accessible in seconds. Strangers become friends, engage in dialogue, exchange knowledge or share a moment. The Internet is an unlimited dimension which allows us to shift horizons, and not just our own: also those of learners, enlarging the experienceable reality at their disposal. Although the web is no true substitute for physical reality, it is a marvellous instrument to complement and support it.

The Internet is principally an infinite source of knowledge. Every click opens the door to a new world. The search engine leads the way, starting with a keyword, sentence or question. Other platforms present specific types of preselected and categorized information: the best example of this is a digital archive which offers universal access to what would otherwise hardly be attainable. Europeana, for example, is a platform via which 'thousands of European archives, libraries and museums share cultural heritage for enjoyment, education and research' (Europeana 2020).

In this chapter I will present a very different form of digital archive, though it too may be considered a trove of cultural heritage. The SHARMED archive catalogues the output media from the workshops carried out throughout the project. It includes: private pictures which children participants chose to share; the written and oral descriptions by which they were accompanied; recordings of ensuing dialogues; and several recordings with translation subtitles. The archive boasts a total of 2,008 items: 1,512 pictures as .jpg, 72 videos embedded as .mp4 and 424 texts in .pdf format.

I will describe the SHARMED archive and explain its uniqueness in both content and flexibility of navigation. I will also contextualize it in an interdisciplinary theoretical framework. Finally, I will put forward just a few suggestions for future use in educational contexts. These are by no means exhaustive or exclusive, but rather a small glimpse of the plethora of possibilities opened up by the comprehensive archive.

11.2 A Dialogic Approach

SHARMED is a project conceived to support educational change, providing pedagogues with the inspiration and instruments for even more inclusive education. According to the SHARMED ethos, *all* students ought to be treated as proactive agents, creators and instigators in a common learning process. By fostering '*genuine* participation' (Hart 1992: 11) SHARMED aims to capture the heterogeneity which is so often claimed to disrupt learning processes, transforming it instead into a valuable opportunity. Diversity is thus a resource which must be freely expressed in order to fulfil its potential. SHARMED fosters the creation of dialogic learning spaces in which differences can defy categories to establish fluid, contingent identities. The SHARMED methodology allows the participants and facilitators to discover the children from new perspectives whilst discovering new worlds.

This dialogic approach flows into SHARMED's digital archive, a crucial output of the project. The specific pedagogical framework is implemented on this digital platform on three different levels:

1. The contents of the archive have been chosen and almost exclusively generated by the children themselves. Their contributions are recognized as cultural heritage worthy of being collected, saved and shown to others. An indirect yet unmistakable message of respectful appreciation has been sent to the children involved in the project. This same message is also sent to the children using the archive, who can view their peers' contributions and recognize that these personal divulgements of children like them are considered valuable. Their own thoughts and memories may therefore also have an intrinsic, possibly underestimated value. As such, SHARMED makes a clear cut with a deficit-centred view upon children: the archive displays and divulges an empowering spectrum of identities, perspectives, backgrounds and situations which can bring forth a variety of skills.

2. The archive is a medium to expand peer-to-peer-learning outside the physical-temporal frontiers of an exchange within the classroom. Digitally shared images, thoughts, information or emotions transcend national borders and time zones to reach and enrich children. The archive is conceived for use by educators who wish to offer their students unique learning experiences, giving them intimate access to other lived experiences. By means of this contact, children are encouraged to independently interpret what they see. They may thus absorb new knowledge and become knowledge creators themselves.
3. A positive approach to diversity is fostered via the use of materials created by peers in another time and space. The children using the archive can develop a differentiated perception of life in other nations, the culture in general and the inhabitant children in particular. The copious media collected enable the users to appreciate international peers in their true heterogeneity. Moreover, browsing this collection makes it possible for the young users to attain varied input regarding specific topics. This increases their ability to perceive the multiplicity of one same phenomenon on a transnational plane.
4. Relatedly, the use of the SHARMED archive brings the true complexity of life a little closer for the students. While content is so often normed and simplified for educational use, the authentic generation of this content by young people establishes both an age-centred interest point and age-appropriate thematic complexity, as understood and presented by the original contributors.

The SHARMED archive aims to give concrete support to teachers willing to make the dialogic learning experience real. On the one hand, educators can employ the original (audio-)visual materials from the archive as educational resources during their classes. On the other hand, they may also be inspired to employ the method in their classes themselves, putting the memories of their own students in the limelight of their didactic activities. In addition to the images submitted by the children, the written accompaniments and the videos in which they described them, the archive also contains videos with longer dialogue sequences which demonstrate the multiplicity of settings harnessed by the eight facilitators in the different classes in Italy, Germany and the UK. Access to these videos allows teachers to grasp how to apply the method in their class, as well as providing the opportunity for critical observation of the facilitation techniques and thus self-reflect.

11.3 A Participatory Archive? Theory and Evidence

SHARMED workshop sessions were based around an ethos of dialogue and therefore, by definition, participation. The subsequent archive is no different. This section outlines the ways in which the SHARMED archive is far from a dusty digital shelf. Instead, it enables interaction, participation and synergetic communication. This two-way mode of digital input is best summarized by the then innovative trend, now key principle and buzzword from the digital revolution at the turn of the millennium: 'Web 2.0' (O'Reilly 2005). While this has become a matter of course in the plethora of social media platforms available, in the context of data logging and processing it is considered a postmodernist turn in archival theory (Cook 2001).

Once locked away for private use, first publications of archival records were made in the course of the Enlightenment in the eighteenth century (Gallner-Holzmann 2020: 383) and new technological advances show a near incredible capacity to refresh and revise this ideological aspect of archiving: access. If knowledge is power, access to information a precondition for equality. Over the course of history, archives have supported processes of democratization. One prominent example comes from the French Revolution, during which archives facilitated a forum for airing grievances as permission to use archives was secured by law as a right for citizen (Lange et al. 2004: 16–17, 26). The digital revolution provides an even larger repository of knowledge, the paradigm-changing possibilities of which are nigh endless. In particular, the evolution of the participatory and social web allows the easy publication of user-generated content, which has led to the creation of what it could be considered global participatory archivism. The revelation of a multiplicity of perspectives, meanings and contexts has turned from radical to trend. Traditional archiving practices are challenged: the user becomes an active participant in the coproduction of knowledge and historical understanding (Eveleigh 2015). More and more organizations and institutions harness this possibility to include those voices traditionally excluded by means of participatory archives (Flinn 2010, 2011). It is precisely in this vein that the idea of creating an open, dynamic SHARMED repository was conceived, establishing a digital possibility for children to let their voices be heard. More challenging, however, was the incorporation of the SHARMED principles of inclusiveness and empowerment into the archive. Precisely these two principles correspond to the dimensions used by Farrington and Bebbington (1993: 105 cited Rolan 2017: 201) to measure participation in the context of sustainable development intervention projects. Their model has been embraced by Rolan (2017: 201–2) to analyse the degree of participation in innovative digital archives. *Inclusiveness*, measured as breadth, is defined as the possibility for the various stakeholders to engage with the archive; *empowerment*, measured as depth, is defined as the extent to which the stakeholders involved may exercise agency. Both aspects must be considered in relation to all stakeholders and all record-keeping activities: appraisal, creation, documentation, preservation, access control and disposal of records (Rolan 2017: 198).

In order to locate the SHARMED archive within the two planes of empowerment and inclusiveness, the record-keeping activities must first be examined and explained. To do so, the section below adopts a definition of records, presents Rolan's 'participatory record keeping and archiving continuum model'[1] and outlines the activities as reorganized into macro-phases.

Records are defined by Rolan (2017: 198) as traces of activity which have value to individuals, organizations and/or societies, 'whether that be for a nanosecond or millennia' (McKemmish 2001: 336). After being *created* – if appraised – they are *captured*, *organized* and *pluralized*. Though the items may be altered in some manner, their storage with metadata supports the transferal of the originally intended meaning into the archive (Rolan 2017: 198). However, the real transfer of any form of original meaning via a database or archive is contestable (Yeo 2007). The new context and new audience will (nearly) always unwittingly alter the message (Cook 2001: 6). Finally, the delineation of rights of access to the records for different user-groups is a prerequisite for the dissemination of the content. In the context of online archives, this phase may blur with the pluralization phase, which brings the items farther away from their creators (Rolan 2017: 207).

11.3.1 Phase I 'Create' (Appraisal and Creation)

The records collected in the SHARMED archive are traces of memories, many directly of the children involved and several of their family histories as a whole. Another key unit of archival are the records of the activities which took place in 2017. Texts, video-recordings and some of the pictures were created by the children themselves during the project, the remainder of the pictures were selected by the children for the project.

1. The picture which they presented in the first or second workshop and the one that had been created during the project: The children were requested to choose a picture which represented a memory which is important to them and which they would like to share with their classmates.
2. The written narrations of their memories were to be filled in standardized form. Nonetheless, the very general and open questions in the form permitted the children to freely decide what to write and how. The children were asked to write about the history of the image, to describe it, to explain why the picture was important to them and to write down their associations with it.[2]
3. The oral narrations of their memories occurred in two different ways: in some cases, this was in the context of the active plenary facilitation process with the whole class. In other cases, this took place directly in front of the camera, with a minimum of facilitator input. When the oral description occurred in context of a facilitated plenary dialogue along with the whole class, the narration was significantly influenced by the other people present, even though the role of the facilitator was to support the children in displaying their agency, which did appear to take place the majority of the time.
4. Some videos represent dialogue sequences which took place during the workshop. They were chosen by the international SHARMED team which acted as curator of the archive. These videos represent scenes which are particularly pertinent from an educational, pedagogical perspective.

The participation of the children was permitted to flourish via the selection or creation of the pictures, as well as in the written and oral narration of the memories linked to them. Their latent agency was displayed in its full glory thanks to these narratives. The contents were of course generated by the children and, to a lesser extent, the facilitators. The curators themselves are only responsible for the selection of the longer dialogue sequences presented in the archive. This interweave of curator and generator reinforces the breadth of participation according to Rolan, as well as the depth of participation, thanks to the interweave of displays of child and adult agency. It must, however, be noted that the archive is inherently incomplete, as not all pictures presented during the project could be archived, nor could all written or oral contributions. The children's parents and guardians played the role of gatekeepers, as they were able to decide upon whether images and written descriptions could be published, as well as whether children could be filmed.

The SHARMED Participatory Digital Archive

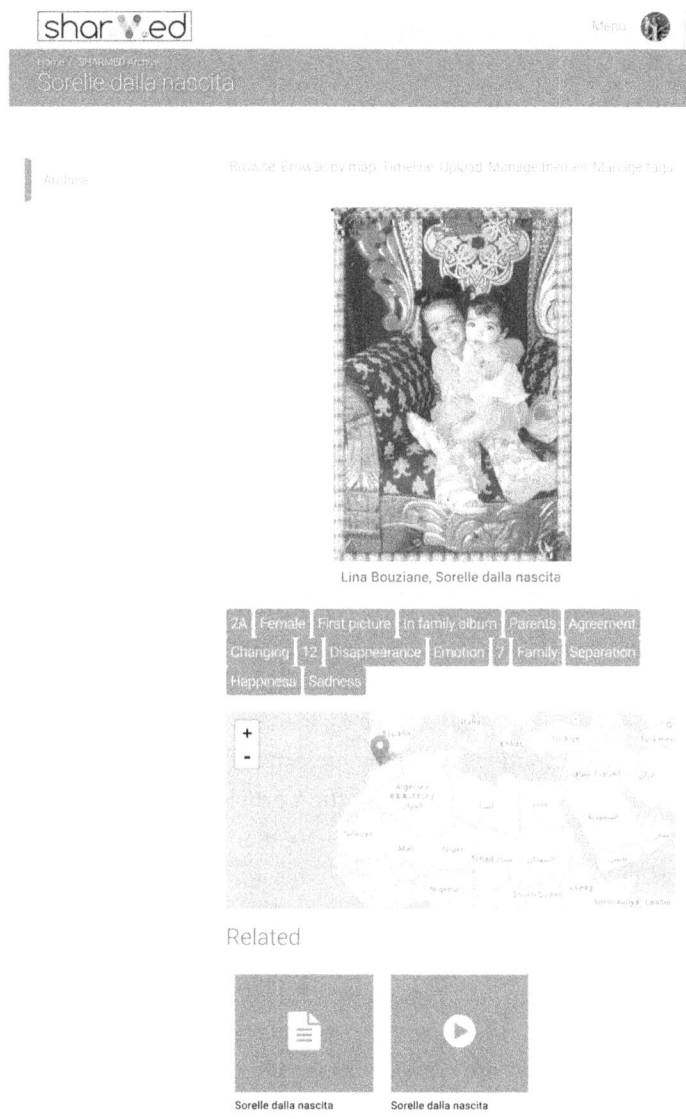

Figure 11.1 Picture, connected to the files with the written and oral descriptions.

11.3.2 Phase II 'Capture' (Documentation and Preservation)

The 1512 images contributed by children participants form the majority of the database. These are labelled with both the original titles, as given by the participant, as well as tags assigned by the curator team in order to enable thematical visual searches or connections. Further key metadata are linked within the remaining records: pictures are linked with their written descriptions (and oral descriptions, if available) and in several cases also to the dialogues which arose from them. In this manner, the original intended meaning can be transmitted to the contemporary users of the archive. These warmly invited viewers may engage with a personal context and explanation to which they might otherwise not be granted access.

It ought to be noted that the majority of the documentation (selection and submission of images, written contextualization and explanation, verbal contextualization and explanation) was carried out by the youths themselves. Only the process of uploading the records into the archive, organizing and labelling them was carried out by the international curator team. In this second phase of the 'record keeping and archiving continuum model', inclusion was therefore broad in relation to the initial documentation. The preservation activities, on the other hand, were rather narrow regarding inclusion: children were not granted access to or responsibility for uploading their images into the archive, nor were their teachers. An original proposal of the SHARMED project was to transfer this responsibility to the teaching staff as a way of physically shifting the sense of archive authorship away from the research staff and into the classrooms in which the project was carried out. This would have made the results more tangible for the students whose contributions made the project possible. Unfortunately, the lack of time at the disposal of the teaching staff (a problem common to all countries and year groups) led to the decision in favour of time-efficiency. The uploads were thus carried out by the curator team. Nonetheless, the record-keeping activities in which the children could participate allowed them to act autonomously. That meant that participation in relation to documentation was both broad and deep, while being rather narrow with regards to the matter of preservation.

The archive itself is based upon a Moodle platform which the curators developed themselves in cooperation with a team of professional programmers. The interface was thus tailored to their needs, rendering it easy to use for the curators. The technical framework necessary for inserting all the data and metadata and creating a network of connections was programmed according to their needs and feedback, giving them an active role in the structural shaping of the archive. Following the multidimensional model of inclusiveness as outlined above, participation on this plane was very deep, although its wideness varied.

11.3.3 Phase III 'Organize' (Access Control)

The organization phase was undertaken solely by the curators of the archive, though it was strongly influenced by overarching ethical and data protection

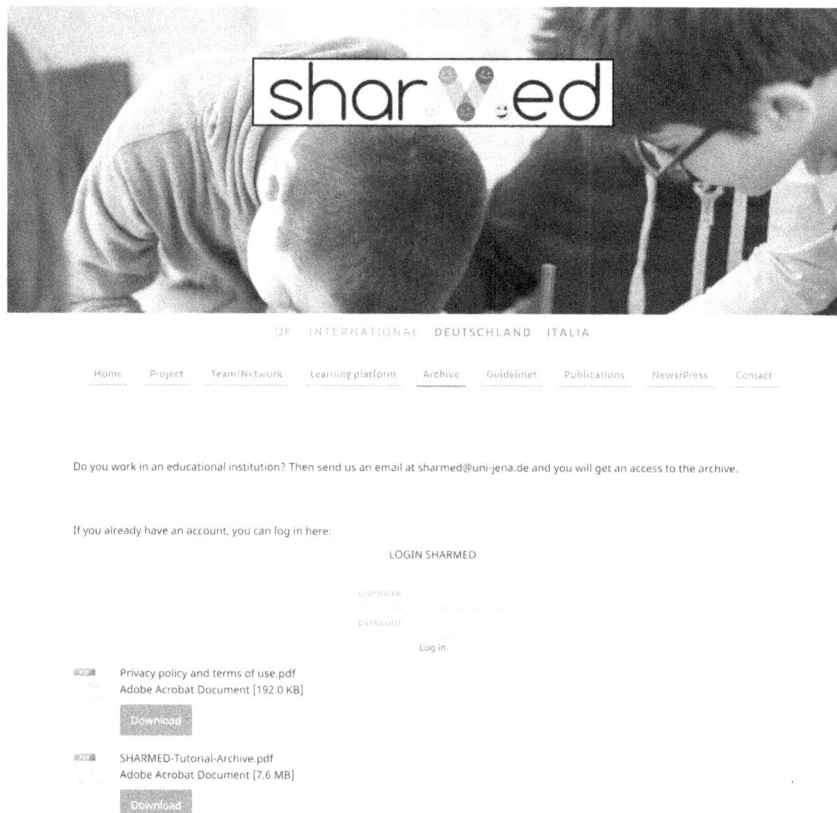

Figure 11.2 Access to SHARMED archive.

issues as well as by the permission issued (or not issued) by the parents and guardians of the children. The unusually sensitive type of records – private pictures and stories of children – had a clear impact on the decision-making process. To protect privacy rights and unequivocally circumvent potential abuse of these records, the curator team took the decision to regulate access. Potential users must register and show credentials as belonging to an educational or academic institution and are individually, manually approved. Login data may be requested by pedagogues working in official educational organizations and institutions only. These approved users then gain access via an individual password.

By token of the restricted user profiles who may gain access, participation in relation to the access is quite narrow on the inclusion scale and shallow with regards to the empowerment scale. The curator team, in dialogue with external experts regarding ethical regulations, saw this restriction as unavoidable due to the nature of the records. It was therefore not possible to follow through with the original SHARMED project plan to create an archive to which all stakeholders would have extensive access.

11.3.4 Phase IV 'Pluralization' (Availability of Records)

The pluralization phase describes the way in which the primary users – those with granted access to the archive – distribute the contents of the archive, whether in the classroom or via the university lecture hall. Those who are shown the contents by the primary users then become secondary users, who increase or 'pluralize' the number of individuals benefitting from access. The primary users, it must be noted, are the ones who decide which elements of the archive they show to whom and in which context, giving them an autonomy in transmitting and interpreting meaning. So far, the primary users of the SHARMED archive have been limited to teachers, researchers and university lecturers. Neither the children involved, nor their parents or guardians, nor other children have attained independent access to the archive. Participation is therefore not particularly narrow, as access is not just restricted to the original research and curation team but rather awarded to a large and varied professional groups in educational contexts, and anyone can search for, find and apply for access to the archive. Conversely, the level of participation is also not particularly broad. In contrast to the original plan for the records, no other stakeholders are permitted access, not even the protagonists whose contributions form the entirety of the data. The curator team accepts the reasons which made this necessary; however, this significantly restricts the possibility for broad participation. This is further reflected in the shallow empowerment experienced by the users: although the users are free to view and employ the records for educational purposes, they are not able to upload their own input.

The initial conception of the SHARMED archive was as a dynamic, growing platform where new images and memories could be uploaded autonomously

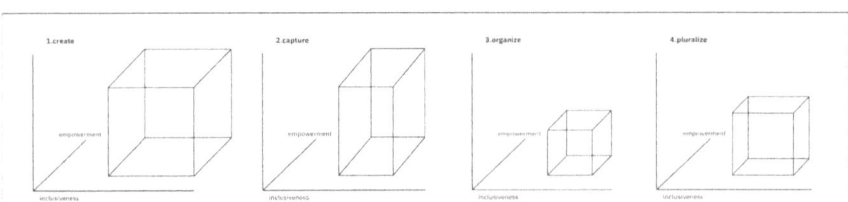

Figure 11.3 Degree of participation in SHARMED archive.

by educators all over Europe. Regrettably, the time-bounded financial support (2016–2018) of the project rendered the long-term supervision, moderation and technical maintenance necessary for the management of such a system unfeasible. In particular, the risk involved in the upload of new material from further minors would have fallen into the responsibility of the archive providers, including the due obtainment and management of permission. This constituted another reason for the non-implementation of the original plans for the archive. Nonetheless, even the continued possibility of retrieval poses several challenges: as Huvila (2008: 27) points out, both the technical upkeep and the capacity (as well as permission) to maintain or process the data must be secured long-term. Fortunately, registration requests will be maintained and supervised for the foreseeable future thanks to the involvement of the Department of Intercultural Communication at the University of Jena. The department were not just active members in the research team but are also a managing institution for the educational platform, Glocal Campus, in which SHARMED archive is hosted. All efforts are made to ensure the longevity of the archive.

Rolan's model refers to a continuum, which implies a circularity and thus reciprocity of record-keeping activities. This is not realizable in the context of the SHARMED-archive as the users cannot become creators of new digital records.[3] Although this online participation is not possible, an independent adaptation of the concept is actionable and the archive remains an important tool for fostering participatory processes offline. These would be led by the primary users of the archive who can support their students to become creators of tangible records in material archives.

According to the circumstances outlined above, the SHARMED archive could be described as a hybrid form between Shilton and Srinivasan's 'participatory archive' and Huvila's 'radical participatory archive'.[4] The engagement of the users is the common aspect, most clearly represented by the term 'participatory'. However, there are two central differences between the models. The first one relates to the localization of participation: in the participatory archive participation is fostered '*around* instead of *within* the archive' (Huvila 2008: 26), thus limiting the role of the user as a creator or curator. In contrast, the radical participatory archive foresees the user as engaging in all archival activities, becoming creators and curators themselves in the context of a collaborative management of the tasks. The curation itself is therefore 'decentralized' (Huvila 2008) in the second model. The second difference between the two models refers to their scope: Shilton and Srinivasan's participatory archive aims to obtain voices from local communities which are coherent and complementary, in order to build archives which reconstruct their heritage or identity. Huvila's model, on the other hand, considers the diversity of the authors as resources for guaranteeing the construction of multiperspectival archives (ibid.).

Due to the unusual nature of the records which it collects, the SHARMED archive limits the participation of the users within the archive and awards curators most of their traditional authority. In this sense, it is not a radical participatory archive, even though the principle of exploring the multiperspectivalism of diversity strongly resembles the ethos of a radical participatory model. While neither interactions nor negotiations of meaning can take place within the archive itself, these tenets remain at the core of the archive's source, as well as its purpose. Radical participatory archives must also reach a critical mass of users in order to operate, as it is these who ensure the interaction and negotiations (ibid., 30). In the case of the SHARMED archive, however, the emergence of a strong user community or a collaborative culture amongst them is not a prerequisite for its success. Despite this, the primary users of the archive remain the key to its impact: these individuals must be satisfied with both the content and the support received if they are to pluralize the records by involving secondary users. Usability is therefore a crucial challenge for digital contemporary archives, in particular for (radical) participatory ones and thereby also for the SHARMED archive.

11.4 Usability

Under the 'traditional archival paradigm' (Huvila 2008: 25), the central aim of the archival process was preservation in and for itself. Usability only recently became a priority, revitalizing the historical linkage to democratization processes: 'records of the people, by the people, and for the people' (Ketelaar 1992). Digitization has led to the development of new record-keeping practices, further influenced by the emergence of a common expectation of universal *access* to all information (Mulrenin 2002: 87–8). In the interest of digital inclusion, accessibility has become an all-important attribute of websites and platforms, although the search for optimal universal accessibility and usability continues (W3C 2021). From a post-modern perspective, this accessibility does not just refer to the actual possibility of using an archive but rather granting access implies an invitation to the users to apply their own interpretations. This amounts to what can effectively be considered an 'attitude' (Menne-Haritz 2001: 61), culminating in Huvila's concept of 'radical user orientation' (2008). In close connection to the radical participatory archive model presented above, this term refers to a broader understanding of usability, the word *use* referring to 'a deeper level of involvement in the sense of actual participation in the archive and in the archival process' (ibid., 25). However, it must be added that the entire principle of *user orientation* is quite radical in practice, if not in terminology. Previously, users were perceived of as archival experts who would be able to act autonomously, know precisely what they are looking for, be able to express this in archival terms and also then be capable of dealing with the records independently (ibid., 16). The trend from the 1990s onwards to reject implausible images of users as experts, both in archival practice and in the scientific community (ibid.), has fostered the development of more easily accessible and usable archives and thus rendered them attainable for a wider public: not to mention more appealing. Moreover, the very medium of digitization is a highly valuable quality for an archive: it is rendered potentially[5] available beyond local and temporal boundaries. *Accessibility* and *usability*, however, depend upon the holistic design of the created archival system, which involves technical, graphic, linguistic and conceptual aspects (Conti 2012: 278–82). A digital archive is simply a space in which users can be encouraged to engage with its digitized material (Grünberger 2014: 64), all of the aforementioned design aspects dictating the extent to which this will be effective.

One key aspect of usability is the *findability* of the records. This is humorously and adeptly demonstrated in the following example:

> Imagine yourself outside an art gallery in a far-off city, with a collection you don't know well. You enter the building to find a small, drab lobby with an attendant at a desk. The attendant asks you to enter your query on a small slip of paper. Not knowing the collection, and not seeking anything in particular, you write down something arbitrary and pass it over. The attendant disappears for a moment before returning with a line of artworks sitting on trollies. These are paraded, ten at a time, through the lobby.
>
> (Whitelaw 2015: 1)

This imaginary scene makes evident the frustration that guests of a digital collections feel when they would like to enter and explore it, though the only access is by search query. Following Drucker (2013), Whitelaw describes this vexation in order to highlight the importance of considering findings not just from the fields of information retrieval and human-computer interactions when conceiving the design of an archive, but also from the Humanities in general. Whitelaw argues the importance of configuring a 'generous interface' which offers the users various manners in which to explore the archive and proposes four principles to follow when designing a digital archive (Whitelaw 2013: 7):

1. Show first. Don't ask
2. Provide rich overviews
3. Provide context
4. Show high quality primary content

So that users might explore the collection, they must be capable of orientating from their very first encounter with the archive. They ought to attain an instant understanding about the collection and its organization and be able to find the various records in an intuitive way (ibid.). To avoid influencing the users and their interpretation, it is important to embed the records in their original context and refrain from adding non-context appropriate content (ibid., 5).

These four categories offer a fitting structure under which to present the SHARMED archive. In advance it must be stipulated that not just the aforementioned skills of the web developers and the requirements of the SHARMED curator team were considered during the construction of the archive. Throughout the conception phase, the image of a final primary user remained teachers located in different European countries who would become archive users to find inspiration or material to use with their students. The perspectival focus taken in the conception phase was, therefore, that of teachers.

11.4.1 Accessibility

The SHARMED archive is a Moodle integrated archive for multimedia data, the structure of which is based on the platform Glocal Campus which hosts numerous international projects related to education and research. Specific plug-ins added the desired features to our archive. This was possible because the basis, Moodle, is an open-source learning management system compatible with any standards compliant browser and without licensing fees. It can therefore be used at any time and on any device directly in the browser, without accessibility or consistency problems. The open-source approach optimizes data security and user privacy. Boasting 213 million users worldwide, it is the most widely used learning platform and would therefore be familiar to many potential users (Moodle 2021).

On the SHARMED website,[6] users are invited to send a request to obtain access to the archive. Once this is granted, they receive their personal login credentials along with a short tutorial file which summarizes all features of the archive and how to utilize them. The login details can be entered via the same web link, upon which the user is redirected to Glocal Campus. This welcome page hosts a short introduction as well as a forum for messages, questions or requests. A .pdf file outlining the terms of use, privacy policies and community standards is also embedded in this page. Inside the archive, videos and pictures can be watched directly in the browser. The texts as written in the forms have been uploaded as .pdf files. These are displayed in an open format which invites the user to browse while enabling them to narrow the scope in terms of medium type, geographical location or record ID as well as via pre-programmed key words, as explained in more detail below. Whitelaw's first criterion of 'show first. Don't ask' is thus fulfilled on a variety of planes.

11.4.2 Findability

The archive offers four different paths for searching within the records, each of which provides a rich overview as recommended in Whitelaw's second criterion.

Visual Search

Once opened, the archive users immediately see the records with their titles. While videos and texts are represented by a general standardized symbol, the pictures are previewed in small format. One click upon the chosen item opens a new page. The record is then displayed above an interactive map with a pin on a contextualizing location as selected by the child. On this same page, the user can find shortcuts to all other records related as well as tags. These tags relate to the eleven categories chosen by the curator team to organize the records.

Search Filters

Users can select the records based upon one or more categories. Only the main and sub-keywords and the topics of the videos which are listed in the 'Process' grouping on the website were selected by the curator team. All others were assigned by the children themselves or are related to the context in which the records were collected. These can be used to filter the results.

i. Media type: image, video or text.
ii. Class: organized by country and region to accommodate the different school systems.
iii. Main keywords: animal, ceremony, changing, character, close persons (not family), emotion, event, family, friend, holidays, leisure, me, objects, place or sport.

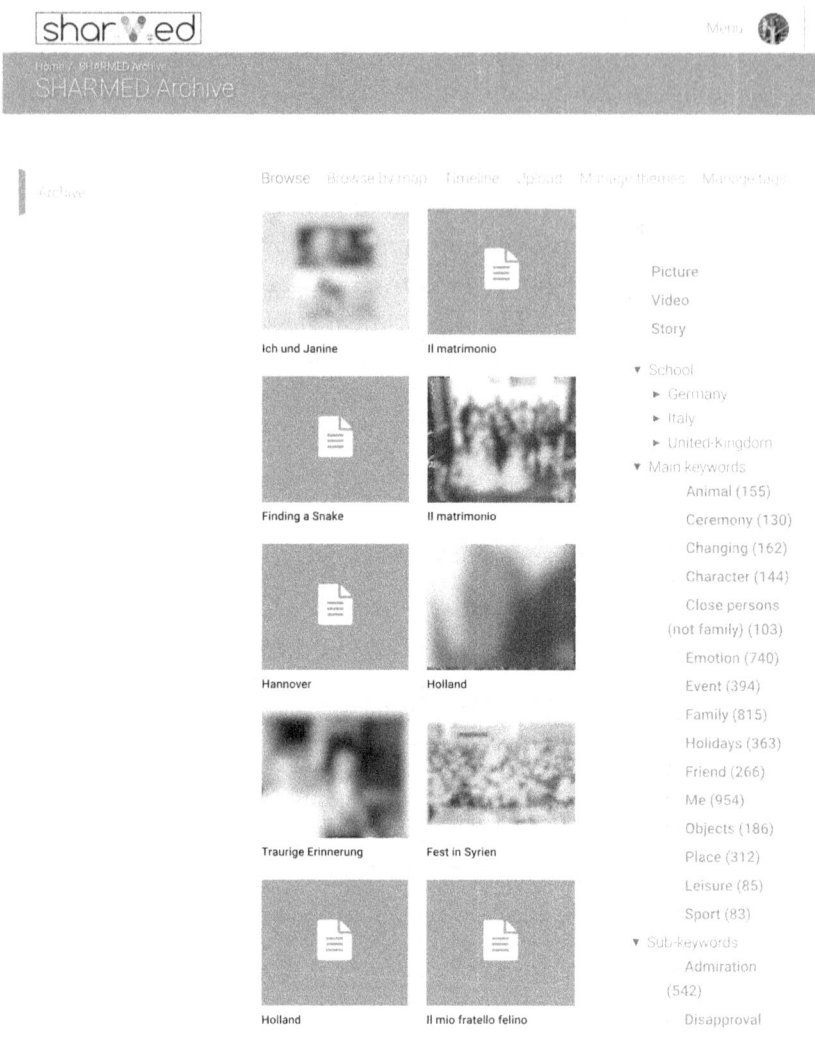

Figure 11.4 Visual search (left); search filters (right).

iv. Sub-keywords: admiration, disapproval, agreement, disagreement, appearance, disappearance, birth, death, conflict, peace, departure, return, meeting, separation, happiness, sadness, comfort or discomfort.
v. Gender: female, male, other.
vi. Age: 8, 9, 10, 11, 12, 13, 14 or 15.
vii. Class: 1, 2, 3, 4, 5, 6, 7.
viii. Author: child, parents, close person, other or unknown.

ix. Process (only for videos): narratives of the family, narratives of the self, personal life, stories, stories of history or stories of migration.
x. Picture: first picture or second picture.
xi. Photograph found: in family album or online.

Browse by Map

Users may also navigate the records using an interactive map into which they may zoom in or out. Shortcuts to all pictures are provided via pins. Users click on the desired pin to open the chosen record. This provides a geographical contextualization of and connections between the records.

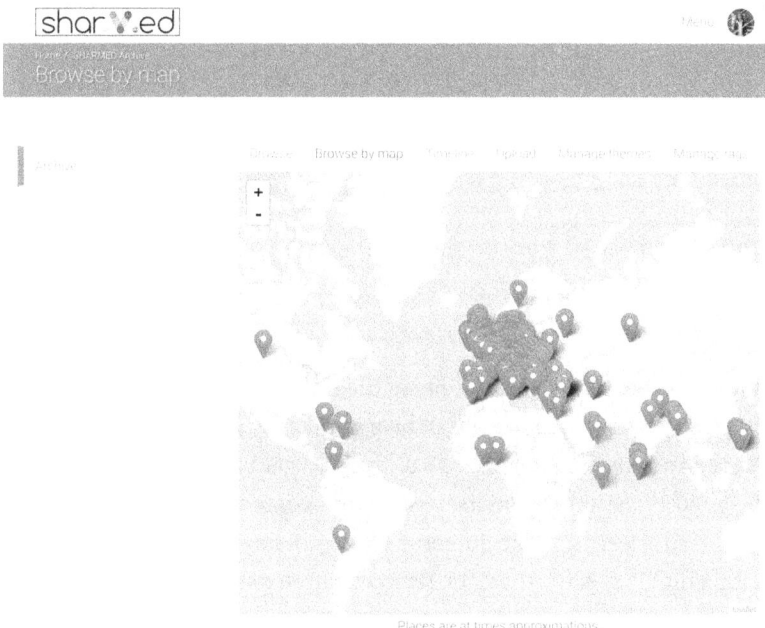

Figure 11.5 Browse by map.

Browse by Timeline

Users can also search by scrolling along timeline bar. This bar starts with the oldest picture, dated back to 1920, and ends in 2017 when the records were uploaded. Above the timeline they can see a preview of the picture assigned to this temporal position, along with its title. The images are hyperlinked shortcuts to the records.

Figure 11.6 Browse by timeline.

11.4.3 Flexibility

Flexibility is given by the accessibility of the records through different pathways, as this allows users to explore the archive in the way which best suits their goal. Each type of access is connected to a different organization of the records which are clustered in various manners: based upon content or upon geographical or temporal characteristics. The numerous different keywords offered in the filters allow for a highly specific thematic reorganization of the records. This flexibility is closely connected to Whitelaw's third principle, 'provide context', both in a narrower as well as in a broader sense: linking records according to the class and school membership of their authors can accentuate the social context in which they were presented or created. Simultaneously, the possibility to organize the records in an individually desired pattern allows for their generational contextualization, useful for the interpretation of the records. Finally, the visual interconnectedness of records regarding individual memories plays an important role: the images are frequently accompanied by the description children proffered in oral and/or written form. This linkage permits users to tread closer to the original meaning of the picture and find a wealth of information related to the record and its author. The SHARMED archive collects the memory traces of hundreds of children and composes a truly specialized and rich knowledge pool. Multiple clusterability fosters high flexibility of use, consequently users are supported in configuring unique learning processes.

The learning experiences made possible by the SHARMED archive are both multitudinous and distinctive. The examples provided here offer a brief glimpse of the potential the records hold and are by no means exhaustive. One option would be to compare the original records with other archives or media collections, as well as with private artefacts or memories of students involved in new workshops run by a primary user. Alternatively, the timeline could be utilized to search for historical primary sources. Several pictures carry true historical value, representing the participants' (great-) grandparents in their bygone lived experiences. Another option would be to diversify sources for Geography or History lessons thanks to the world map which localizes the records. The personalized nature of the content also makes it highly suitable for fostering intercultural competence. Relatedly, foreign language learners of German, Italian or English may click on the corresponding option in the search filters to obtain records based upon their age group or interests, thus bringing the target language closer to them in terms of relatability as well as providing authentic materials of broad scope.

In line with the suggestions above, it would be possible for the students to navigate the archive themselves, the autonomy permitting them to browse and select text and media sources independently. This may be particularly pertinent for project-based learning in which the students engage in exploratory and enquiry learning. Whether in plenary, groups or individual work, the students could be posed with research questions, the answers to which can be found in the archive. However, the teachers could also pre-select the materials which they put at their students' disposal. The images would provide an element of immediacy, as students can zoom in and discover meaningful details. These images also provide the possibility for a quite different form of engagement: navigating the picture preview function on the archive's start page, the teacher and students can choose pictures to adapt into new artworks, potentially even connecting them with their descriptions. Inspiration can be taken from the book *SHARMED Archive. A Selection* (Ballestri et al. 2018) which consists of some of the pictures and texts from the archive. It can be found within the archive in its entirety, an excerpt is also available on the public SHARMED website. Finally, the teachers may also find themselves in the role of a student, most notably in the context of teacher training and professional development courses. The videos available under the 'process' category offer an intimate view of fascinating classroom interactions, many of them subtitled. These interactions are a precious resource, particularly for future teachers.

11.4.4 Authenticity

As far back as the mid-nineteenth century, British school inspectors recommended using original historical sources for educational purposes. By the end of the nineteenth century, schools and archives in both Belgium and in Germany were cooperating. In the mid-twentieth century, the French *service educatif* institutionalized cooperation between schools and archives (Gallner-Holzmann 2020: 384). These examples demonstrate the growing recognition for authentic primary historical resources rather than ones normed or simplified for use in the classroom. These stimulate exploratory learning, foster deeper associations with the topic discussed, enable the learner to enter the imaginary world of the original situation in a way that brings them closer to the reality. They also challenge and strengthen the student's ability to interpret contexts and narratives as well as evidencing elements of inherent bias or perspectivity in the sources, whether through cultural fissures or selectivity of access. In this way, the pupils can learn from an early age that texts must be questioned and viewed critically, enabling them to develop their own opinions. Furthermore, successful archival pedagogy with original sources brings students closer to processes of history: it is not just something to be studied, but rather the pupils themselves can *make* it (Schaller 2019: 102).

An important goal in working with original sources is also to convey a critical awareness of history by training media and judgment skills (ibid., 103). Thus, the archive has the task of conveying the importance of the original and the genuine (Aspelmeier 2019: 104). In this context, the archive offers opportunities for lifelong learning, propounding knowledge that extends beyond the subject itself. Identity-related forms of archival work, such as researching family history, can also arouse extracurricular curiosity about history (ibid., 106). Archival pedagogical work is intended to bring historical elements closer to young people, in an experiential, sensory and personalized manner. The pupils should experience history as open, multiperspectival and somewhat contradictory: while it may feel spatially or biographically close, it is also distant, at the very least in a temporal sense (Lange et al. 2004: 47–8).

In the age of the Internet, teachers and students have primary historical sources at the tips of their fingers, offering them a variety of representations of history. It boasts a plethora of digital resources related to all disciplines, enabling lifelong learning in both formal and informal educational settings. The SHARMED archive is one such digital resource. Even though it is not a particularly prestigious collection of historical fragments, it is a unique collection which displays authentic material. In this respect it satisfies Whitelaw's fourth principle 'show high quality primary content'. The content is of high quality in the sense that it is idiosyncratic, personal and therefore pedagogically and educationally valuable: the relatability of content is a key factor in all educational analysis of its effectiveness (Klafki 1991: 270).

The relatability of the content is primarily established by the youthful sources of the records. The archive collects pictures and memories of peers, written and told by them personally. This creates a personal connection to knowledge for the users, bringing the lived experiences closer to their own world and thus rendering it easier to imagine how these memories would smell, taste or feel. In language classes, working with memories written and/or told by children in the country of the target language stimulates curiosity to discover the content. Once motivation has increased, so too does the absorption of new content. These records are not just appealing didactic material but also content-rich ones: the pictures, the texts and the videos transmit significantly more information than standard foreign language textbooks, also in a much more immediate manner. Genuine access to various topics can be afforded so as to inform, sensitize or both. One prime example is the variety of pictures and narratives about religious rituals and symbols. By utilizing these materials, teachers can foster intercultural dialogue and assist the children in acquiring correct information, an indispensable skill in order to resist racist discourses and fake news. The high-quality content also provides ample scope for children to learn how to deal with different types of media, an important element of media competence (Borries 2008: 100). Moreover, SHARMED actively invites teachers to get to know the SHARMED method and try it out in their own classes. The children would therefore create their own media outputs to further develop their skills. The learning process is thus entirely student-centred, beginning with the analysis of the archive sources and ending with a tangible individual achievement.

11.5 Conclusion

The SHARMED project is characterized by a dialogic approach that puts the children themselves at the centre of learning processes. Their own memories as educational content and their agency foster an anti-hierarchical culture of participation. The project pushes forward the development in education towards inclusiveness and the compendious archive came to be one of the most important outputs of the project. The SHARMED archive collects the products of the workshops carried out in three countries and is offered up as a source of inspiration for teachers across Europe on the one hand, on the other hand offering tangible and unique educational materials which teachers can employ in their classroom activities.

This chapter has analysed the archive from various perspectives, embedding it in different theoretical frameworks. Firstly, it was shown how the dialogic approach deeply shapes the archive, which was originally planned to be as participatory as possible. Secondly, the limiting impact of the short-term nature of the funding as well as the particularly sensitive data upon participation *within* the archive was discussed, although conceptual and technical efforts have been made to ensure as much participation *around* it as possible. Finally, specific attention was given to its generous interface which aims to foster usability through guaranteeing accessibility, optimizing findability, offering flexibility and conquering with its authenticity.

The innovativeness of the SHARMED archive can be summarized in three core aspects:

1. It is an educational platform which builds strong synergies between the physical and the digital dimension, making one the source of inspiration of the other.
2. It carries on the historical goal of democratization of public archives and simultaneously promotes the democratization of education: the epistemic authority of children is recognized and valued.
3. It offers inspiration in the form of tangible didactic materials and supports teachers in designing child-oriented learning processes.

The archive holds a wealth of knowledge and an abundance of educational possibilities, yet the user rates of this innovative child-generated archive remain modest. Coming exclusively from the perspective of the children, it runs counter to the established process of utilizing normed materials, specifically designed or simplified for use in the classroom. The question to be posed is: Are educators ready to take children seriously as a source of valuable, educational knowledge in their own right?

Notes

1. Rolan's model is a further development of the Records Continuum Model, revisited also under the perspectives of the new technologies by its own authors (Upword et al. 2011).
2. The questions in the form are following: Do you have a title for this picture? Where did you find it? Where was it stored? Who took it? Where was it taken? When? (If you don't know the exact date, the year is enough) In what circumstances was it taken (i.e. holidays, ceremony …)? Please describe this picture: what/who is on this picture? Why is this picture important to you? What does it remind you of?
3. As a cyclical perspective cannot be taken, more specific differentiation between the terms *record keeping* and *archiving* are not discussed here. These issues are explored in more detail in Rolan (2017: 198).
4. Huvila (2008) discussed both a participatory archive model and a participatory archive. Although the similarity of the terms may appear confusing, the model is differentiated on account of its radical user orientation.
5. The Covid-19 pandemic has shown that the Digital Divide is a challenge which must be overcome (Iyengar 2020).
6. https://www.sharmed.eu/uk-international/archive-1/

12

Conclusion: General Reflections on SHARMED as Innovative Pedagogy

Claudio Baraldi, Erica Joslyn and Federico Farini

12.1 Introduction

This final chapter considers the educational and societal implications of SHARMED. The complexity and the varied outcomes of this project demand non-linear and interwoven reflections about its achievement and its European impact. First, in this concluding chapter we reflect on the mosaic of results that have emerged from the different parts of the project to draw a number of connected conclusions about this three-country SHARMED project. This also includes comparisons between different European settings, which is important to assess the possible expansion at European level, and the impact on multicultural contexts and intercultural communication, which was a fundamental requisite of the SHARMED project. Second, this chapter charts the final methodological applications and tools of practice that have emerged from SHARMED and that are designed to promote innovative pedagogies and support further intercultural education research. Finally, this chapter provides a summary of the germane features of SHARMED that would be appropriate for those seeking to conduct similar educational research and interested in transforming schools in communities of dialogue.

12.2 Social and Cultural Contexts of the Project

The multicultural social contexts found within schools proved to be crucial in providing effective underpinning for SHARMED activities. Four key variables (see Chapter 2 for more details and data) were clearly common across all three countries while also enabling sufficient local flexibility:

1. *The way school systems are organized:* Different ways of organizing education in schools have an impact on timetables and accessibility. In relation to SHARMED, for example, the desynchronization of school activities proved more problematic across country borders and less problematic in national or local settings. In this case solutions were sought through partnership and understanding the potential for accessing schools during the school year amid different country practices. Through partnership with schools SHARMED was able to link accessibility to schools with school expectations in relation to pedagogical practice.
2. *Pedagogical expectations in schools (in particular among teachers)*: Schools and teachers tended to organize a project like SHARMED in a way that was designed to avoid disturbing regular teaching activities. Often, projects like SHARMED are seen as experiments that should not disturb regular teaching. SHARMED recognized that changing these traditional expectations depended on local school systems and, more importantly, on the degree of distance between teaching on the one hand and on the other hand, dialogic and participatory approaches – which were fundamental to the SHARMED project. The project experienced both low and high distances – with each having advantages and disadvantages. In the SHARMED project, low distance was clear in the Italian settings, where non-curricular activities may be rather frequent in primary schools, but also in some secondary schools. Low distance enhanced the acceptance of the proposed activities, but it also created some 'competition' with teachers, who are interested in stressing their own competence. In SHARMED this competition was productively transformed through enhancement of new classroom activities. High distance was clear in the UK setting, where the school system is based on testing and performance. In the England perspective, teachers were very interested in dialogic and participatory approaches but the challenge of integrating new and different practices alongside regular and statutory requirements called for further partnership working compared to Italian schools. The German settings presented more nuanced and differentiated characteristics, with both 'warm' interested teachers who were keen to be involved alongside 'cold' reluctant teachers who were more hesitant because of the 'disordered' nature of dialogic and participatory pedagogies. In all cases, partnership working with schools and teachers to achieve an appropriate balance of pedagogical expectations became a recurring practice across all three European countries – working with the unique characteristics of three different education systems.

3. *Fostering and maintaining children's interest:* While expectations in schools and among teachers depended on local approaches to teaching, children's expectations often depended on the quality of the proposed forms of communication, specifically on the style and mode of the facilitator. In all settings, children considered their participation in SHARMED as a positive experience and only a marginal minority considered this experience as negative. A more interesting account that deserves some reflection is that children most often enjoyed participatory features when they were involved in the less visible roles. For example, they preferred being the audience for classmates' stories and pictures, while those aspects requiring more leading participation, such as presenting pictures, telling stories and exchanging ideas, were considered more taxing. In general, children's interest and involvement were successfully maintained throughout the project. Generally, evaluation by children was very positive and in Italian and English settings almost all children showed enthusiasm for the experience, though some more were observed in the English setting. However, both at the level of participation during the activities and by children's direct evaluations the English students had more concerns. Various factors contributed to the positive experience including, being able to have fun, having opportunities to express opinions, discovering things about others, doing and learning something, feeling respected, appreciated and involved were the most frequent reasons given for their positive evaluations. Evaluations showed that children particularly appreciated classmates' supportive behaviour and many felt comfortable with their facilitators. In Italy, the percentage of children who felt very comfortable with their facilitators was much higher than in the other settings. Only a marginal minority (very marginal in Italy) felt uncomfortable with facilitators. Facilitators were described as open to children's interests and feelings (a majority in Italy) and facilitators were perceived as friends (a majority in England). According to children's evaluations in the German settings enthusiasm was lower and more differentiated, although children's participation during the SHARMED activities was noticeably energetic. These differences between countries may be explained by the different ways of facilitating classroom interactions. In Germany, facilitation included some normative orientations and managing conflict was less controlled. This finding was frequently evidenced by the perception of facilitators and teachers. In England, facilitation worked very well for many aspects, particularly in enhancing new narratives and securing interlacements

between narratives. However, English facilitators sometimes provided praise and comments which were at times interpreted as judgements in response. Facilitation in Italy was seen to be very effective in avoiding normative and judgemental scenarios by providing mediation of conflict and in enhancing agency and dialogue.

Another interesting reflection relates to the type of school and participant's gender in relation to involvement and engagement in the project.

Throughout the SHARMED project and in all three countries, children in primary schools attended and engaged in these activities more frequently than children in secondary schools, and female students were involved in the activities more frequently than male students.

4. *Establishing social, cultural and educational characteristics of migration processes and settlements*: Given the multicultural context of this project, a common approach to the characteristics of migration and settlement was essential for the success of cross-country comparisons. For example, in relation to both children's language competence and their motivation for participating. This proved more complex in Italy and Germany compared to England. In England, despite having migrant communities from a wide range of different countries there was a shared spoken language – English. Thus, in England the impact of language was minimal and the exchange of experiences in the classroom was easier and confidence in the SHARMED processes was based on common understanding and acceptance. As a consequence, in England, no negative evaluations were received regarding the spoken language, probably due to the overall high competence of all children in the use of the English as a first or second language.

   In contrast, in Italy and Germany there were more linguistic differences and stronger cultural differences and as a consequence the impact of language difference was greater. The differences in evaluations between native speakers and children with mainly other languages were rather nuanced in Germany and Italy, where discovering and learning were high but personal expression was seen as more difficult. Interestingly, however, in Italy facilitators were more frequently appreciated by non-native speakers compared to native speakers. Analysis of SHARMED activities shows that the impact of cultural and linguistic differences can be mitigated by careful and competent handling of the facilitation process. In some cases, for example facilitation can transform difficulties in self-expression while if not competently handled, facilitation can be too rigidly structured, thereby compounding dialogic difficulties and leaving insufficient space for self-expression (see also Chapter 7). Therefore, it became important to conduct, in all three countries, a careful evaluation of the cultural and linguistic context; this evaluation was coupled with the careful and competent use of facilitation (see below).

12.3 Types of Activities and Methodology of Facilitation

The SHARMED project was based on standardized activities in the different settings and with standardization the project was able to compare and evaluate activities across countries and settings. An important feature of the activities was the greater genuine interest from schools in oral activities – from both students and teachers. According to participating teachers, written texts were considered to be less useful than oral narratives and dialogue in achieving the objectives of a SHARMED project. While the SHARMED methodology was designed to provide greater preference to visuals and narratives, participating teachers felt that current school systems did not provide sufficient opportunity to involve children in high-quality oral narratives, rather than working with written texts.

Evaluations by children also showed that most children preferred to listen to their classmates' stories and look at their photographs, rather than to participate actively in questions (see Chapter 2). Significantly, however, this preference was not visible through the video-recordings of the activities, which showed most children as very active participants – particularly in the Italian and English settings. In England, for example, children were very enthusiastic when engaging in the many opportunities for self-expression provided by the SHARMED activities. This was particularly striking as the English schools were strongly oriented towards academic performance. Video recordings of the English settings demonstrate more active participation and rather less of listening to and looking at. As discussed in Chapter 9, children quickly embraced the project's idea of photographs as a pivot for the production and sharing of narratives and explaining experiences, emotions, points of view. This was very important pedagogically because when children observed similarities in their personal and family memories, even if those happened in different contexts, learning about others was combined with the promotion of empathy and personal expression.

This kind of active participation around intercultural activities helped to cement the importance and success of the SHARMED project. For SHARMED, classroom pedagogical management was fundamental for developing innovative practice during the project – in particular managing initiatives and conflict that could negatively impact intercultural exchanges. The evidence gained through video recordings of classroom practice shows highly successful classroom pedagogical management. Interestingly, however, children's written evaluations, for example in English settings, perceived conflicts that were not at all visible in these recordings (see Chapters 2 and 8). Again, there appears to be a mismatch between the children's declarations in the questionnaire and the evidence in video-recordings, at least for the English settings. In contrast, in Italian settings, conflict appeared to be more evident in the recordings and these were largely interpreted as children holding 'different views'. Comparative analysis demonstrated that there were different perceptions of what conflict is and that meanings and interpretations very much depended on local contexts. It could be that in the more statutory-controlled school context in England the expression of different and contrasting views may be more muted.

The use of facilitation was an underpinning feature of the SHARMED project with a methodology designed around shared and common principles agreed by all project partners. These principles included (a) promotion of active participation, (b) soliciting conversational dialogue and (c) avoidance of normative actions. However, given differences in school contexts in the three countries, variations in the style of facilitation were encouraged so long as these three principles were maintained (see Chapter 9). This consideration was important to ensure that a particular style of facilitation was not imposed on any setting. For example, it was interesting that the German facilitators decided to introduce a series of standardized activities, while the Italian and English facilitators followed more flexible methods. During the SHARMED project, the recordings of differences in style and method of facilitation were useful to understand the nature of facilitation in the different settings and how these differences solicit different levels of participation and dialogue.

It is interesting to note the different approaches of participation and dialogue that emerged from the facilitators' choices and style and their implication for children's active participation. Variations in the form of facilitation are connected to contextual variables: facilitators' personal styles, pre-existing network of peer-relationships in the classroom, the social and cultural contexts of adult–children interactions. The crucial pedagogical observation is that different forms of facilitation have different effects on children's agency.

A first, more obvious, contextual variable could concern the grade of education where facilitation takes place. However, whilst children's active participation seems to be higher in primary schools than in secondary schools, this is more influenced by the form of facilitation and the micro-context of the classrooms than the grade of education.

The form of facilitation typical of most Italian settings is based on a variety of supporting and enhancing actions, which are provided in different turns of talk. Facilitation develops as combination of questions and formulations, enriched through minimal feedback and sparse comments. This form of facilitation is most effective in enhancing expansions of personal stories, thus promoting a community of dialogue based on a great number of narratives, often linked to the same photograph and developing contingently.

The form of facilitation more frequent in English contexts is based on a wide variety of actions such as formulations, comments, personals stories and appreciations, combined in single turns of talk. Comments and appreciations display facilitators' engagement in the interaction, promoting children's stories even when facilitators' turns are sometimes extended. This form of facilitation is effective in enhancing a community of dialogue through interlacements, based on facilitator's long and personal stories, followed by several children's interlaced contributions.

German contexts were characterized by a form of facilitation based on linear exchanges between the facilitator and a single child at a time, followed by facilitator's invitation to contribute addressed to other children. This form of facilitation is connoted by minimal feedbacks (continuers, repetitions and acknowledgement tokens), rare direct questions and formulations. Invitations to talk at the end of a dyadic exchange with the narrating child connoted this form of facilitation, which appears to be effective in enhancing a community of dialogue based on children's autonomous contributions, without facilitators' coordination. However, it can encounter difficulties when children's are hesitant or reluctant towards active participation

The Italian and English forms of facilitation are based on facilitators' intense activity of co-construction of narratives. The difference between the two forms of facilitation is a difference between contingency of turn-by-turn co-construction of narrative (Italian settings) and ordered sequence of complex turns and interlaced narratives (English settings). The form of facilitation typical of German settings is closer to established styles of facilitation, underpinned by questions and active listening with minimal feedback to enhance the autonomous voice of children with reduced involvement and collaboration of the facilitator.

The diversity in the form of facilitation can be explained as the consequence of three different interpretations of children's participation. First, participation was interpreted as co-construction, in which the facilitator is continuously involved through questions and formulations. This is related to the form of facilitation most common in Italian settings. Second, participation was interpreted as uttering more or less long, individual (personal) narratives, actively promoted by other participants' questions and comments, and confirmed through open appreciation. This seems to underpin the form of facilitation characterizing English contexts. Third, participation was interpreted as children's autonomous individual (personal) contributions, very loosely solicited and based on established techniques. The form of facilitation typical of German settings appears to be based on this interpretation.

These different interpretations were largely, based on personal styles, influenced by theoretical approaches and influenced by educational and cultural contexts. For example, a facilitator in Italy explained his work as based on the intention of avoiding any normative action and counting on the contingent, personal involvement of children and himself. This interest in contingent situations, based on personal feelings and attitudes, shaped his style. While this was a risky approach for both facilitator and for children, children's assessment showed that this style worked better than any other during the SHARMED project. It was perceived as genuine and attentive. Its 'cost' was that while narratives were systematically co-constructed so that the children were (and felt) constantly supported in their verbal action, the produced narratives were rather fragmented. Moreover, dialogue was much more frequent between the facilitator and the child, though the facilitator made efforts to involve the other children. Working on contingent situations and personal involvement means avoiding 'forced' dialogue but can also result in the loss of some opportunities to enhance dialogue.

A further example in England were facilitators who made use of strong supportive speech in which they combined positive feedback, personal comments and personal stories. This type of facilitation effectively enhanced both children's participation and interlacements among children's narratives, so that children uttered frequently longer and complex narratives and sequences of narratives. However, on a less positive note, children frequently reverted to hierarchical relations. Analysis suggests that this behaviour may have been influenced by the local context. Comparison of these two examples shows that different facilitative pedagogic approaches can yield equally productive outcomes.

In contrast, facilitation in Germany was based on a much less active style, including active listening, punctuated by short and infrequent questions. In this approach, facilitators encouraged the direct involvement of other children to create questions and give comments. This approach proved more limiting, particularly for children with migrant backgrounds who had fewer opportunities to express themselves not least because of language barriers (see Chapter 7). This style of facilitative pedagogy demonstrates the need to promote active inclusion as a feature of facilitative practice.

Facilitation is a very versatile methodology, since it may be applied to enhance children's agency in different ways and contexts. Facilitation can be used to propose a reflexive approach, focusing on *the way* in which the communication process is produced in educational contexts. Facilitators can clarify opportunities for children's active participation, both enhancing their narratives and supporting their autonomous initiatives. Facilitation can enhance and support the expression of relevant, complicated, unclear or delicate information and manifestations of intentions. Facilitation can also include conflict mediation when delicate issues and children's initiatives create relational problems in the classroom. In a nutshell, SHARMED has shown that facilitation is a valid method to create a community of dialogue in the classroom.

12.4 Project Outcomes

Ultimately, some of the most important outcomes of the SHARMED project are the series of products, which were planned and designed as a sustainable feature of the project. These products were designed as a means of explaining and disseminating innovation beyond the involved schools and in particular at the European level. SHARMED has developed these tools for further applications. They included a training package, both face-to-face and online (MOOC, Massive Online Open Course) (see Chapter 10), guidelines for the activities, an evaluation package, an archive and a learning platform (see Chapter 11). All these tools are available on the SHARMED website, though the archive is password protected for ethical reasons and can be only visited (after permission) by educational institutions and organizations.

At the end of the project, the SHARMED website has been filled with important materials to promote download and active participation, and communication of results in networks and organizations has been improved.

These outcomes are provided for future applications in schools and other educational contexts. They may be seen as the tools that SHARMED proposes for the construction of communities of dialogue in European (and non-European) schools, based on teachers' awareness of the importance or enhancing (migrant) children's agency and narratives of personal cultural trajectories.

12.5 Final Reflections

The final reflections on the SHARMED project lead to the following conclusions about the dissemination and replication of projects based on SHARMED methodology.

The first conclusion concerns the effectiveness of SHARMED methodology. Photographs proved to work well as a pivot for the narration of memories encrypted in the photographs or related to them, as discussed in Chapters 3 and 4. SHARMED's idea that the possibility to share personal memories can motivate participation and dialogue was confirmed by the analysis of data.

The evaluation of SHARMED activities also confirms the validity of the interpretation of narration as a potential context for children's agency. SHARMED aimed to create favourable contexts for children's choices in the production of narratives, and children embraced this opportunity displaying children's agency and authority responding to facilitators' elicitation and taking autonomous initiatives to access and produce knowledge. As illustrated by Chapters 5 and 6, children quickly engage with the opportunity to make choice in the construction of narratives that presented their personal and cultural trajectories to the facilitator and the classroom.

It is very important to evaluate the context of the activities (using the evaluation package developed by SHARMED and available via the project's website), regarding the composition of the class, schools' organization of teaching, teachers' motivation and involvement of parents. The experience of the SHARMED project suggests that contextual features, the type of migration and the children's attitude to be involved (again on the basis of the context) can be different in different situations; these situations are often related to local, rather than national, contexts.

Facilitation of children's participation and dialogue through use of photographs can have important effects, in multicultural classrooms. How children with migrant backgrounds are included is an important variable; if they are not sufficiently included the activities may fail to achieve an important objective.

Creating favourable contexts for children's choices in the production of narratives was the main aim of facilitation. Although facilitation took different forms, consequently to facilitators' style and other contextual variables, it successfully promoted children's agency across all contexts. As suggested in Chapter 9, facilitation can be adapted to different contexts, increasing sustainability and impact of SHARMED methodology. The sustainability of

SHARMED is supported also by the archive and the other tools available on the website (see the section 'Project outcomes', this chapter; Chapters 9 and 11) that can be utilized to implement SHARMED-like projects.

SHARMED is based on a learning-by-doing process that can be adapted to specific conditions. The tools developed by the SHARMED project can be particularly useful for this adaptation.

Facilitation can effectively promote children's agency; however, children's agency can lead to conflicts (see Chapter 8) that demand the facilitator to mediate between different perspectives. Facilitation promotes participation by offering children opportunity for autonomous choices rather than through adult-centred communication. This makes facilitation a complex way of enhancing participation that cannot be left to goodwill and enthusiasm. In light of the complexities of facilitation, training for the use facilitative methodology is very important; SHARMED approach to training was presented in Chapter 10.

The evaluation of SHARMED activities suggests that facilitation can successfully create favourable conditions for the development of community of dialogue, based on agency and hybridization of identities through interpersonal communication. SHARMED activities proved to be beneficial not only for children with migrant backgrounds; rather, SHARMED engaged all children in the dialogic construction of personal and cultural trajectories.

References

Abdallah-Preitcelle, M. (2006), Interculturalism as a paradigm for thinking about diversity, *Intercultural Education*, 17 (5): 475–83.

Alanen, L. (2009), Generational order, in J. Qvortrup, W. Corsaro and M.S. Honig (eds), *The Palgrave Handbook of Childhood Studies*, 159–74, Basingstoke: Palgrave.

Allen, S., Whalley, M., Lee, M. & Scollan, A. (2019), *Developing Professional Practice in the Early Years*, Milton Keynes: Open University Press.

Alred, G., Byram, M. & Fleming, M., eds. (2003), *Intercultural Experience and Education*, Clevedon: Multilingual Matters.

Artamonova, O. (2017), Teacher's ethnic teasing: Playing with ambiguity and exploiting in-group communication, *Discourse and Society*, 29 (1): 3–22.

Aspelmeier, J. (2019), Geschichte selber erkunden – GeschichtsdidaktischeÜberlegungen zu Chancen und Grenzen Historischen Lernens im und mitdem Archiv, *Archivar. Zeitschrift für Archivwesen Neue Tendenzen in der Archivpädagogik*, 2: 105–8. Available online: http://www.archive.nrw.de/archivar/hefte/2019/Ausgabe-2/Archivar-2-2019.pdf (accessed 3 January 2021).

Balibar, Ê. & Wallerstein, I. (1991), *Race, Nation, Class: Ambiguous Identities*, London/New York: Verso.

Ballestri, C., Baraldi, C., Iervese, V. & Vincenzi, M., eds. (2018), SHARMED Archive. A selection. Available online: https://www.sharmed.eu/app/download/9696447884/Sharmed-Book.pdf?t=1547246160 (accessed 3 January 2021).

Bamberg, M. (2005), Narrative discourse and identities, in J.C. Meister, T. Kindt and W. Schernus (eds), *Narratology beyond Literary Criticism*, 213–37, Berlin: de Gruyter.

Bamberg, M. (2011), Narrative practice and identity navigation, in J.A. Holstein and J.F. Gubrium (eds), *Varieties of Narrative Analysis*, 99–124, London: Sage.

Bantock, G. (1970), *Freedom and Authority in Education*, Whitstable: Latimer Trend & Co.

Baraldi, C. (2012), Participation, facilitation and mediation in educational interactions, in Baraldi, C. and Iervese, V. (eds), *Participation, Facilitation, and Mediation. Children and Young People in Their Social Contexts*, 66–86, London/New York: Routledge.

Baraldi, C. (2014a), Children's participation in communication systems: A theoretical perspective to shape research, *Soul of Society: A Focus on the Leaves of Children and Youth. Sociological Studies on Children and Youth*, 18: 63–92.

Baraldi, C. (2014b). Formulations in dialogic facilitation of classroom interactions, *Language and Dialogue*, 4 (2): 234–60.

Baraldi, C. (2015a), Promotion of migrant children's epistemic status and authority in early school life, *International Journal of Early Childhood*, 47 (1): 5–25.

Baraldi, C. (2015b), Intercultural communication systems and discourses of cultural identity, *Applied Linguistics Review*, 6 (1): 49–71.

Baraldi, C. (2019a), Using formulations to manage conflicts in classroom interactions, *Language and Dialogue*, 9 (2): 193–216.

Baraldi, C. (2019b), Poisoning children: A reflection on the social constraints of children's agency and narratives of sexual abuse, *Childhood*, 26 (2): 153–68.

Baraldi, C. (2020), Roots ad problems of universalism. The concept of children's agency, in C. Baraldi and L. Rabello de Castro (eds), *Global Childhoods in International Perspective: Universality, Diversity and Inequalities*, 15–32, London: Sage.

Baraldi, C. & Cockburn, T., eds. (2018), *Theorizing Childhood. Citizenship, Rights and Participation*, Basingstoke: Palgrave.

Baraldi, C. & Corsi, G. (2017), *Niklas Luhmann. Education as a Social System*, Dordrecht: Springer.

Baraldi, C. & Iervese, V. (2010), Dialogic mediation in conflict resolution education, *Conflict Resolution Quarterly*, 27 (4): 423–45.

Baraldi, C. & Iervese, V. (2017), Narratives of memories and dialogue in multicultural classrooms, *Narrative Inquiry*, 27(2): 398–417.

Barthes, R. (1980), La Chambre claire: Note sur la photographie, *Cahier du cinéma*, Paris: Gallimard/Éd. du Seuil.

Benjamin, W. (1997), *Tesi sul concetto di storia*, Einaudi, Torino (Über den Begriff der Geschichte, in: *Die Neue Rundschau*, 1940).

Berntsen, D. & Rubin, D. C., eds. (2012), *Understanding Autobiographical Memory; Theories and Approaches*, Cambridge: Cambridge University Press.

Bjerke, H. (2011), It's the way to do it. Expressions of agency in child-adult relations at home and school, *Children & Society*, 25: 93–103.

Bolten, J. (2015), *Einführung in die Interkulturelle Wirtschaftskommunikation*, 2nd edn, Göttingen: Vandenhoeck & Ruprecht.

Bolton, G. (2010), *Reflective Practice: Writing and Professional Development*, London: Sage.

Borries, B. von (2008), *Historisch Denken Lernen – Welterschließung statt Epochenüberblick Geschichte als Unterrichtsfach und Bildungsaufgabe*, Opladen: Barbara Budrich Verlag.

Bowling, D. & Hoffman, D., eds. (2003), *Bringing Peace into the Room*, San Francisco: Jossey-Bass.

Breinig, H. & Lösch, K. (2002), Introduction: Difference and transdifference, in H. Breinig, J. Gebhardt and K. Lösch (eds), *Multiculturalism in Contemporary Societies: Perspectives on Difference and Transdifference*, 11–36, Erlangen: Univ-Bibliothek.

Brown, R. & Kulik, J. (1977), Flashbulb memories, *Cognition*, 5 (1): 73–99.

Burke, P. (2013), *Testimoni oculari – Il significato storico delle immagini*, Rome: Carocci.

Bush, B. R. & Folger, J. (1994), *The Promise of Mediation: Responding to Conflict through Empowerment and Recognition*, San Francisco: Jossey-Bass.

Byrd Clark, J.S. & Dervin, F., eds. (2014), *Reflexivity in Language and Intercultural Education*, New York: Routledge.

Cable, C. & Miller, L. (2011), A new professionalism, in Miller, L. and C. Cable (eds), *Professionalization, Leadership and Management in the Early Years*, 147–62. London: Sage.

Chernyshova, E. (2018), Explicitation sequences in conversation: Some considerations on formulations, candidate inferences and grounding, *Travaux neuchâtelois de linguistique*, 68: 51–8.

Clayman, S.E. & Loeb, L. (2018), Polar questions, response preference, and the tasks of political positioning in journalism, *Research on Language and Social Interaction*, 51 (2): 127–44.

Coffield, F., Moseley, D., Hall, E., & K. Ecclestone (2004), *Learning Styles and Pedagogy in Post-16 Learning: A Systematic and Critical Review*, London: Learning & Skills Research Centre. Available at: https://www.leerbeleving.nl/wp-content/uploads/2011/09/learning-styles.pdf (accessed 10 June 2021).

Colwell, J. (2015), *Reflective Teaching in Early Education*, London: Bloomsbury.

Conti, L. (2012), *Interkultureller Dialog im virtuellen Zeitalter. Neue Perspektiven für Theorie und Praxis*, Münster/Berlin: Lit Verlag.

Conway, M.A. & Pleydell-Pearce, C.W. (2000), The construction of autobiographical memories in the self-memory system, *Psychological Review*, 107: 261–88.

Cook, T. (2001), Archival science and postmodernism: New formulations for old concepts, *Archival Science*, 1 (1): 3–24.

Curtis, N. ed. (2010), *The Pictorial Turn*, London: Routledge.

Davies, B. (2014), *Listening to Children. Being and Becoming*, London: Routledge.

Department for Education (2017), *Statutory Framework for the Early Years Foundation Stage*. Available at: www.foundationyears.org.uk/files/2017/03/EYFS_STATUTORY_FRAMEWORK_2017.pdf (accessed 24 March 2019).

Dervin, F. & Liddicoat, A.J., eds. (2013), *Linguistics for Intercultural Education*, Amsterdam: John Benjamins.

DESTATIS (2020), 'Überbelegung von Raum´, *Destatis Statisches Bundesamt*. Available online: https://www.destatis.de/Europa/DE/Thema/Bevoelkerung-Arbeit-Soziales/Soziales-Lebensbedingungen/Ueberbelegung.html (accessed 15 December 2020).

Dewey, J. (1933), *How We Think: A Restatement of the Relation of Reflective Thinking to the Educative Process*, New York: D.C. Heath.

Dewey, J. (1966), *Democracy and Education*, New York: Free Press.

Dinoi, A. (2012), *Lo Sguardo e l'Evento*, Firenze: Le Lettere.

Douglas, K.B. (1998), Impressions; African American first-year students' perceptions of a predominantly white university, *The Journal of Negro Education*, 67 (4): 416–31.

Drucker, J. (2013), Performative materiality and theoretical approaches to interface, *Digital Humanities Quarterly*, 7 (1). Available online: http://www.digitalhumanities.org/dhq/vol/7/1/000143/000143.html (accessed 3 January 2021).

Europeana (2020), About us. Available online: https://www.europeana.eu/en/about-us (accessed 3 January 2021).

Eveleigh, A. (2015), *Crowding Out the Archivist? Implications of Online User Participation for Archival Theory and Practice*, PhD thesis, London: UCL. Available online: https://www.nationalarchives.gov.uk/documents/research/eveleigh-amm-phd-2015.pdf (accessed 3 January 2021).

Fail, H., Thompson, J. & Walker, G. (2004), Belonging, identity and third culture kids. Life histories of former international school children, *Journal of Research in International Education*, 3 (3): 319–38.

Farini, F. (2011), Cultures of education in action: Research on the relationship between interaction and cultural presuppositions regarding education in an international educational setting, *Journal of Pragmatics*, 43 (8): 2176–86.

Farini, F. (2014), Trust building as a strategy to avoid unintended consequences of education. The case study of international summer camps designed to promote peace and intercultural dialogue among adolescents, *Journal of Peace Education*, 11 (1): 81–100.

Farini, F. & Scollan, A. (2019), *Children's Self-Determination in the Context of Early Childhood Education and Services: Discourses, Policies and Practices*, Dordrecht: Springer.

Farrington, J. & Bebbington, A. (1993), *Reluctant Partners? Non-governmental Organizations, the State and Sustainable Agricultural Development*, London: Taylor & Francis.

Finkenauer, C., Luminet, O., Gisle, L., El-Ahmadi & Van Der Linden, M. (1998), Flash- bulb memories and the underlying mechanisms of their formation; toward an emotional-integrative model, *Memory & Cognition*, 26: 516–31.

Fisher, W. (1987), *Human Communication as Narration: Toward a Philosophy of Reason, Value, and Action*, Columbia: University of South Carolina Press.

Flinn, A. (2010), An attack on professionalism and scholarship? Democratising archives and the production of knowledge, *Ariadne 62*. Available online: http://www.ariadne.ac.uk/issue62/flinn (accessed 3 January 2021).

Flinn, A. (2011), Archival activism: independent and community-led archives, radical public history andthe heritage professions, *InterActions: UCLA Journal of Education and Information Studies*, 7 (2). Available online: https://escholarship.org/content/qt9pt2490x/qt9pt2490x.pdf?t=lm235y (accessed 3 January 2021).

Gallner-Holzmann, K. (2020), Visualisierung und Didaktisierung digitaler Archivbestände. Perspektiven zur Gestaltung offener Lernräume für historisches Lernen, *Zeitschrift MedienPädagogik 17 (Jahrbuch Medienpädagogik)*: 373–99. Available online: https://doi.org/10.21240/mpaed/jb17/2020.05.15.X (accessed 3 January 2021).

Gardner, R. (2001), *When Listeners Talk: Response Tokens and Listener Stance*, Amsterdam: Benjamins.

Gay, G. (2000), *Culturally Responsive Teaching: Theory, Research and Practice*, New York: Teachers College Press.

Gibbs, P., ed. (2015), *Transdisciplinary Professional Learning and Practice*, London: Springer.

Giddens, A. (1984), *The Constitution of Society*, Berkeley-Los Angeles: University of California Press.

Glaister, K.W. & Falshaw, J.R. (1999), Strategic planning still going strong, *Long Range Planning*, 32 (1): 107–16.

Glenberg, A.M. (1997), What memory is for, *Behavioral and Brain Sciences*, 20 (1): 1–19.

Goodwin, C. & Heritage, J. (1990), Conversation analysis, *Annual Review of Anthropology*, 19: 283–307.

Gourevitch, P. & Morris, E. (2009), *The Ballad of Abu Ghraib*, New York: Penguin Books, cited in: J. Tucker, Entwined Practices; Engagements with Photography in Historical Inquiry, *History and Theory*, Theme Issue 48 (Dec.).

Grant, C.A. & Portera, A., eds. (2011), *Intercultural and Multicultural Education. Enhancing Global Interconnectedness*, New York: Routledge.

Grünberger, N. (2014), Räume zum Flanieren, Spielen und Lernen. Überlegungenzur Gestaltung von Bildungs- und Lernräumen im Kontext kulturellerEntwicklungen, in K. Rummler (eds.), *Lernräume gestalten – Bildungskontexte vielfältig denken*, 56–67, Münster: Waxmann.

Guillherme, M. (2012), Critical language and intercultural communication pedagogy, in J. Jackson (ed.), *The Routledge Handbook of Language and Intercultural Communication*, 357–71, London: Routledge.

Gundara, J.S. (2000), *Interculturalism, Education and Inclusion*, London: Paul Chapman.

Gundara, J.S. & Portera, A. (2008), Theoretical reflections on intercultural education, *Intercultural Education*, 19 (6): 463–68.

Harper, D. (2010), Talking about pictures; A case for photo elicitation, *Visual Studies*, 17 (1): 13–26.

Harré, R. & Van Langenhove, L., eds. (1999), *Positioning Theory*, Blackwell: Oxford.

Hart, R. (1992), Children's participation: From tokenism to citizenship, *Innocenti Essays* 4, Florence: UNICEF International Child Development Centre. Available online: https://www.unicef-irc.org/publications/pdf/childrens_participation.pdf(accessed 3 January 2021).

Harrington C. F. & Lindy, I. E. (1998), The use of reflexive photography in the study of the freshman year experience, *Journal of College Student Retention: Research, Theory and Practice*, 1 (1): 13–22.

Harrison, K. (2002), Scholar or Baller in American Higher Education? A visual elicitation and qualitative assessment of the student athlete's mindset, *National Association of Student Affairs Professional Journal*, 5 (1): 66–81.

Helms, M.M. & Nixon, J. (2010), Exploring SWOT analysis; where are we now? *Journal of Strategy and Management*, 3 (3): 215–25.

Hendry, R. (2009), *Building and Restoring Respectful Relationships in Schools*, London/New York: Routledge.

Heritage, J. & Clayman, S. (2010), *Talk in Action. Interactions, Identities, and Institutions*, Chichester: Wiley-Blackwell.

Heritage, J. & Raymond G. (2005), 'The terms of agreement: Indexing epistemic authority and subordination in talk-in-interaction', *Social Psychology Quarterly*, 68 (1): 15–38.

Heritage, J. & Watson, R. (1979), Formulations as conversational objects, in G. Psathas (ed.), *Everyday Language: Studies in Ethnomethodology*, 123–62, New York/London: Irvington.

Herrlitz, W. & Maier R., eds. (2005), *Dialogues in and around Multicultural Schools*, Tübingen: Niemeyer.

Higgins, E. T. (1996), Knowledge activation; Accessibility, applicability, and salience, in E.T. Higgins and R. W. Kruglanski (eds.), *Social Psychology; Handbook of Basic Principles*, 195–211, New York: The Guilford Press.

Hochschild, A.R. (1983), *The Managed Heart*, Berkeley: University of California Press.

Hoerl, C. (2007), Episodic memory, autobiographical memory, narrative; On three key notions in current approaches to memory development, *Philosophical Psychology*, 20: 621–40.

Hofer, C.W. & Schendel, D. (1978), *Strategy Formulation: Analytical Concepts*, St. Paul: West Publishing Company.

Hosftede, G. (1980), *Culture's Consequences*, Beverly Hills & London: Sage.

Holliday, A. (1999), Small cultures, *Applied Linguistics*, 20 (2): 237–64.

Holliday, A. (2011), *Intercultural Communication and Ideology*, London: Sage.

Holliday, A. (2013), *Understanding Intercultural Communication. Negotiating a Grammar of Culture*, London: Routledge.

Holliday, A. & Amadasi, S. (2020), *Making Sense of the Intercultural. Finding DeCentred Threads*, London: Routledge.

House, J. (2013), Developing pragmatic competence in English as a lingua franca: Using discourse markers to express (inter)subjectivity and connectivity, *Journal of Pragmatics*, 59: 57–67.

Huq, R. & Amir, A. (2015), When the tokens talk: IRF and the position of acknowledgement tokens in teacher-student talk-in-interaction, *Research on Youth and Language*, 9 (1): 60–76.

Huvila, I. (2008), Participatory archive: Towards decentralised curation, radical user orientation, and broader contextualisation of records management, *Archival Science*, 8: 15–36. Available online: https://doi.org/10.1007/s10502-008-9071-0 (accessed 3 January 2021).

Iervese, V. (2016), Altro che invisibili. Il paradosso delle immagini degli immigrati, *Zapruder*, 40: 130–9.

Iervese, V. (2017), *Engrammi ed exogrammi della fotografia contemporanea*, in M. Manni e L. Panaro (ed.), 30–9, Ravenna: Montanari.

Iyengar, R. (2020), Education as the path to a sustainable recoveryfrom COVID19, *Prospects*, 49: 77–80. Available online: https://doi.org/10.1007/s11125-020-09488-9 (accessed 3 January 2021).

Jackson, J. (2014), The process of becoming reflexive and intercultural: Navigating study abroad and re-entry experience, in J. S. Byrd Clark and F. Dervin (eds), *Reflexivity in Language and Intercultural Education*, 43–63, London: Routledge.

James, A. (2009), Agency, in J. Qvortrup, W. Corsaro and M.S. Honig (eds), *The Palgrave Handbook of Childhood Studies*, 34–45, Basingstoke: Palgrave.

James, A. & James, A.L. (2004), *Constructing Childhood. Theory, Policy and Social Practice*, Basingstoke: Palgrave.

James, A. & James, A.L. (2008), *Key Concepts in Childhood Studies*, London: Sage.

Joslyn, E. (2017), *Resilience in Childhood: Perspectives, Promise and Practice*, London: Macmillan Palgrave.

Keevallik, L. (2010), Minimal answers to yes/no questions in the service of sequence organization, *Discourse Studies*, 12 (3): 283–309.

Kelly, B.T. & Kortegast, C.A. (2018), *Engaging Images for Research, Pedagogy, and Practice; Utilizing Visual Methods to Understand and Promote College Student Development*, Sterling, VA: Stylus Publishing.

Ketelaar, E. (1992), Archives of the people, by the people, for the people, *South African Archival Journal*, 34: 5–16.

Klafki, W. (1991), *Neue Studien zur Bildungstheorie und Didaktik. Zeitgemäße Allgemeinbildung und kritisch-konstruktive Didaktik*, 2nd edition, Basel/Weinheim: Beltz.

Kirby, P. (2020), Children's agency in the modern primary classroom, *Children & Society*, 34: 17–30.

Kirova, A., Prochter, L. & Massing, C. (2019), *Learning to Teach Young Children*, London/New York/Oxford: Bloomsbury.

Kitchen, W.H. (2014), *Authority and the Teacher*, London: Bloomsbury Academic.

Klocker, N. (2007), An example of thin agency: Child domestic workers in Tanzania, in R. Panelli, S. Punch and E. Robson (eds), *Global Perspectives on Rural Childhood and Youth: Young Rural Lives*, 83–94, London: Routledge.

KMK (2013), *Interkulturelle Bildung und Erziehung in der Schule*. Available online: https://www.kmk.org/fileadmin/veroeffentlichungen_beschluesse/1996/1996_10_25-Interkulturelle-Bildung.pdf (Accessed 15 December 2020).

Kotler, P. (2000), *Marketing Management*, Upper Saddle River, NJ: Prentice-Hall.

Kramsch, C. & Uryu, M. (2012), Intercultural contact, hybridity, and third space, in J. Jackson, *The Routledge Handbook of Language and Intercultural Communication*, 211–25, London: Routledge.

Lange, T., Lux, T. & Mayer, U. (2004), *Historisches Lernen im Archiv. Methoden Historischen Lernens*, Schwalbach: Wochenschau-Verl.

Langford, M. (2001), *Suspended Conversations. The after Life of Memory in Photographic Albums*, Montreal and Kingston: McGill-Queen's University Press.

Larkins, C. (2019), Excursions as corporate agents: A critical realistic account of children's agency, *Childhood*, 26 (4): 414–29.

Latz, A.O. (2012), Understanding the educational lives of community college students; A photovoice project, a Bourdieusian interpretation, and habitus dissonance spark theory, *Current Issues in Education*, 15(2): 1–19.

Learned, E.P., Christiansen, C.R., Andrews, K. & Guth, W.D. (1969), *Business Policy: Text and Cases*, Homewood: Irwin.

Leonard, M. (2016), *The Sociology of Children, Childhood and Generation*, London: Sage.

Leung, A., Chiu, C. & Hong, Y., eds. (2011), *Cultural Processes; A Social Psychological Perspective*, Cambridge: Cambridge University Press.

Lindon, J. & Trodd, L. (2016), *Reflective Practice and Early Years Professionalism: Linking Theory and Practice*, London: Hodder.

Luhmann, N. (2000), *Organisation und Entscheidung*, Opladen: Westdeutscher Verlag.

Luhmann, N. (1995), *Social Systems*, Stanford: Stanford University Press (v.o. 1984).

Mahon, J. & Cushner, K. (2012), The multicultural classroom, in J. Jackson (ed.), *The Routledge Handbook of Language and Intercultural Communication*, 434–48, London: Routledge.

Mandelbaum, J. (2012), Storytelling in conversation, in J. Sidnell and T. Stivers (eds), *The Handbook of Conversation Analysis*, 492–508, London: Wiley.

Maoz, I. (2001), Participation, control, and dominance in communication between groups in conflict: Analysis of dialogues between Jews and Palestinians in Israel, *Social Justice Research*, 14 (2): 189–208.

Margutti, P. (2010), On designedly incomplete utterances: What counts as learning for teachers and students in primary classroom interactions, *Research on Language and Social Interaction*, 43 (4): 315–45.

Matthews, H. (2003), Children and regeneration: Setting and agenda for community participation and integration, *Children & Society*, 17: 264–76.

Mayall, B. (2002), *Towards a Sociology for Childhood: Thinking from Children's Lives*, Buckingham: Open University Press.

McCarthy, M. (2003), Talking back: 'Small' interactional response tokens in everyday conversation, *Research on Language and Social Interaction*, 36: 33–63.

McDonald, M. (1999), *Marketing Plans*, Oxford: Butterworth-Heinemann Press.

McKemmish, S. (2001), Placing records continuum theory and practice, *Archival Science*, 1 (4): 333–59. Available online: https://link.springer.com/content/pdf/10.1007/BF02438901.pdf (accessed 14 June 2021).

Mehan, H. (1979), *Learning Lessons*, Cambridge: Harvard University Press.

Menne-Haritz, A. (2001), Access—The reformulation of an archival paradigm, *Archival Science*, 1 (1): 57–82. Available online: http://dx.doi.org/10.1023/A:1011508016557 (accessed 3 January 2021).

Mercer, N. & Littleton, K. (2007), *Dialogue and Development of Children's Thinking*, London: Routledge.
Mitchell, W.J.T. (2005), *What Do Pictures Want?; The Lives and Loves of Images*, Chicago: The University of Chicago Press.
Moline, S. (2011), *I See What You Mean*, Portland: Stenhouse.
Moodle (2021), *About Moodle*. Available online:https://docs.moodle.org/310/en/About_Moodle (accessed 3 January 2021).
Moosa-Mitha, M. (2005), A difference-centred alternative to theorization of children's citizenship rights, *Citizenship Studies*, 9: 369–88.
Moran-Ellis, J. (2013), Children as social actors, agency, and social competence: sociological reflections for early childhood, *Neue Praxis*, 43 (4): 323–88.
Morrison, F., Cree, V., Ruch, G., Winter, K.M., Hadfield, M. & Hallett, S. (2019), Containment: Exploring the concept of agency in children's statutory encounters with social workers, *Childhood*, 26 (1): 98–112.
Moyles, J. (2006), *Just Playing?*, Milton Keynes: Open University Press.
Muftee, M. (2015), Children's agency in resettlement: A study of Swedish cultural orientation programs in Kenya and Sudan, *Children's Geographies*, 13 (2): 131–48.
Mulchay, L. (2001), The possibilities and desirability of mediator neutrality – Towards an ethic of partiality?, *Social & Legal Studies*, 10 (4): 505–27.
Mulrenin, A., ed. (2002), *The DigiCULT Report: Technological Landscapes for Tomorrow's Cultural Economy*. Brussels: European Commission, Directorate-General for the Information Society. Available online: https://www.digicult.info/pages/report2002/dc_fullreport_230602_screen.pdf (accessed 3 January 2021).
Nair-Venugopal, S. (2009), Interculturalities: Reframing identities in intercultural communication, *Language and Intercultural Communication*, 9 (2): 76–90.
Nelson, K. (1993), The psychological and social origins of autobiographical memory, *Psychological Science*, 4: 7–14.
Nelson, K. & Fivush, R. (2004), The emergence of autobiographical memory; A social cultural developmental theory, *Psychological Review*, 111: 486–511.
Norrick, N. (2007), Conversational storytelling, in D. Herman (ed.), *The Cambridge Companion to Narrative*, 127–41, Cambridge: Cambridge University Press.
Norrick, N. (2012), Remembering for narration and autobiographical memory, *Language and Dialogue*, 2 (2): 193–214.
Norrick, N. (2013), Narratives of vicarious experience in conversation, *Language in Society*, 42: 385–406.
Nutbrown, C. (2012), *Foundations for Quality: The Independent Review of Early Education and Childcare Qualifications*. Available at: www.gov.uk/government/uploads/system/uploads/attachment_data/file/175463/Nutbrown-Review.pdf (accessed 23 September 2015).
O'Connor, C. & Michaels, S. (1996), Shifting participant frameworks: Orchestrating thinking practices in group discussion, in D. Hicks (ed.), *Discourse, Learning, and Schooling*, 63–103, Cambridge: Cambridge University Press.

O'Reilly, T. (2005), *What Is Web 2.0. Design Patterns and Business Models for the Next Generation of Software*. Available online: http://www.oreillynet.com/pub/a/oreilly/tim/news/2005/09/30/what-is-web-20.html (accessed 3 January 2021).

Oswell, D. (2013), *The Agency of Children. From Family to Global Human Rights*, London: Routledge.

Panaro, L. (2009), *Rileggere l'immagine. La fotografia come deposito di senso*, Carpi: APM.

Panofsky, E. (1939), *Studi di Iconologia*, Einaudi, Torino.

Pashler, H., McDaniel, M., Rohrer, D., & R. Bjork (2008), Learning styles: Concepts and evidence, *Psychological Science in the Public Interest*, 9 (3): 105–19.

Peräkylä, A. (2019), Conversation analysis and psychotherapy: Identifying transformative sequences, *Research on Language and Social Interaction*, 52 (3): 257–80.

Picard, C., Sargent, N., Bishop P.J. & Ramkay, R. (2015), *The Art and Practice of Mediation*, Edmonton: Montgomery.

Piller, I. (2007), Linguistics and intercultural communication, *Language and Linguistic Compass*, 1 (3): 208–26.

Portera, A. (2008), Intercultural education in Europe: Epistemological and semantic aspects, *Intercultural Education*, 19 (6): 481–91.

Qvortrup, J., W. Corsaro & M.S. Honig, eds. (2005), *The Palgrave Handbook of Childhood Studies*, Basingstoke: Palgrave.

Ramsbotham, O. (2010), *Transforming Violent Conflict. Radical Disagreement, Dialogue and Survival*, London: Routledge.

Reed, B. (2005), Reading the records continuum: Interpretations and explorations, *Archival Manuscript*, 33 (1): 18–43. Available online: https://www.records.com.au/pdf/Reading_the_Records_Continuum.pdf (accessed 3 January 2021).

Rolan, G. (2017), Agency in the archive: A model for participatoryrecordkeeping, *Archival Science*, 17: 195–225. Available online: https://doi.org/10.1007/s10502-016-9267-7 (accessed 3 January 2021).

Rubin, D.C. (2006), The basic-systems model of episodic memory, *Perspectives on Psychological Science*, 1: 277–11.

Samuel, R. (1996), *Theatres of Memory, Past and Present in Contemporary Culture*, vol. 1, London: Verso Books.

Schaller, A. (2019), Anspruch und Wirklichkeit. Archivpädagogik inDeutschland heute, *Archivar, Zeitschrift für Archivwesen Neue Tendenzenin der Archivpädagogik*, 2: 102–5. Available online: http://www.archive.nrw.de/archivar/hefte/2019/Ausgabe-2/Archivar-2-2019.pdf (accessed 3 January 2021).

Schell, A. (2009), Schools and cultural difference, in H. Kotthoff and H. Spencer-Oatey (eds), *Handbook of Intercultural Communication*, 303–21, Berlin: Mouton de Gruyter.

Schön, D.A. (1987), *Educating the Reflective Practitioner: Towards a New Design for Teaching and Learning in the Professions*, San Francisco: Jossey-Bass.

Scollan, A. (2009), Academic and vocational progression routes for early years practitioners working towards 'Early Years Professional Status' (EYPS). *Extended Services and Early Years Conference*, London, 23 January.

Scollan, A. & Farini, F. (2021 forth.). From enabling environments to environments that enable: Notes for theoretical innovation at the intersection between environment and learning, *An Leanbh Óg. The OMEP Ireland Journal of Early Childhood Studies*.

Seedhouse, P. (2004), *The Interactional Architecture of the Language Classroom: A Conversation Analysis Perspective*, Oxford: Blackwell.

Seuren, L.M. & Huiskes, M. (2017), Confirmation or elaboration: What do yes/no declaratives want?, *Research on Language and Social Interaction*, 50 (2): 188–205.

SHARMED Archive accessed at https://www.sharmed.eu/uk-international/archive-1/

SHARMED final project training MOOC accessed at https://www.sharmed.eu/uk-international/learning-platform/mooc

SHARMED guidelines for 'training the trainers', accessed at https://www.sharmed.eu/uk-international/guidelines/guidelines-for-sharmed-like-projects

Sharpe, T. (2008), How can teacher talk support learning?, *Linguistics and Education*, 19: 132–48.

Shier, H. (2001), Pathways to participation: Openings, opportunities and obligations, *Children & Society*, 15: 107–17.

Sinclair, J. & Coulthard, M. (1975), *Towards an Analysis of Discourse. The English Used by Teachers and Pupils*, Oxford: Oxford University Press.

Siraj-Blatchford, I. & Hallett, E. (2014), *Effective and Caring Leadership in the Early Years*, London: Sage.

Skarbø Solem, M. & Skovholt, K. (2019), Teacher formulations in classroom interactions, *Scandinavian Journal of Educational Research*, 63 (1): 69–88.

Somers, M.R. (1994), The narrative constitution of identity: A relational and network approach, *Theory and Society*, 23 (5): 605–49.

Spencer-Oatey, H. & Franklin, P. (2009), *Intercultural Interaction. A Multidisciplinary Approach to Intercultural Communication*, Basingstoke: Palgrave.

Sternhouse, L. (1983), The relevance of practice to theory, *Theory into Practice*, 22 (3): 211–5.

Stewart, K.A. & Maxwell, M.M. (2010), *Storied Conflict Talk. Narrative Construction in Mediation*, Amsterdam: John Benjamins.

Stoecklin, D. & Fattore, T. (2017), Children's multidimensional agency: Insights into the structuration of choice, *Childhood*, 25 (1): 47–62.

Sutton, J. & Williamson, K. (2014), Embodied remembering, in L. Shapiro (ed.), *The Routledge Handbook of Embodied Cognition*, 315–25, London: Routledge.

Tilly, C. & Tarrow, S. (2007), *Contentious Politics*, Boulder: Paradigm Publishers.

Ting-Toomey, S. (1999), *Communication across Cultures*, New York: The Guilford Press.

Tupas, R. (2014), Intercultural education in everyday practice, *Intercultural Education*, 25 (4): 243–54.

Upward, F., McKemish, S. & Reed, B. (2011), Counterpoint archivists and changing social and information spaces: A continuum approach to recordkeeping and archiving in online cultures, *Archivaria*, 72: 197–237. Available online:https://archivaria.ca/index.php/archivaria/article/view/13364/14672 (accessed 3 January 2021).

Voutilainen, L., Henttonen, P., Stevanovic, M. Kahri, M. & Peräkylä, A. (2019), Nods, vocal continuers, and the perception of empathy in storytelling, *Discourse Processes*, 56 (4): 310–33.

W3C (2021), *Accessibility Standards Overview*. Available online: https://www.w3.org/WAI/standards-guidelines/#intro (accessed 3 January 2021).

Walsh, S. (2011), *Exploring Classroom Discourse: Language in Action*, London: Routledge.

Whitelaw, M. (2013), Towards generous interfaces for archival collections, *ICA Congress Brisbane*. Available online: http://mtchl.net/assets/Whitelaw_ICA_GenerousInterfaces.pdf (accessed 3 January 2021).

Whitelaw, M. (2015), Generous interfaces for digital cultural collections, *DHQ: Digital Humanities Quarterly*, 9 (1). Available online: http://www.digitalhumanities.org/dhq/vol/9/1/000205/000205.html (accessed 3 January 2021).

Wierzbicka, A. (2006), The concept of 'dialogue' in cross-linguistic and cross-cultural perspective, *Discourse Studies*, 8 (5): 675–703.

Williams, D. (2002), Postscript: Reflective practice: Writing and professional development, *Journal of Medical Ethics*, 56 (1): 179–201.

Williams, H.L., Conway, M.A. & Cohen, G. (2008), Autobiographical memory, in G. Cohen & M.A. Conway (eds), *Memory in the Real World* (3rd ed.), 21–90, Hove: Psychology Press.

Winslade, J. & Monk, G. (2008), *Practicing Narrative Mediation: Loosening the Grip of Conflict*, San Francisco: Jossey-Bass.

Winslade, J. & Williams, M. (2012), *Safe and Peaceful Schools*, Thousand Oaks: Corwin Press.

Wong, J. (2000), Repetition in conversation: A look at 'First and Second Sayings', *Research on Language and Social Interaction*, 33 (4): 407–24.

Wyness, M. (1999), Childhood, agency and education reform, *Childhood*, 6 (3): 353–68.

Wyness, M. (2013), Children's participation and intergenerational dialogue: Bringing adults back into the analysis, *Childhood*, 20 (4): 429–42.

Yeo, G. (2007), Concepts of record (1): Evidence, information, and persistent representations, *The American Archivist*, 70(2): 315–43. Available online: https://www.jstor.org/stable/40294573?seq=1#metadata_info_tab_contents (accessed 14 June 2021).

Zupnik, Y.-J. (2000), Conversational interruptions in Israeli-Palestinian 'dialogue' events, *Discourse Studies*, 2 (1): 85–110.

Index

active participation 2, 7, 13, 21, 68, 69, 70, 71, 74, 78, 86, 92, 162, 164, 165, 169, 177, 178, 180, 186, 187, 221, 222, 223, 225
agency 4, 7–8, 13, 21, 32, 47, 64, 68, 86, 87–8, 91–3, 95, 99, 105–6, 113, 114, 117, 123, 124, 148, 149, 153, 154, 156, 162, 168, 169, 174, 176, 184, 197, 198, 214, 220, 222, 225–7
archive
    access(ibility) 193, 195, 196, 197, 200, 201, 202, 204, 205, 206, 210, 212, 213, 214
    digital 193, 194, 197, 205
    findability 193, 205, 207, 214
    flexibility 210, 211, 214
    participatory 196, 203, 204, 214
    usability 204, 205, 215

bilingual children 16

children speaking only a foreign language at home
    communication with adults 21
    communication with peers 21
    communication with teachers 21
children with a first language other than the national
    Communication with peers 21
    Communication with teachers 24
children's initiatives 13, 88, 91, 93–4, 96, 99, 100, 103, 105–6, 135, 148, 153, 180, 186–7, 225
circularity 133, 149, 203
community/communities of dialogue 2, 6, 8, 12, 67, 86, 87, 91, 105, 133, 148, 149, 153, 161, 162, 163, 164, 170, 171, 177, 178, 179, 217, 223, 225, 227
conflict 2, 8–9, 13, 26, 78, 116, 133–4, 135, 136, 139–49, 166, 169, 222, 227

conflict mediation 8–9, 133, 134, 135, 141, 144, 148–9, 169, 220
    narrative mediation 9, 135
    transformative mediation 135
coordination 91, 94–6, 105–6
culture 51, 115, 116, 117, 123, 124, 128, 131, 195, 204, 214

dervin 3, 116
dialogue 3, 8, 10, 13, 19–20, 22, 23, 32, 61, 64, 65, 78, 95, 105, 106, 117, 134, 153, 161, 163, 164, 176, 180, 183, 193, 220, 221, 222, 224, 226
discrimination 114, 115

emergent listening 177
empowerment 1, 2, 4, 8, 114, 117, 135, 143, 196, 197, 201, 202
epistemic authority 7, 92, 93, 176, 214
essentialism 3, 115, 119, 128
ethical research 11–12

facilitation 2, 6, 7–8, 9, 67, 71, 74, 78, 82, 86–8, 91, 93, 94, 99, 105–6, 114, 117, 119, 125, 126, 128, 129, 131, 133–5, 143–4, 148–9, 153–4, 156, 160–4, 167, 169–71, 173, 176–82, 184, 186–91, 195, 198, 219–27
facilitative actions 8, 86, 87, 153, 164, 174, 181, 184, 186
facilitative pedagogy 7, 8, 12, 13, 179, 183, 185, 224, 225
Fisher 4, 47, 65, 145
focused questions 68, 69, 71, 72, 86, 101, 119, 122, 131, 154, 156, 157, 160
formulations
    combined with questions 87, 154, 160, 162, 223, 224
    definition of 77–8
    as developments 78, 79, 80, 96, 125, 137, 142, 154
    as explications 78, 81, 100, 120, 154, 156

heritage (John) 7, 77, 92
hierarchical 6–7, 92, 176, 224
holiday 3, 4, 79, 115, 116, 131

identity/identities
   cultural 2, 3, 4, 6, 33, 79, 117, 131
   hybrid 3, 33, 203, 227
   multiple 117, 122
   negative 133, 134, 135, 136, 138–41, 144, 146, 148–9
   personal 51, 54, 57, 59, 122, 129
images/pictures 29–31, 33, 42, 45
intercultural
   communication, 2, 3–4, 114, 115, 116, 130, 180, 183, 217
   competence 13, 116, 130, 131–2, 211, 213
   dialogue 1, 213
   education 11, 115, 217
   learning 9, 194, 195, 206, 211, 212, 213, 214
invitations
   to ask 70, 160
   to expand 44, 69
   to talk 38, 67–8, 70, 72, 86, 160, 223

knowledge 9, 18, 33, 48, 49, 56, 74, 76, 78, 84, 86, 87, 88, 91, 113, 114, 116, 163, 164, 173, 174, 176, 177, 179, 180, 181, 186, 189, 191, 193, 195, 196, 211, 212, 213, 214, 226

learners as experts 177
listening
   active 59, 75–7, 79, 119, 120, 124, 154, 161, 223, 224
   double 135, 144, 149
Luhmann 8, 31, 133, 134

massive open online course
   phase 1 183
   final version 185
memory/memories 1, 2, 5–6, 9, 30–4, 37, 42, 44, 45, 47, 48–9, 54, 57, 59, 63, 75, 77, 101, 124, 164, 173–4, 175, 178, 179, 183, 187, 194, 195, 197, 198, 213, 226
   flashbulb memories 33–4, 37–8
migrant background 1, 2, 9, 17, 21, 22, 25, 26, 115, 129, 131, 164, 170, 225, 226, 227

minimal answers 71, 76
minimal feedback
   acknowledgment tokens 76–8, 79, 160, 223
   continuers 74–7, 79, 154, 160, 223
   repetitions 75–6, 119, 160, 175, 223
mode
   declarative 33, 34, 35, 37
   emotional 36
   semantic 36
model 197, 200, 203, 204, 215
multicultural
   classroom 1, 4, 153, 226
   community 1
   settings/contexts 2, 170, 217, 220

narratives
   definition of 3, 4–6, 47–9, 58, 64–5
   adversarial 135
   alternative 8, 133, 135, 139, 140, 144, 146, 148, 149
   condensed 30
   co-construction/co-production/co-narration 30, 32, 33, 38, 48, 50, 54, 58, 59, 61, 64, 65, 67–74, 79–81, 119, 148, 154, 169, 174, 223, 224
   declarative 49
   interlaced 56, 59, 63–4, 169, 219, 224
   metanarratives 5, 51, 55, 143
   Ontological 5, 50, 51–2
   personal 10, 135, 189, 224
   public 5, 48, 51, 52–5
   related to photographs 30, 31, 32, 33–4, 43, 44–5
   semantic 49
   support of 86, 87, 103, 117, 119, 131, 153, 187
   third-person 56
   transgressive 50
   valuing 74–7
   vicarious 41, 55
Nelson 33, 49
Norrick 4, 5, 30, 47, 49, 50, 59, 65

open questions 68, 71

parents speaking at least an additional language
   engagement with education 25
   integration 24

parents speaking only the national
    language 17
personal contributions
    as displacements 83–4
    as stories 82
personal learning networks 185
personal cultural trajectories 3, 4, 114,
    116, 119, 122, 128, 131, 162, 164,
    225–7
photographs (use of) 2, 5–6, 10–11, 13,
    30–2, 38, 40–4, 49, 119, 163–4
photo-elicitation 31
prejudices 129

racism 115, 116
RARA Key model 188, 189
reflectivity
    on action 179, 181
    of learning 177
    of practice 178
Right to tell/narrate 7, 11, 49, 50, 58, 86, 105
Rubin 32, 49

skills 115, 116, 126, 124, 132, 194, 206,
    212, 213
small cultures 4, 79
Somers 4, 5, 47, 51, 143
storytelling 5, 47, 48, 49, 50, 59, 61, 63, 65
survey
    description of 10

age-based differences 22
attitudes to dialogue 19
background-based differences 1
country-related differences 26
gender-based differences 23
participants 15, 17
problems of communication 18
relationships 19, 21, 22, 24, 25, 26
SWOT analysis 181, 188

teacher-centred education 176
tellability 48, 50
three-turn sequences 78
training 117
    face to face 183, 184
    guidelines for 185
transition between primary and secondary
    school 25
trigger 30, 32, 33, 43, 47, 55, 57
tripartite turns at talk 78

unique learners 175

visual, auditory and kinaesthetic
    methodology,
    for auditory learners 175
    for kinaesthetic learners 176
    or visual learners 175

Winslade 8, 9, 134, 135

www.ingramcontent.com/pod-product-compliance
Lightning Source LLC
Chambersburg PA
CBHW062139300426
44115CB00012BA/1982